Drugs, Intoxication and Society

ANGUS BANCROFT

D0066895

polity

First published in 2009 by Polity Press

Polity Press
65 Bridge Street
Cambridge CB2 1UR, UK

Polity Press
350 Main Street
Malden, MA 02148, USA

ISBN-13: 978-0-7456-3533-0
ISBN-13: 978-0-7456-3546-0 (pb)

A catalogue record for this book is available from the British Library.

Typeset in 11 on 13 pt Scala
by Servis Filmsetting Ltd, Stockport, Cheshire
Printed and bound in Great Britain by
MPG Books Ltd, Bodmin, Cornwall

The publisher has used its best endeavours to ensure that the URLs for external websites referred to in this book are correct and active at the time of going to press. However, the publisher has no responsibility for the websites and can make no guarantee that a site will remain live or that the content is or will remain appropriate.

Every effort has been made to trace all copyright holders, but if any have been inadvertently overlooked the publishers will be pleased to include any necessary credits in any subsequent reprint or edition.

For further information on Polity, visit our website: www.polity.co.uk

Contents

Detailed Contents

Acknowledgements

Thanks to Emma Longstaff for suggesting I write a book on this topic and for her support and patience.

The following people were of invaluable assistance while this book was in preparation: Kim Masson; Nick Prior; Jennifer Fleetwood; Anna Leppo; Donald MacKenzie; Steve Kemp; Sue Renton; John Arthur and Crew; Craig Reinarmann; staff of the UC Santa Cruz Sociology Department; José, little José, Dan and Frances in Santa Cruz, USA; staff and students past and present of the University of Edinburgh Sociology Department; the University of Edinburgh School of Social and Political Studies for funding a semester-long sabbatical during which I laid the groundwork for this book; and, in particular, all the students who have taken my course in the Sociology of Intoxication.

The vignettes at the start of chapters 1 and 3 are fictionalized, but based on real-life events. The vignette at the start of chapter 5 is a true account. The quote from Thomas McKeown in chapter 4 came via J. Walton (2000), *The Faber Book of Smoking*, London, Faber and Faber.

Preface

We are used to discussing drugs and alcohol as social problems, in terms of criminality, addiction, violence, misuse and risk. Few accounts, however, look at the other side of the story and give proper consideration to their role in dispensing pleasure, inspiration and solace. This book aims to show how a more comprehensive, alternative understanding could be reached. It focuses particularly on the experience of intoxication, which to date has been a neglected area of the literature in this field. Throughout the book, five main arguments are developed.

First, it shows how distinctions between categories of drugs, and between substances that are defined as 'drugs' and those that are defined as 'medicines', 'foods' or 'intoxicants', are largely arbitrary and a function of social power, not chemistry. It looks at the category of 'drugs' in the broadest possible way, including substances as diverse as heroin, cannabis, cigarettes, coffee and Viagra. It also examines how the history of drugs and alcohol has been a spiral of moral panic and myth-making which has made these malleable categories appear solid and immutable.

Second, it looks at the experiences of intoxication, arguing that these are likewise not ingrained in the pharmacological properties of the substance, but are shaped by culture, environment and individuals' characteristics, experiences and expectations. Drug users must *learn* to use their substance of choice for pleasure, or for other purposes. Neither problems nor pleasures are 'fixed' or 'innate' in the drug's chemistry.

Third, the book argues that blame for drug problems is far too often heaped on drugs as the source of harm while far less attention is paid to the individual and social problems that may have contributed to their use. In this way, drugs offer explanations for problems we would rather not account for in other ways, especially if it meant doing something about them. Some drugs, such as those prescribed by doctors, are also used to ameliorate some of the problems generated for individuals by the stresses of modern life, including problems associated with the use of other drugs. In both senses, then, they provide chemical solutions for social problems.

Fourth, and closely related to the above points, it is argued that the definition of, and proposed solutions to, the 'drug problem' have been used to control and stigmatize the most vulnerable. In this sense, drug problems can also be useful. Defining a drug and its users as a social problem allows for controls to be exercised over both. Drug controls are most familiar in the form of prohibition – banning some substances outright. However, power works most insidiously not by banning some substances and leaving others to the free market, but by shaping the material context of intoxication – the scenes and settings in which drugs and alcohol are consumed and the forms in which they are made available to users.

Finally, the book explores the idea of the 'pharmaceutical society', one that develops medicines for a range of conditions, and promotes conditions for its products to treat. Recently, addiction has been generalized to a whole range of human behaviours, and, as smoking and overeating have also become 'social problems', they have come to be described in terms of addiction. Developments such as these may presage a new phase in the history of drug use. Individuals are allowed and encouraged to use drugs to enhance their sexual performance, concentration at work and performance in social interactions with others. This is not merely the creation of a generation of shiny happy people, but a development in prosthetic culture – using drugs to extend and develop the self. Drugs are objects in a culture of intoxication, a culture that is constantly changing and developing. They can never be wholly good or bad, an unsustainable distinction. They are what we make them.

The book is written in a way that will make it useful to those who are studying drugs and society for the first time as well as those with some experience in this field. It cuts to the heart of issues that are so often obscured by political agendas, moral panics and taboo, looking afresh at drugs and alcohol use in clear and direct language. The book thoroughly explains technical details and puts the facts about drugs firmly in their social context. It offers people's stories and case studies, historical perspectives and extracts from fiction so as not to lose sight of the people and society behind the smokescreen of the 'drugs problem'. As well as guiding readers through a close and reasoned consideration of the whole range of issues surrounding alcohol and drugs, this book presents original arguments and perspectives that will be of interest to more experienced researchers and practitioners also.

1 Defining Drugs in Society

A woman sits forward on her high-backed leather chair, putting together a joint with the swift, blasé confidence of a children's TV presenter demonstrating how to create a jewellery box for Mummy out of an egg carton and coloured paper. She deftly pulls three thin cigarette papers out of their silver packet, licks two of them and sticks them together to form a longer paper, strengthening it with the third. Holding her creation in one hand, she crumbles some cannabis pollen and tobacco into it, spreading the mixture evenly along. With both hands, she rolls the paper over into a tube and seals it with her tongue. Finally, she shreds the cover of a report on her desk to make a small mouthpiece in the form of a thin cardboard tube, which she inserts into one end.

Her work done, she holds the joint between her lips to light it, and takes half a breath. The tobacco flares, burning the crumbs of cannabis pollen. Smoke – a mixture of carbon dioxide, nicotine, cannabinoids and particulates – pours down her throat. She pauses and takes the joint out of her mouth momentarily, and then breathes in deeper, pulling smoke throughout the alveoli of her lungs. A burning sensation caused by the old, dry tobacco she had used – the last of a prehistoric packet of forgotten provenance in her desk drawer – spreads across her chest. She holds the smoke in her lungs for a moment, allowing the cannabinoids and nicotine to be absorbed into her blood, breathes out slightly and then takes the smoke back in again into her now constricted airways.

She finally exhales fully, slowly letting the smoke drift out of her mouth, in a pleasingly sensual stream. She reflects on her preference for smoking joints mixing cannabis and tobacco, which go together like red wine and Christmas cake. She likes the mixture of nicotine kick and cannabis high. The only time she does not feel guilty about smoking tobacco is when it is mixed into a joint. She begins to feel light-headed as her mind reacts to the action of smoking, its taste, smell and sensation, and the more rapid effect of the nicotine, which kicks in before the chemical action of the THC from the cannabis begins to do its work. She puts her feet up on her desk and observes with quiet satisfaction the view from her office overlooking the centre of London. Flipping open her mobile with one hand, she texts her dealer to arrange the purchase of three grams of cocaine for that night's dinner party, and then calls her boyfriend to ensure he has bought sufficient beer and wine for the evening.

What's the problem? Why this book?

Drugs are evil. Drugs will fry your brain and turn it into Swiss cheese. Drugs will make you into a rapist or a rape victim. Drugs are for mugs. In Western societies, we are bombarded with messages from celebrities, politicians, teachers, public health specialists and social scientists telling us that we are one puff or one pill away from certain disaster. Yet at the same time we appear to be the most drug-aware and drug-experienced society in history. Millions of people of all backgrounds around the world take illicit drugs regularly and unremarkably (Hammersley, 2005), and many countries, mainly in Northern Europe, have developed their own speciality in extreme alcohol intoxication. The preceding vignette describes a common enough end-of-week ritual in many places: the casual use of an illicit substance, the preparation for an enjoyable social evening by 'sorting' out a shareable amount of cocaine and ensuring sufficient alcohol is laid in, the combination of different substances and the normalized fashion in which illicit recreational drug use constitutes part of the routine of (in this case) a young professional couple. This everyday occurrence coexists with bemusement among non-drug users as to what on earth drugs are for and why anyone would want to use them.

A recent British television advert for an illicit drugs-awareness campaign shows a cheeky-faced boy, aged about eleven or so, wearing shorts and sporting a question mark on his head. He pops up in various scenes where adults have taken, are taking, or are about to take unspecified but presumably illicit drugs, and asks precocious and slightly irritating questions of them. He bounces up and down on a tired woman's bed, asking 'How long are you going to feel like that for?' He leans over the partition wall of a seedy public lavatory, asking two men who are chopping what is presumably cocaine on the toilet seat, 'What does that actually smell like?' He inquires of a woman in a dance club who appears to be having a serious mascara problem, 'What's wrong with your face?' The advert captures the faint ludicrousness of intoxicant use when seen through naive eyes, but only insofar as it is similarly bizarre and opaque as most adult behaviour when viewed by children. The bafflement applies to illicit drugs and to other ambivalent vices like smoking and drinking alcohol.

Children tend to be very opposed to illicit drugs, tobacco and alcohol use up to the age of puberty (Johnson and Johnson, 1995), although there are many young children who are far more aware of the nature and effects of illicit drug and alcohol misuse than their nearest and dearest, or anyone else, gives them credit for (Barnard, 2005). Between then and around about age fifteen, the perspective of many appears to flip and becomes much more positive (Fuller, 2004). At around that age many will start to experiment with almost anything they can get their hands on. They come to welcome and enjoy what was previously mysterious and frightening (Leigh, 1999). The pre-adolescent bafflement at the strange things that adults and older children will voluntarily do to themselves for apparent enjoyment is an attitude present in many academic and policy accounts, although, for many, less prone to softening over time.

A large number of academics and policymakers never reach the epiphany experienced by so many adolescents. How on earth, they ask, would somebody snort a dental/ocular anaesthetic in order to expose it to their mucal membrane, drink the fermented juice of rotting plants used as fuel, preservative and sterilizing agent, to the point of serious motor and mental impairment, or ingest the smoke of a plant cured to preserve its very strong and quite toxic pesticide? Surveying the human wreckage caused by cocaine, alcohol and cigarettes, and many other intoxicants, it seems as if it would be better had the substances in question never been discovered, or had never been put to their recreational use by whatever enterprising souls first plumbed their powers over the psyche.

Health education campaigns that address the alcohol drinker, the cigarette smoker and the illicit drug user illustrate that wreckage. A young working everywoman talks to camera, describing how she likes to go out with the girls at the weekend and enjoy 'a few drinks'. Her monologue is interspersed with footage of her drinking shots and alcopops with her friends, throwing up in a nightclub sink, and finally falling over in the street (Portman Group, 2004). An emotionally charged real-life advert shows a mother in her early forties who is dying from lung cancer. Her daughters talk movingly about their pain and anger at their mother, as they plan her funeral and prepare for life without her (Department of Health, 2006). A series of pictures shows a crack-cocaine user, teeth falling out and skin almost transparent, staring with a look of detachment at the observer (Metropolitan Police Service, 2004).

Such apparently self-inflicted damage by those who presumably knew the consequences before they began is commonly explained in terms of addiction, ensnarement, peer pressure, mindless conformity, personality defects, psychological maladaption, deviance, anomie, desperation, fragmented communities, broken homes and bad examples. Almost any explanation is entertained, save one of a common desire to be intoxicated. The massive counter-evidence is often dismissed, that of healthy and controlled heroin users, social drinkers, casual cocaine users, and – perhaps more salient – the many people who have been through serious episodes of heavy and chaotic drug and alcohol use in their lives, but who have simply stopped in the course of time and without outside intervention, a process recognized by many drug workers as that of 'maturing out' of problem drug use.

The attention paid to intoxication's collateral damage is not just disgusted fascination with the bizarre and outlandish, but an awareness that in illicit drug and alcohol problems the observer sees an aspect of themselves. A sociologist would normally assume that such widespread social repulsion was evidence for the existence of a marginalized or deviant minority whose habits outrage the righteousness of the comfortable majority, in this case, those who use psychoactive substances to take the quick route to happiness. This would be followed by a statement about how, to some extent, the habits of outsider or alien groups are always inexplicably transfixing and disgusting, whatever the reality of their lives might be. The tricky issue about cannabis, ecstasy, cocaine, alcohol, tobacco and other drug use is that, frequently, what we find disgusting and repulsive is some aspect of ourselves. There is the very particular, metaphysical self-hatred that accompanies the worst hangovers; the sense of being unable to stop oneself pulling another cigarette from the packet; the hidden dependence on painkillers and anti-depressants; the parent who hides her drink from her family in the washing machine; the heavy ecstasy user's midweek emotional crash.

Despite attempts to present these problems as solely the preserve of the damaged, and not of ordinary people taking part in everyday activities, great desire and great disgust exist in the same society, and frequently in the same person. In this, the drug problem is surprisingly persistent. The image of cultural, religious or ethnic arrivistes often softens over time. Deviant subcultures dissipate into statements of fashion. Immigrant minorities find their niche, intermarry or become part of the local colour. In contrast, the problems of intoxication come round again and again, historically. Intoxication is a feature of social life that attracts and repels, often at the same time. It becomes a social problem that can never be solved, and triggers various crusades and wars against alcohol, drugs and tobacco that have no end in sight.

About intoxication

> Man, being reasonable, must get drunk;
> The best of life is but intoxication.
> Lord Byron, *Don Juan*, II.179 (1819)

Whether smoking cigarettes, drinking alcohol and coffee, or taking illicit drugs, for the majority of society's members, some kind of intoxication is a regular, often daily practice. All the same, 'the aim of artificially inducing a change in one's consciousness is considered by many to be immoral' (Becker, 1967). In all societies there exist sets of objects and practices that their members imbue with the power to change the world and the self, or, rather, the relationship between the two. Such practices may involve curses, prayers, incantations, meditation, psychotherapy, ritual scarring, holy charms, holy water, relics and mystical places. Some rely for their impact on faith, ritual and promise. Others work more directly on the psychophysiology of the human organism, while retaining more than a dash of faith in order to be effective. It is a particular set of objects and practices that is the concern of this book, psychoactive substances and the rituals and habits associated with them. These are chemical substances, including illicit drugs, alcohol, tobacco and pharmaceuticals, which are used to manage, maintain or change the experience of the self in the world by working on a direct relationship between internal states and external experiences. All of those discussed in this book have at various times attracted controversy and condemnation, their users subject to ridicule, shame or stigma; and have also been hailed as the saviour of the human condition, as vital oil on the wheels of social life, panacea for all ills. There is in biology a well-known phenomenon, hormesis, whereby a substance or exposure can be toxic in a high dose, but beneficial at a low dose. Intoxicants are the sociological equivalent, except that the relationship to dosage and form is arbitrary. Each substance is a poison in one form and context, and, in a different time and place, is a cure. In relation to Howard Becker's assertion, those that are seen as involving the effortless alteration of states of consciousness are treated with suspicion, although such altered states are no different from the controlled ecstasy of a Whirling Dervish.

Explaining why and how certain substances come to acquire their particular status as poisons or cures is one purpose of this book, which will explore society's contradictory and muddled relationship with intoxication. For example, in many societies, especially those of Western Europe and North America, one intoxicant of long-standing use, tobacco, is being slowly but surely driven to the edge of the acceptable. In the UK, it is illegal to smoke anywhere but in one's own home, in prison as an inmate, or in the street. In some jurisdictions in the USA, one also may not smoke in one's home if living in an apartment, or in specified open public spaces. At the same time, a raft of new semi-medicinal pharmaceuticals is in development, which will in theory make us work harder, feel more sociable, concentrate better, and keep us awake and alert, the same attributes that were once lauded upon cigarettes. Chemical intoxication of one kind or another is not, as a society, something we appear to be prepared or able to walk away from. Our personal and societal demand for it grows even as one substance is abandoned for another.

Intoxication is not frequently regarded as a subject on which the social sciences can or should have much to say. After all, if one drinks, one gets drunk. Where is the puzzle that needs to be solved there? The effects are most commonly thought of as consisting of the chemical-physiological effect of a substance, and although users are themselves frequently aware of the importance of psychological mindset and social setting (Zinberg, 1984), these last two are often treated as secondary to the form of the substance, its composition, and its interaction with the human organism.

Psychologists, anthropologists, sociologists and others can comment on the aftermath and the impact on society, but are presumed to have little to say about the process of intoxication. As has been suggested, social studies of licit and illicit substance use have tended to confine themselves to their problematic, subcultural, criminogenic or deviant aspects. Little attention is paid to the content and construction of the experience itself, which seems to be thought of as off-limits, self-explanatory, or irrelevant. We social scientists see it as our job to explain why someone might choose to take a drug, but think that we can leave the effect of the drug to biology. It is frequently the case that the closest we get to thinking about what it is like being drunk or high is when we discuss withdrawal symptoms, or people's motivations for seeking solace in illicit drugs and the bottle. However, there is also a venerable tradition of challenging or countering this problem-oriented approach, to which this book attempts to add.

This is because intoxication is a significant feature of social life, very closely integrated into how we go about our daily lives, from the endless cups of tea and coffee taken from sunrise to sunset, cigarette breaks throughout the working day, the swift pint after work, the bottle of wine with dinner, the cannabis joint smoked at night, the weekend ecstasy pill or line of cocaine, or the Viagra before bedtime. They fit into the patterns of modern life, as social practices and cultural rituals, involving pleasure and desire, suffering and resistance. The status given to an intoxicant used in a particular context profoundly affects how we approach each substance, the way it is used, the intoxicant effect of it, and the regulatory regimes users have to navigate, conform to, or subvert and undermine.

Sweet poisons of misuse

Bacchus, that first from out the purple grape
Crushed the sweet poison of misused wine
John Milton, *Comus* (1634)

How many drugs do you take? Many? Enough? Everything available? One religiously? None at all? I count six different psychoactive substances in varying amounts in a normal day for me. Some I like to think of as morning drugs, some workday drugs, and some evening drugs. I purchase one in a pharmacist, two at a supermarket, one from the newsagent, one from an off-license and another is more acquired than purchased (South, 2004). People who pronounce themselves as having a drug-free lifestyle may take the same number or more, but not categorize them as drugs.

What, then, is a drug? It is possible, in a blasé manner, to say that all substances that have a psychoactive effect are drugs. Whether whisky, cocaine, cannabis or Ritalin, they are all absorbed into the bloodstream, whence they proceed to rearrange the mental furniture, the molecules bouncing around the brain like excited pinballs. The United Nations Office on Drugs and Crime (UNODC) defines a drug as 'a substance that people take to change the way they feel, think or behave' (Office on Drugs and Crime, 2007). This is an all-encompassing definition, which would include chemical substances that are not within the remit of the UNODC, like tobacco and alcohol. However, its notion of 'changing' how one feels, thinks or behaves is tricky. Would that include restoring normal service? Or does it purely refer to changes away from the mental status quo that apply? Some drugs are used to restore balance, to make the body/mind conform to an ideal of normality. Would an addict taking heroin to feel normal, capable of everyday interaction and activity, therefore not be using it as a drug? Some anti-depressant medicines correct an imbalance of serotonin whether or not the person receiving the treatment has inherited that particular chemical imbalance in their brain. Is that then altering brain activity in a drug-like way? We turn to the United Nations for clarification:

> What is the difference between medicines and drugs?
>   People take medicines if, for example, they have a headache or an illness like bronchitis. Medicines are legal, which means that you can get them through a doctor or buy them in a supermarket or a pharmacy. But when people use drugs, they are generally healthy and do so to forget their prob-lems, feel happy and stay awake longer, among other things. Drugs are illegal, which means that if you get caught, the police will be involved and you might face criminal charges. (UNODC leaflet, *Questions Kids Might Have About Drugs*, 2007)

No definition or system of classification is disinterested, and most reasons given for their existence turn out to be rationalizations rather than explanations. The UNODC's attempt to explain to children how exactly drugs differ from medicines is akin to the type of explanations given by adults to children that are not intended to enlighten, but to make them realize that asking further questions is pointless. One can imagine a persistent child responding, 'Yes, but what *actually* is the difference?' (or, 'So how do I avoid getting caught?'). Within it is an admission that some substances have some of the characteristics of 'drugness' without being socially accredited as drugs, for little reason other than that is what the grown-ups have decided.

The word 'drug' does not designate a set of chemicals based on their molecular structure (Becker, 2001). There are no pharmacological cat-egories of 'illicit drugs', 'licit drugs' and 'medications'. They are social categories constructed because as a political community we have come to treat some substances differently from others, depending on who uses them, how and for what.

The availability of coffee and tea in the workplace is allowed and encouraged as it is seen to enhance concentration and productivity, and keeps my chin off my desk. Likewise my morning aspirin fights off my headache from the previous night's indulgence and allows me to show up to work on time and reasonably coherent. Smoking is legal but restricted. If I am to enjoy a mid-morning cigarette I have to join a few other holdouts in a windswept corner of campus, where our shame can be exposed to the disapproving eyes of passers-by. Drinking alcohol is confined not by law but by convention to outside the working day, venerated in the traditional lunchtime or after-work drink. Both alcohol and tobacco products are heavily taxed in most countries when used for the purpose of intoxication, signalling both the puritanical disapproval of the government for these pastimes, a desire for demand control in the public interest, and, less charitably, the same government's eye on the main chance when it comes to a ready supply of cash. Thanks to its illegal status, cannabis, like heroin, ecstasy, amphetamines and cocaine, is governed by no formal regulatory structure at all.

These legal and institutional categories are of the nature of self-fulfilling statements. Heroin, cocaine and ecstasy are illegal drugs because . . . they are illegal. Some anti-drug campaigning bodies, like the Partnership for a Drug-Free America, try to piece together a bio-pharmacological basis for the category of illicit drugs, on the basis that illicit drugs operate on the limbic system of the brain and therefore are potentially subverting of free thought. Illicit drugs do operate on this system, but so do many other activities, like sex or exercise. It is an *ex post facto* justification, since no substance was made illegal because it operated in this way. 'Drugs' are a social category. As 'drugs', to the Western eye, connotes one particular category – that of illicit psychoactive substances – they are differentiated here from 'intoxicants', of which they are a subcategory. Drug categorization is in part a function of power. Defining alcohol as a drug is resisted by the alcohol industries, which see it as in their interest to avoid the stigmatizing connotations of drugs and the form of state regulation that would accompany it.

Intoxicants are substances that affect the human organism when ingested. Substances are not the same as their chemical constituents. Each substance has a status accorded to it depending on its form, when and where it is used, why, and by whom. The same *chemical* can make its appearance as a different substance depending on these factors, and can have a very different intoxicant effect. A rose by any other name does not smell as sweet. The language we use to describe them – to do things with them – alters what they do and, effectively, what they are. Heroin and amphetamines are psychoactive substances that have licit and illicit uses, usually under different names. Alcohol can be an industrial fluid, a sterilizing, purifying agent, a fuel, and an intoxicant. It serves potentially any of these functions but rarely more than one at the same time. The economic, psychological and social functions performed are not the same. Each and every observed aspect of intoxicant use is a product of history, culture, social structure and attitudes, but is disguised in the concepts we use to describe them; addiction, drug abuse, drunkenness, recreational drug use or medication and the catch-all of 'drugs' itself. Cultural products disguise the conditions of their production. They embody social power and are imbued with social characteristics, possessing qualities such as demonic, classy, addictive, medicinal or potent.

However, these attributes are never consumed passively. We absorb them into our selves, developing a taste for intoxication, becoming skilful users, then using our skills to display distinction (Bourdieu, 1984), which may be according to class, social status, sex, ethnicity, region, or the myriad markers of difference created in human societies. For example, philosopher Roger Scruton argues that the intoxication of wine is markedly different from that of other drugs and other drinks, as the intoxication derives in part from the drinker's appreciation of the wine, not merely its chemical effects, vinous intoxication being virtuous intoxication (Scruton, 2007). The pace, ritual, reflection and refinement involved in drinking good wine makes it a rational, revelatory intoxicant, transforming the self in the act of consumption. Attributing this quality solely to wine is an act of distinction, of separating one's own, socially valid, intoxication from others and in the process devaluing other vehicles of self-transformation, reflection and ritual.

The scope of this book is mainly about illicit drugs but it is also concerned with alcohol, tobacco and any 'intoxicant' because they are linked, but not interchangeable. The link is in what they do. They are used to alter, manage or change the self in the world (Partanen, 1981). Within that statement there are many specifics. They modify behaviour, for instance, being used to perform better in response to institutional requirements as in taking amphetamines to help with exam revision. They mediate social relations, so that drinking alcohol in rounds is a sign of convivial sociability. They can enhance collective emotional experience. Intoxication is positive, not in the sense of being an unalloyed good, but of adding to experience rather than, as commonly claimed, simply taking away reason, inhibitions and repression. What that does not explain is how this state of affairs came to exist at all, and why it is that intoxicants intoxicate at all.

Why do drugs work?

Oh that men
Should put an enemy into their mouths to steal away
Their brains. That we should, with joy, pleasance,
Revel and applause, transform ourselves into beasts!
　　　　　　　　Shakespeare, *Othello*, II.iii. 1443–6

How is it that there exists a set of what were initially naturally occurring substances that have the often fortuitous and sometimes disastrous effect of altering the behaviour of highly evolved mammals in uncontrolled ways? We know a fair amount about how psychoactive substances work on the body and brain, the mechanisms and pathways involved, and current knowledge is increasing all the time. 'How' and 'why' are different questions. Why drugs 'work', why there should be a set of plants and substances derived from them that intoxicate *homo sapiens* and many other life forms, is fairly speculative. One evolutionary perspective, put forward by Randolph Nesse and Kent Berridge, is that the use of psychoactive substances is the result of an unfortunate environmental mismatch (Nesse and Berridge, 1997). Just as our bodies have evolved to deal with scarcity, and so we have no mechanism to stop eating ourselves to death in an environment of superabundance, the presence of drugs in the environment is a kind of seductive easy way out that allows individuals to short circuit the brain's reward/avoidance circuitry.

These are the mechanisms that evolved to ensure humans can and will compete for mates, that we then have sex and produce offspring, that we hunt, forage to provide food, drink and shelter to give them the best possible survival chances so that our genetic inheritance will be passed on, and that our progeny will be strong enough to compete against others. Returning the favour when we are old and weak is a fruitful benefit for us as individuals, but is not written into the evolutionary contract. These mechanisms work by creating positive mental states through chemical processes in the brain, as spurs to and rewards for action. Monkeys with higher social status in their group, for instance, have been shown to have higher serotonin levels than those further down the simian social ladder. Artificially raising the serotonin levels of subordinate male monkeys can lead to their becoming dominant in their group (Raleigh et al., 1991). Dopamine regulates the work-effort-reward balance. Although far more complex than my clunky terms 'reward mechanism' and 'circuitry' suggest, this operates as an elaborate economy of exchange, feedback and incentive.

This suggests that psychoactive chemicals present in the environment, or produced and created by humans for their effects, add hyper-inflation to this biochemical economy. They mostly work by causing the brain's chemical balance to alter, either releasing more neurotransmitters such as serotonin or dopamine, rather like a government central bank printing too much money, or blocking the re-uptake of what is already there, like reducing the supply of goods. Drugs allow positive emotional states to be achieved or negative emotional states to be avoided, irrelevant of the presence of the stimuli these mechanisms developed to respond to. The human organism frustrates its genetic inheritance by invoking an, in these terms, false state of being by using drugs. I can feel like I would after a successful day's foraging, fornicating or fighting while remaining on my sofa watching television, by dint of using heroin to activate my forebrain and brain-stem systems to give the hedonic reward of achieving an optimal state for genetic survival. A drug user can feel and act like Lord of the Jungle while retaining lordship over the remote control. Drugs work, then, through a process of biological legerdemain, allowing us the feelings of acting on the basic evolutionary imperatives of survival and reproduction when we are not (Newlin, 2002). It also applies to substances that are used to interfere with negative states, which might include tranquillizers and anti-depressant medicines. As negative states also have their evolutionary advantages – for instance, signalling danger – those drugs that medicate out normal negative feelings are also potentially maladaptive.

Drug use is in these terms inherently pathological. Human beings who use drugs, which, as I suggested, are a majority of us, stand accused of helpless selfishness, and of hijacking evolutionary reward/defence mechanisms to benefit our own personal happiness, benefiting our brains at the expense of our genes, which is what those brains are in fact adapted to protect. This state of affairs emerged because psychoactive substances are relatively novel when viewed in an evolutionary timescale, and we have not had the many generations required to select avoidance of them. Like baby turtles crawling the wrong way along the beach towards artificial light, when they should be aiming for the moon and guiding themselves towards the sea, modern psychoactive substances pull our instinctive responses and actions away from the reproductive imperative.

In fact, psychoactive substances of one kind or another have been present since prehistory, and their use does not seem to have interfered greatly with the rise of civilizations and the dominance of the human race over competitor species. The mismatch theory focuses on what is quite a historically and culturally specific form of drug use, the consumption of purified or artificial psychoactive chemicals, whereas most drug use throughout the world is and has been relatively mundane and unspectacular, for instance, in the consumption of tobacco, betel, opium, khat, coca leaf and coffee. The theory has a lot of difficulty explaining drug use among more successful social groups. Its implication is that drug use is more likely among those lower down the social hierarchy as they will have more negative states to deal with and are more likely to end up there, given that drug use will be providing false rewards instead of real ones, with little effort. This is based on a misconception. The efforts to produce and obtain illicit drugs are extensive, and do not indicate a generalized social pathology among drug users. In fact, better-off drug users tend to expend much less effort obtaining either drugs or the resources to pay for them. The theory tends to take the distorted and partial picture of illicit drug use as being the preserve of the poor and marginal at face value. According to these lights, we should be ruled by a class of ascetic puritans. In fact, drug and alcohol problems historically were as likely to emerge among the middle and upper classes as among the poor. Cocaine and hashish usage in the West were popularized by sections of the Victorian and Edwardian elites.

In this, as in many perspectives on drug use, drugs can only be destructive, of personalities, social order and morality. That drugs might enhance self and experience, and even one's survival chances, and provide stability in users' lives (Moore and Miles, 2004), is not considered a possibility. Mismatch theories like this, and there are many equivalents in the social sciences, also have difficulty accounting for, or do not attempt to account for, the use of drugs that do not confer feelings of power, sexual confidence or even well-being on the user. Hallucinogens are notoriously challenging to the user, often demanding an effort of self-control. It is hard to fit LSD or Ibogaine use into this schema, for instance, or that of Ketamine, a dissociative that produces in the user a sense of becoming dissociated from their body. They work on the same biochemical systems as the more hedonistic substances but do not appear to generate reward sensations and can be in fact quite disturbing – if satisfying, revelatory or otherwise worthwhile – experiences. The evidence from use of these drugs indicates that intoxication is about much more than mindless fun.

Recognizing some of these criticisms, R. J. Sullivan and E. H. Hagan (2002) posit an adaptive evolutionary account that incorporates the fact that humans and other mammals have coexisted with and used psychoactive substances for many millennia. All these substances are cultivars, selected for their psychoactive properties. Agricultural crops were grown specifically to produce alcohol with; cannabis, opium and coca plants were selected over generations for those which yielded the greatest psychoactive effect. Plants evolved neurotransmitter analogues as a defence – for instance, the nicotine found in the tobacco plant is a pesticide, and mammals evolved mechanisms to use these defences to their advantage. The membranes on the inside of the mouth may have developed to allow such chemicals to be extracted and not bypassed or rejected. In addition, there are many cultural and behavioural adaptations that allowed chemicals to be extracted from plants during consumption, such as chewing coca leaves with wood ash or lime, or making tea from dried and rolled leaves with boiled water. Most humans who consumed plants with psychoactive properties did not consider them to belong to a category of drugs, and many do not today, but rather thought of them as foods, with positive, energizing, symbolic or religious properties. In periods of scarcity, humans found that they could save time and energy by eating plants containing neurotransmitter analogues, rather than seeking foodstuffs containing the precursors for endogenous neurotransmitters.

Psychoactive substances are more than brain-fuel analogues, though, and they have conferred their own advantages to the species that have grazed them. Ethanol is ubiquitous in ripe fruit. It is hormetic, conferring advantages at small doses although poisonous in large quantities, and was something that animals, including our evolutionary forebears, adapted to (Dudley, 2001). The adaptive evolutionary perspective goes some way towards explaining why there are substances that interact with complex organisms in apparently contradictory ways. This still tends to downgrade the intoxicant experiences themselves, for which there appears to be no evolutionary explanation and which are rated here as something of a by-product. If they are evolutionary by-products, then, as is the case with many human cultural activities, it is the by-product that has become the main thing. Whatever view is taken of our evolutionary inheritance, intoxicants are part of a long-standing attempt to manage the relationship between self and the elemental world. So if there is a symbiotic relationship between the human organism and psychoactive substances it is two-way – and humans have worked on drugs far more extensively than they have worked on us.

Conclusion

The ways in which drugs 'work' for people, and people work for drugs, will be explored throughout the book. There is, however, a leap to be made here, between drug use as a practical activity rooted in biology, and intoxication as a practice – something pursued in and of itself with its own logics, narratives, experiences – which seems to be more fruitfully examined in terms of history, culture and society. We are talking about human activities, on a human scale, that have to be understood in human terms, taking into account all the frailties, cruelty and shortsightedness of human behaviour, but also its unbounded art, generosity and ingenuity. The path that the evolutionary perspective starts us down leads us to understand that behaviour is not meaningless. Taking illicit drugs, smoking tobacco or drinking alcohol are not unfortunate foibles that would not be part of an ideal world. They are embedded in every other force shaping human behaviour, be it material, cultural, habitual, emotional, personal or historical

2 Drugs and Alcohol in Historical Perspective

The sun-god Ra ruled over mankind for many thousands of years. Taking human form, he grew old. Men laughed at his silver frailty and broke his laws. The Goddess Hathor was sent to punish mankind, who had blasphemed against the majesty of Ra. Joyfully she slew them, and she waded in the blood of mankind. Ra softened towards those that she had not slain and resolved to protect the remnants against her, for she was intoxicated by destruction. He sent messengers to find mandrakes. They were given to the women who were crushing barley to make beer. Seven thousand vessels were filled with the sleep-inducing beer, which was poured in the fields of heaven. Hathor in the morning came to the fields full of blood-red beer and 'joyful was her face because of it . . . merry was her heart, she came to a condition of drunkenness, she knew not mankind'. Ever after men drink sleeping-beer at Hathor's festival.

Destruction of Mankind, Egyptian Eighteenth Dynasty. Adapted from a translation by E. A. Wallis Budge, 1904

Useful problems: the inescapable usefulness of drugs and alcohol for society

[. . .] a wise government puts fines and penalties on pleasant vices. What a benefit would the American government, not yet relieved of its extreme need, render to itself and to every city, village and hamlet in the States, if it would tax whiskey and rum almost to the point of prohibition! Was it Bonaparte who said that he found vices very good patriots? He, "got five millions from the love of brandy, and he should be glad to know which of the virtues would pay him as much." Tobacco and opium have broad backs, and will cheerfully carry the load of armies, if you choose to make them pay high for such joy as they give and such harm as they do.

Ralph Waldo Emerson, *Society and Solitude* (1904 [1870])

Illicit drug use is one strand in humanity's long quest for intoxication, from brewing to distillation to pharmacology, dream molecules of delight and menace. Its history could be written as a continuous upward curve, Whiggish progress towards an ever more refined use of chemicals to manage and change the self, or, as a Toryish fall from grace, society tipping over the edge of its chemical catastrophe graph. Many histories of drugs and alcohol in Western societies combine both, hinging around a shift from merriment to miserability casued by the Promethean quest for intoxication. Whether written in the eighteenth or the twenty-first centuries, they point to a similar shift in drinking and drug taking. Accounts of drinking hark back to a golden age when ruddy-cheeked folk clunked together flagons of sweet beer or wine while taking a break from gathering in the harvest. They are then contrasted with the contemporary scene, in which drunken women abandon babies and morality, and men sink into vice. Literary accounts in the nineteenth century shift from the comical drunk to the tragic alcoholic. In the twenty-first century, commentators compare the mellow use of cannabis by children of the Flower Generation in the 1960s with the skunk-damaged youth of today. At some point, and each account differs in precisely when and where this happened, inebriety becomes deviance, anti-social, an addiction, requiring surveillance and possible coercive intervention. These narratives are part of the formation and definition of the drug and alcohol problems as public problems.

The apparent increase of intensity, immediacy and diversity in the form of drug availability disguises the subtle way in which intoxication has become, and is continually recreated as, a public problem, generative of policies, institutions and conflicts, reframing the context in which drugs and alcohol are taken. The modern era is marked by the emergence of public problems, matters of public concern that become the basis for state action, a category of behaviour and/or of people that demands public action to deal with it (Gusfield, 1981; Gusfield, 1996). Public problems demand our attention, our concern, our resources, our money, our time and energy (Best, 2008).

Personal troubles and deviant desires have not always been approached in this way, and still only some personal difficulties are defined as public problems. The development of public (or social) problems indicates a distinct development in drug and alcohol control – a process whereby objects and practices become the subject of public concern. There have been illegitimate desires throughout history. Some kinds of substance use by some people, especially women and the young or poor, were always objectionable. As in the *Destruction of Mankind*, women could make beer but were not supposed to drink it. A Roman woman could be legitimately killed by her husband for drinking wine. Restrictions, both formal and informal, of this kind can be found throughout recorded history. The notion of there being such things as substances routinely denied to *any* member of society has appeared at a relatively recent historical moment and set of circumstances. This involved the emergence of a category of psychoactive substances. including previously disparate objects – alcohol, cocaine, cannabis, opiates – that only in the past 100 years or so started to be seen as possessing some common moral and physical attributes. This development could not have taken place without the emergence of the modern notion of society as an abstract community of theoretically equal individuals, to which the sociologically driven notion of public problems contributes (Beck, 1978).

A society is defined by those entities it chooses as its opposites. In the post-modern, relativistic West we try desperately not to define conflicting ideologies or nations as enemies, even when we are at war with them. We are more and more reluctant to scapegoat individual types, as would have happened in the nineteenth and much of the twentieth centuries – when the sexually loose woman, the homosexual, the drunkard and the indigent poor were all targets of society's wrath. The nation-state and international bodies like the European Union and the United Nations now increasingly cohere around public problems as the basis for collective action (Ashworth, 1990), of which the drug problem is one, including the environment, poverty, crime, terrorism and health.

The example of poverty shows how public problems function. In the nineteenth century and before the poor were mainly of interest to the ruling class as the source of nightmares, as threats to the social order. Poverty as a condition defined in abstract, bureaucratic terms – by means tests or established rights to support – came into being along with the welfare state towards the end of the nineteenth century and into the twentieth. Likewise, the problem of crime is distinct from the existence of specific crimes. It was knitted together by the creation of a police force whose target was 'crime', as the target of the welfare state was and is 'poverty', along with the identification of criminal types and classes (the homosexual, the recidivist, the deviant and so on). Scientific knowledge is brought to bear on, and constructs, the problems of order, health, poverty, health, crime, drugs, alcohol and so on, and in so doing establishes the 'reasonable' (hence, reasoned) point of view, the accepted frame of reference for the problem, to which all right-thinking people adhere. Despite its humanitarian instincts, the objects of public problems are depersonalized. The welfare state, the health-care system and other bureaucracies established to deal with public problems construct and define the roles that their charges play. This is positive power that produces individuals as subjects of surveillance and management systems.

The control of intoxicating substances as a set, rather than the haphazard targeting of individual substances, is historically novel. The modern bureaucratic systems that govern substances are closely aligned with the governance of individuals. Control of intoxicants and intoxication has become a matter of the governance of subjects and the production of subjectivities, through various systems, including taxation, health care, public health, education, criminal justice and civil regulation. It was an integral part of the rise of new, bureaucratic forms of social control and regulation that marked the modern era, and the systems of reflexive governance characteristic of late modernity. The individual citizen's consumption of psychoactive substances, especially illicit drugs but also alcohol and tobacco, what is consumed, where and how, have become a matter for public policy. With the recent panic about obesity, the same process seems to be happening with food. The psychic life of populations is considered to be a matter for state power and international treaty. The complex of regulations and controls around psychoactive substances goes beyond mere 'prohibition', the system whereby some substances are made illegal to possess. Focusing on systems of prohibition, though relevant, can blind us to the wider transformation of the relationship between individuals and society, as mediated through the 'drug, tobacco and alcohol problems'. There has been a historical change from laissez-faire acceptance of the sale and consumption of drugs like opium, along with concern about some of the problems caused for individuals, to a situation where individual difficulties form part of the drug problem. Public problems are inescapably useful, not because they are beneficial as such, but because they provide powerful narratives for individuals to understand their experiences, and they form a legitimating basis for public policy and state action, integrating with other forms of social control, and, in a time when political elites are suffering a catastrophic loss of trust and credibility, they provide a way for politicians to reconnect with the public and answer the ubiquitous demand that they 'do something'.

Refined relief: ordering drugs and intoxication

We allude to the simple desire for stimulation, – in the words of another, 'that innate propensity of mankind to supply some grateful means of promoting the flow of agreeable thoughts, of emboldening the spirit to perform deeds of daring, or of steeping in forgetfulness the sense of daily sorrows.' No climate and no soil is without some product of its own which furnishes, at man's bidding, a stimulating ingredient to meet this universal want.

F. E. Oliver, *The Use and Abuse of Opium* (1872)

It is 1884 and a gentleman feels in need of a pick-me-up. Drinking oneself into oblivion is the habit of the wretched working classes. Opium smoking is dilettante and has the whiff of Oriental vice. Its liquid cousin, laudanum, is for poets and their hangers-on. Cocaine infusions have the endorsement of the Pope and Queen Victoria. They are refined relief, medicinal really, neat, effective, and Godly. He reaches for the bottle.

Every picture to be drawn of intoxication, like this one, portrays an intoxication order, a coding and arranging of intoxication by gender, geography, nationality, class, ethnicity, sex, sexuality, and form of governance, all of which are located in and operate on the body of the user. These orders are partly encoded in the substance itself and partly in the conditions of its production and consumption. Both elements – the nature of the substance and its prevailing conditions of use – are historically produced. In each period in recent history there have been vices that are endorsed – that proffer refined relief – usually as alternatives to alcohol, and those that are reviled when taken by the wrong sort of people. Many current 'demon drugs', like cannabis, cocaine and heroin, came into widespread use in this way, as refined relief. It has been the case that 'drug pioneers' are as likely, or more likely, to be found among the elites as the masses – at least, those that end up in the historical record are.

A society produces, and restricts, available choices for an individual, choices about what intoxicants there are and what intoxication itself is. It distributes those choices by material wealth, cultural capital and power relationships; and through ritual, custom, price mechanisms, legal restrictions and cultural practices. It also renders some forms, for some people, utterly beyond the pale. What differs for modern societies is the systematic way in which this is done, through appeal to constructed, felt abstractions embedded in the self, such as risk, health and addiction. Drugs are one such abstraction. A discourse around drug use is created that defines drug users as certain kinds of subject – increasingly, subjects without agency, driven by a combination of alienation and appetite.

One of the significant established features of today's intoxication order is the construction of a unified category of 'drugs', which includes very different substances, but partially excludes alcohol, pharmaceuticals and cigarettes. In the late nineteenth century there were no drugs. There were opiates, cocaine, beer, spirits, cannabis and ether, but these objects were not recognized as belonging to a single category. There were no illicit drugs, as every substance that is now by law supposed to be kept out of the hands of the consumer was freely available. Neither was there a recognizable category of medicines, as in substances prescribed by a doctor or obtained from a pharmacy. Opioids and cocaine found their way into tonic drinks and patent medicines, which were sold rather like 'buzz' drinks are today, and filled the place now taken with tranquilizers and anti-depressants (DeGrandpre, 2006).

> The catholicity of the Temperance movement is remarkable. It links together in a fraternal bond of union, people of every nation, irrespective of colour, education, politics or religion, and through the agency of these bodies, the peoples of the earth are being linked together not only to drive the means of intoxication from the commerce of the world, but to secure peace and goodwill among nations. (Guy Hayler, International Prohibition Federation, *Prohibition Advance in All Lands* (1913), quoted in Schrad, 2008)

For much of the nineteenth century and into the early twentieth century, it was alcohol, and mainly spirits, that was the subject of societal controversy, held responsible for many ills. Ardent spirits (distilled liquors like whisky) were responsible for the condition of starving, ragged-clothed children, and weeping, bruised wives with empty pantries. The temperance movements made sure alcohol was a live political issue in the UK, the USA and elsewhere, particularly Nordic Europe and Russia. They were very powerful, transnational social and political movements. As their name suggests, temperance movements did not, for much of their existence, demand that the sale of alcohol for personal consumption should be made wholly illegal. Prohibition was more of a twentieth-century innovation, typical of a 'public problems' approach that involves state-directed action. Rather, the voluntaristic approach of temperance activists involved moral exhortations demanding that men show restraint in drinking, tavern owners repent, and women abjure them to do so. For a long time spirits, rather than alcohol as such, were seen as the problem. Beer was not in these terms an alcoholic drink.

Since then, the category of drugs has been radically altered and reordered. Alcohol appeared to be in nearly terminal condition in some countries during the inter-war period, outlawed entirely in the USA, Finland and Russia. Now it is a 'non-drug'. Not wholly unrelated to that development, cocaine, opium and cannabis have been elevated to the status of demon drugs, whose fundamental chemical character is so dangerous that vaunted liberties and laws of supply and demand can and should be abrogated so that citizen and society should not be exposed to them. In the first half of the twentieth century, the modern mythic structure of the drug problem was established. It is that there is a set of substances so seductive and dangerous that human beings cannot control themselves when exposed to them – chemicals that take away human agency, autonomy and reason; people will be driven to degradation, crime and the abandonment of moral principle and social obligation. Alcohol was too diffused, too normative, to perform this role. Temperance ideology saw the danger to a man's soul from drinking 'demon rum' in a saloon, away from hearth and family. Now, the soul sits in the brain, whose biopharmacology can be irreparably damaged by demon drugs. Molecules rather than morality rule our world, but they are as fearsome and unforgiving as a Revivalist God was. Like all systems of belief, there are origin myths.

Narratives and origin myths in drug histories

There are three narratives or, rather, three types of narrative, in drug history: chemical, economic and socio-cultural. All have some truth to them. They capture the history of individual substances but also tell their own story of the development of drugs as a singular but fuzzy category. In themselves they document humanity's changing relationship to its substances of sensation. First, there are those that focus on the discovery of the chemical structure of each substance, the source of its potency and its action on the human body and mind, which are slowly revealed over many years as scientific understanding progresses and new substances are developed. Human development is only admitted into this narrative in terms of the discovery of new drugs or new techniques for taking them, for instance, the chemical rush of the late nineteenth and early twentieth centuries. This gives the impression that we as a society are working towards an ever more perfect chemistry set for the mind, developing a picture of the brain as a chemical factory. There is a feedback loop here, in that scientific knowledge is used to develop new substances, the experience of which then reshapes that knowledge, but those experiences are partly subjective and socially shaped, so that knowledge is always socialized and in part structured by how drugs, drug use, intoxication and the drug problem are defined and understood.

Discoveries change how we think of drugs, the body and the brain. For instance, the refinement of morphine from opium in 1805 by Friedrich Wilhelm Adam Sertürner laid the foundations for understanding of the brain as a chemical factory, as it could be seen how refined and later altogether new drugs had more direct and specific effects. Opioid receptors in the brain were identified in 1973 (Brownstein, 1993), indicating the mechanisms by which opiates had a psychoactive effect. These narratives culminate in the drug 'unified field theory', positing a common set of mechanisms in the brain through which drugs have their effects (Robbins and Everitt, 1999). This involves not just the specific receptors and neurotransmitters that are activated by drug ingestion – endocannabinoids, dopamine, endomorphins, the 'party pooper' monoamine oxidase B – but also a sense that these mechanisms could and should be conceived as part of a functional whole. What this does is shape how users think of and report on their drug use, altering the body–mind–drug relationship, which changes with the emergence of 'drugs' (and 'addiction', 'withdrawal' and so on) as single categories and experiences.

The combination of chemistry and drug-user practice has revolutionized intoxication and turned most members of society into users. Social histories consider the development and diffusion of drugs and drug-use practices. There were two psychoactive revolutions in the development of the modern world. The first psychoactive revolution was of the late sixteenth to early eighteenth centuries. This involved the spread of tobacco, cocoa, tea and distilled alcohol (Matthee, 1995). Then there appears to have been a second, occurring in the nineteenth century, involving opium, cocaine and to a lesser extent cannabis. Much of this was the spread of technique – brewing coffee or chocolate, smoking tobacco, distilling alcohol. Smoking became a general technique for imbibing many drugs over the years – opium, heroin, crack-cocaine, cannabis, methamphetamine – and is almost always associated with intoxicant use rather than medical administration.

Alongside these two narratives, there is one more recent story of a social-cultural fall from grace at a point in the not-quite-distant past, around about the late eighteenth to nineteenth centuries, in which intoxication stopped being merriment and became the slouching beast you see before you today. There may be lamentation of the now widespread use of drugs (Jonnes, 1996) or the damaging effect of the drugs war on drug-using cultures (Davenport-Hines, 2004). This latter narrative forms a central part of the systematic regulation of drugs and to some extent alcohol. It includes the defining of various types of users – the junkie, the alcoholic, the addictive personality, the rake, the lush or the moderate drinker.

These historical narratives intersect and intertwine. They are regularly punctuated by catastrophism; humanity being visited with a scourge upon itself, be it with the application of distillation to alcohol, the refinement of morphine or the invention of heroin, PCP, crack-cocaine or methamphetamine. What this has done is treat intoxication as a divine plague, or a force of nature that, like *el Niño*, is a heartless destructive force that returns every few years. If we understand drug plagues of the past we can put present worries in some perspective; and also rehabilitate intoxication as a productive element of human history and experience.

Social complexity and transformation

When viewed historically, there is always an apparent, though deceptive, arbitrariness to contemporary attitudes and practices. The varied and wildly different uses of intoxicants at different times and places exposes the contingency of our own sets of taboos, stigmas, regulations and prohibitions. The easy conclusion to take from this is that therefore all cultural and societal referents and restrictions are random, with little significance beyond pointing to 'where the power lies' to define their limits. Many features of intoxication, drug use and control are arbitrary, but they are not random, in the sense that there is no material reality to the chemistry and technical practice of intoxication. Academics are terrified of the accusation of Whiggishness – of assuming that all past periods in history are mere preludes to the present. Absolute arbitrariness appears only when intoxication is viewed objectively, out of time, as if all periods of history and all actions were reversible. They are not, of course. Experience is the congealed past. We cannot step out of time and, for instance, uninvent heroin or our knowledge of what it does. History cannot be unwound, at least not without civilization being unwound at massive cost to humanity. There are some step-changes and transformations that build on past developments. One is complexity (Dietler, 1990); the other is the psychoactive revolution, an outcome of technical and social development. The transformation is wrought by growing social complexity and techno-scientific development. Technologies – and psychoactive substances are technologies – are the material residue of social organization and human endeavour, social relations that become embedded in the object.

The evidence of past technological innovations varies. Magic mushrooms require little preparation – just picking, drying and eating. The consumption of cannabis needs a little more processing, through fire, either being smoked or cooked. Alcohol production appears to need a more systematic approach, and a higher level of civilizational development in order for it to be available regularly, and especially outside the harvesting season. The production of alcohol appears to be at a turning point in the history of intoxication. It is an intoxicant that requires a sufficient level of social complexity to be produced outwith the cycles of the seasons and in cooler climes. It needs the domestication of crops, a surplus, and a certain degree of planning, which had to be seen as being worth the effort. In fact, alcohol production is the continuation of a process of crop selection and breeding and the development of effective techniques of intoxication, such as sitting in your specially made yurt and throwing cannabis seeds on to the fire, which made intoxication a state to be sought after. The desire for intoxication has driven human technical and social development.

Alcohol production seems to mark a qualitative change in human history. Alcohol marks the end of the hunter-gatherer society and the beginning of the settled agrarian society. It may have been part of the dynamic that led from one to the other, requiring for its production in any quantity stable agriculture and settled societies. In the form of beer and wine it appears to have been part of a process of emerging, stable social elites, social complexification and regular surpluses (Joffe, 1998), possibly driving the domestication of cereal crops (Braidwood et al., 1953). There is some evidence of the hunger for alcohol driving crop management and cultivation. Domestication of the maize ancestor teosinte was not initially for grain but for its sugar, used to provide for the production of alcohol (Smalley and Blake, 2003). The spread of maize was partly driven by alcohol production. It was not a staple crop converted to the service of alcohol production as a secondary use once an agricultural surplus had been produced, but the opposite. The crop's spread was driven by its use in alcohol production and it then becoming established as a food staple.

There is, then, in human history a long, unsteady process of expanding the horizon of sensation, involving remarkable developments in technical ability and social organization, and also the development of consumption practices. The development of the means of intoxication is only one side. There is also the cultural creation of tastes for experiences, which has been at times an obsession for Western societies. Europe from around the Elizabethan era developed a new taste, the hunger for novel luxury that became a mania for nutmeg, sugar and chocolate. The aristocracy and middle classes of Europe developed a taste for tastes, a hunger for sensual experience. A category of products, *genußmittel* or articles of pleasure (Schivelbusch, 1992), became established in the Western mind, as a driving force and justification for economic and imperial expansion.

The use to which substances are put, the regulation applied to them, and the social and cultural symbolism associated with them, feeds back into their development, changing their internal nature and external form. Alongside this is the creation of a category of at first luxury, and later, luxuriant, products and the leisure time to enjoy them, with which the many forms of intoxication came to be bound up with. It is the intensity of experience that marks out the modern period and the systematic division of intoxication from the legitimate, sober lifeworld. These two elements – production and consumption – developed through, and developed, intoxication.

Fermentation and distillation: the release of the spirit

> Oh wondrous craft of the vices! By some mode or other, it was discovered that water also might be made to inebriate.
> Pliny the Elder, *Natural History* 14.29 (c.AD 77)

The word *chemio* is Arabic for 'concealment' from which we get the word chemistry. Olympiodorus' commentary on Aristotle's *Meteors* describes sailors apparently distilling sea water using sponges to absorb steam, which they then drank from (Morewood, 1824), and F. R. Allchin suggests alcohol was distilled for drinking in India and Pakistan from around 500 BC (Allchin, 1979). The credit for the invention of distillation in its modern form is given to Jabr ibn Hayyan around AD 800. It was used for various pharmaceutical preparations but there is no record of it being used as an intoxicant until the twelfth century. It seems it was Jews and Christians in the Arab world who became the purveyors of distilled alcohol for the purposes of intoxication, finding an extra use for the distillation devices to produce arrack or *araki*, distilled from dates or currants. This corresponds to their marginal social position in Islamic societies, reflecting the social level of drug dealers and suppliers at all times, regardless of how high class their clientele may be.

The development of alcoholic distillation introduced a devilish concept into the world of psychoactive chemistry, of refinements that produced an effectively new substance, transformative of the object, with intoxicating effects magnitudes greater than before. Distillation released the spirit of alcohol – which was again seen as producing a wholly new and useful but dangerous substance. The development of 'modern intoxication' in terms of this step-change could be traced to the distillation of spirits and their popularization. Distillation is the process of separating the constituent chemicals of a substance by their volatility through evaporation and condensation. Alcohols have a lower boiling point than water, so can be separated by heating fermented liquid to the correct temperature and condensing the vapour. The correct temperature is vital. Too low, and methanol – which is toxic when metabolized – will be produced. Higher and the result will be largely water. The discovery of the sweet spot for the desired ethanol must have taken some trial and perhaps tragic error as the two substances are only distinguishable by the sweeter smell of methanol.

When introduced in Europe, spirits were seen as fundamentally different from wine and beer, which were considered to be foods, and still are in some places such as France. An analogy is the difference between guns and bows and arrows; the coming of the gun unleashed unprecedented concentration of power. However tempting, firepower and firewater cannot be so easily and rashly compared. After all, guns, properly handled, can give power over others; alcoholic spirits give power over what? Or whom? Another question, or bone of contention, is that in fact guns did not automatically produce an unprecedented potency. They were good for scaring the natives with a loud bang and flash, but the poor range and accuracy of the musket, not to mention the achingly long time it took to reload while your enemies were charging full pelt at you, meant that it was not an unprecedented leap in firepower. Indeed, the gun and gunpowder had been around for a fairly long time before the techniques of modern warfare fully exploited it or, rather, the techniques of modern warfare exploited the power of a modern society which could command a standing army to kill whenever and whoever it wanted to and in whatever numbers it took. The gun was a tool of that shift in the history of warfare, but the technique was the vital element. Likewise, it is technique along with technology that matters in defining the modern use of alcohol and drugs. Really, technique and technology are inseparable.

This brings us back to alcohol and one of its unique qualities that has contributed to its near ubiquity in human societies. The production of alcohol is a technique of working on plant material. Alcohol can be produced from any plant with a sufficient sugar content that the user can stomach – potatoes, grain, bananas, cacti. It may be that the technique of its use was spread by migration, by cultural exchange, or simply that it was developed in a number of different places at different times. Alcohol production liberated humanity from the plant-specificity of intoxication. It can be produced in most human environments, and does not need the conditions required to grow opium poppies, or for the cannabis sativa plant to yield a high tetrahydrocannabinol (THC) content. It required a certain level of organization, the material for its production, stills and so on, and although this is fairly simple it is not insignificant. Was alcohol production, then, an early universal sign of human culture as a technical civilization? It was a step in the development of human technoculture that stands in a transformative relationship to objects in the natural world. From this point it was not far to the development of morphine and cocaine and, from plant refinements, to wholly new chemicals like heroin.

It could be that the production of alcohol was the inspiration for the production of all sorts of other things. The observation that plants could be subject to a process that produced an intoxicant might have led to further experimentation, such as using lime to release the cocaine in coca leaves. Alcohol introduces the crucial concept of transformative process that humans can apply to plants and other objects of the material world. 'Cooking' is one such process, but it does not produce a new 'thing', a new object, except in the anthropological sense. Brewing does – it produces a liquid with an entirely new property not shared with its constituent ingredients. This is alchemy, making something desirable out of the base elements to hand. This is more alchemical than eating intoxicant plants, raw or cooked. Humans have always known that some plants poison, that plants have 'effects' on them that can be strange or disturbing or deadly, but for humans to produce a liquid that has such an effect places their relationship with the material world at one step above that. It also transforms the drug problem. It is the case historically that distilled spirits kicked off one of the first societal drug – or, more strictly, intoxication – scares, the Gin Craze of eighteenth-century Britain, which ushered in a new kind of culturally and economically determined drunkenness.

Dissolving luxuries: the Gin Craze

> The vast torrent of luxury, which of late years hath poured itself into this nation hath contribute to produce, among many others, the mischief I here complain of.
>
> Henry Fielding, *An Enquiry into the Causes of the Late Increase of Robbers &c. with Some Proposals for Remedying the Growing Evil* (1824 [1751]: 360)

A continuous theme of research into poverty of the past hundred years and more has been bafflement that poor people do not channel their energies in what the observers would approve of as a more productive fashion, that they apparently prefer to blow hard-won and limited resources on superfluous vices – alcohol, bingo, crack-cocaine, cigarettes and dog-racing. Another theme since the eighteenth-century Gin Craze has been the intrusion of a substance into their suffering, producing a narrative of substance abuse to explain social problems. The Gin Craze has been referred to as the first drug scare of modern Europe (Warner et al., 2001) and has been often compared to the crack epidemic in the USA during the 1980s, involving as it did the sudden and widespread availability of a powerful and cheap intoxicant that wreaked havoc among deprived and vulnerable populations. In fact, it has more in common with periodic upsets over excessive drinking, since the British state sought not to effectively suppress it, or could not do so, but to balance the healthy tax revenues it provided with some demonstration of concern for the public good and an attempt to be at least seen to try and limit the social problems associated with it.

Gin was the drink of the poor, the working class and, what is worse, appeared to be mainly sold to facilitate the attempt to get drunk. Much like crack-cocaine in the 1980s, gin was said to cause working-class men and women to choose it over food and the care of their children, to destroy the maternal instinct, the work ethic and all sense of decency. The increase in gin consumption was due partly to ease of supply, but also to the developing desire among the middle and working classes for luxury products that previously had been the domain of the aristocracy, along with coffee, tea, sugar and tobacco. The increase in supply had been engineered by the Westminster Parliament. Wealthy landowners found themselves with a grain surplus and a labouring population able to command relatively high wages. The production of cheap distilled spirits provided a neat solution to both use up the surplus grain and relieve the workers of their ready cash. From 1689, Parliament manipulated the market to encourage domestic production over foreign imports of gin. As now, the mass-market availability of luxuries that were previously the playground of the elite was narrated as a threat not only to their morals but also to the future of society. In Henry Fielding's words, luxury among the poor amounted to a political evil, dissolving the social order. The working classes were and are regarded as congenitally incapable of coping with plenty, while their social betters are born to it.

The Gin Craze was at its most intensive phase from 1720 to 1751. For most of that time, the levels of gin and other spirits consumed per head were high, although not stupendously so, comparing well for instance to those of colonial and post-Revolutionary America later in the same century (Warner, 2004). Historical catastrophes are always a mirror for ourselves, and attempts have been made to find evidence of modern Foetal Alcohol Syndrome in records of the Gin Craze, although the birth of physically vulnerable children in that period is better explained with reference to prevailing environmental conditions of disease and near-starvation (Abel, 2001). In what became a familiar pattern. Gin came to stand in for the problem of poverty and squalor among the poor of London and the rest of England, as, in the 1980s, heroin in the UK came to stand in for post-industrial decline, rising poverty and disintegration of family life. It enabled members of the ruling elite to condemn not the conditions of the poor's misery but the outlet many chose as relief for that misery, establishing this as a public problem.

Various Gin Acts in the Westminster Parliament were ostensibly introduced to take gin out of the hands of the poor. These were mostly unenforceable and had the effect of turning gin drinking into an act of resistance, against a government that at the time was hardly conspicuous for its legitimacy in the eyes of working-class Britons. The eventual fall in gin consumption had a number of causes, including the loosening of the economic pressures that had driven its rise, the Gin Act of 1743 that reversed the damage caused by previous Gin Acts and made gin drinking seem less of an anti-government activity, and the emergence of a culture of self-regulation. In problematizing intoxication as a societal issue, worthy of some kind of intervention, the reaction to the upsurge in gin consumption laid the ground for the later systematization of addiction and drug abuse as public problems (Quan Nicholls, 2003), detached from their background causes (White, 2003), although, as the era of landowners waned and that of industrialists waxed into the next century, an observer could have been forgiven for thinking the opposite. The British state's unofficial policy was not to prohibit but to encourage the use of a drug to solve an economic dilemma for itself. In this case, the drug was opium and the country was China.

Nineteenth-century political economies of intoxication

It may be argued that the entire rise of the West, from 1500 to 1900, depended on a series of drug trades.

C. A. Trocki, *Opium, Empire, and the Global Political Economy*
(1999: xii)

In moneyed societies, drugs and alcohol become commodities, and at times they have driven commodification and recommodification of places and objects. They are not neutral, contentless objects, with a value defined by supply and demand. There are political, material and symbolic economies of intoxication. The development of the modern ordering of drugs and alcohol is intimately intertwined with state formation, globalization, trade and empire – with political economy, distribution sites of production and places of consumption alongside imperial trade.

The rise of the nation-state and the decline of empires went along with closer control over drugs and their use, which corresponded with concern about the damage done to the national and racial soul by drugs and alcohol. For most of the nineteenth century and before, European empires were relatively sanguine about what we would now call the drug trade. The Spanish initially anathematized coca-leaf chewing until they found that South American Indians could be made to work long days in the silver mines with some coca and little food (Mann, 2000). The British Empire was for part of its history a 'drugs empire', facilitating the trading of drugs around the world.

The first drugs wars were not, as drugs wars today are, wars on and against the production and distribution of drugs, but a war to force the importing of drugs. These were the Opium Wars. In the early nineteenth century, opium was in widespread use in China, with many Chinese being heavy users of it. Although it was illegal, the Chinese government could not stamp out its sale and use. The opium was grown in India, then under British control. The opium trade with China helped balance a huge current account deficit caused by the British addiction to tea, which was then grown mostly in China. China refused payment in anything but silver, the Heavenly Kingdom having no need of the manufactures of the Industrial Revolution. The balance of trade was in deficit, a situation that was anathema to the bookkeepers of Victorian Britain.

By 1838, British traders were importing 14,000 tons of opium into China. Two notable traders (in modern parlance, drug smugglers) were the Scots William Jardine and James Matheson. In 1839, the Chinese government blocked the importing of opium and, when the British refused to stop the trade, blocked all trade with them. Victorian Britain did not take kindly to snubs and restraints on its inalienable right to conduct free-market exchange anywhere in the world, and on terms preferable to it. The traditional imperial instrument for dealing with uppity non-Europeans was physical force. Vastly superior armaments and tactics meant an inevitable defeat for the Chinese. The concentration of power that can be projected by a modern state revealed itself in the Opium Wars, where the British won by superior technology and organizational ability. It was a clash between a highly developed medieval state and a brash modern state. For the Chinese, encountering British combined-ops must have been a similar shock to that experienced by the Native Americans when first experiencing the effects of hard liquor. Another war followed in 1856. The conclusion of the wars led to the ceding of Hong Kong to the British and loss of sovereignty for China. The Scots traders founded Jardine Matheson, now an international conglomerate. The Jardine Matheson website disappointingly makes no mention of this fascinating formative episode in its history and only refers to early trade in tea, coal, metals and machinery.

The focus on the opium trade within the British Empire can obscure other political economies, giving the impression that this was an aberrant period in human history, in which a rapacious and unscrupulous economically driven empire foisted an addicting but profitable drug on a weaker state. The Opium Wars were stark in their cynicism, but that should not obscure the existence of other drug trades that were as extensive and valuable in reshaping global trade, economies and landscapes, and which had an impact on the later development of global drug prohibition. The coffee, tea and sugar trades have been as widespread in their effects on developing and developed worlds, and are much more entrenched as well as legitimate.

These drug trades contributed to the rise of globalization and the political and economic pre-eminence of Western Europe (Courtwright, 2001). Psychoactive commerce provided intoxicants in huge quantities. Drugs became commodified. Their production ceased being for local use and became for sale. This went for wine, spirits, tea, coffee, tobacco, opium and, later, cocaine and cannabis. Global commerce spread the cultivation of intoxicants. Vine-growing and wine-making were taken to the Americas, South Africa and Australia during colonization. Although initially mainly for the benefit of the colonizers, later on the products were exported back to the old world, to Europe. It then sustained those colonies, which otherwise might have been unviable. They may also have contributed to the prevailing political culture in the USA, which came to reject the lush intoxications of old empires.

Social order, status and the lamentation of the object

Modernity means the intensification of human power over the natural world and over ourselves. Intoxication is part of this, with the development of more finely tuned or powerful intoxicants – heroin, cocaine, and the very many psychopharmacological substances – and means for delivery, from old favourites like smoke to pills and needles. The shadow of modernity is a pervasive sense of this power being golem-like. In Jewish legend, a golem was a human-like creature created out of mud and dust by a powerful figure such as a Rabbi. In the hubristic version, the golem takes up more and more power from its creator until it is more powerful than him. Not having a soul, it wreaks havoc and destruction. Rather than having a power for ourselves, we have produced powers over ourselves. This involves imbuing objects with characteristics of secular social problems. In a society organized around the sacred, human misfortune is attributed to capricious gods, evil spirits, witches and failure to make the correct holy observances. Objects and practices that are sacred – oracles, relics, taboos, sacred places – have power over human life and death. In a secular society, human miseries are understood in terms of public problems. They also absorb the characteristics of those problems.

A publishing phenomenon of the past decade or so has been the proliferation of popular history books with the name of a commodity as their title – 'Cod' 'Salt' 'Coal'. Although appearing to be a history of the said object in the world, they often attempt to refract world history through the progress of the object. Histories of drugs like opium and cannabis are not so ambitious, and often lament either the object itself, or the way in which it has been turned to socially destructive uses. In contrast, histories of coffee and tea use the opposing narrative, of initial social suspicion turning to widespread acceptance. Histories of smoking used to follow this pattern, recounting with amusement the outrage of James VI at the habit. Since we are in a period where that practice is being transformed, it will soon join the opiums and amphetamines in being recorded as a once functional, now deadly, and near-dead, drug.

This process is written as one of initial naivety and enthusiasm, such as that of Sigmund Freud for cocaine (Freud, 1885), followed by dreadful realization of the sordid truth. Intoxicants do not appear as the driving force of anything, except a brief period of literary history beginning and ending in the nineteenth century, and even then the story is that the stuff of dreams leaves the authors stuffed. Most cultural histories of intoxicants describe a fall from grace, in which the substance in question becomes the carrier for numerous social problems in modern society, its ceremonies shorn of romance or merriment. The bacchanalian orgy becomes the Friday night binge, and although the rituals of the Bacchae would have given modern pedlars of moral outrage dining-out material for life, that is not included in the roster of alcohol problems.

> The Occasion of which Insufferable *Disaster*, after a serious Enquiry, and Discussion of the Point by the Learned of the *Faculty*, we can Attribute to nothing more than the Excessive use of that Newfangled, Abominable, Heathenish Liquor called *COFFEE*, which Riffling Nature of her Choicest *Treasures*, and *Drying* up the *Radical Moisture*, has so *Eunucht* our Husbands, and *Crippled* our more kind *Gallants*, that they are become as *Impotent*, as Age, and as unfruitful as those *Desarts* whence that unhappy *Berry* is said to be brought. (*Women's Petition Against Coffee*, 1674)

In the early modern period in Britain we can see the development of the idea that a particular substance can be subversive of the social and moral order, that it produces political subversion. Coffee took the function that in later times was ascribed to drugs like LSD and cannabis. James VI closed coffee-houses, which were seen (not without reason) as hotspots of political dissent. The drug, coffee, was an integral part of this. The famous women's petition against coffee lamented the decline of English manhood in the seventeenth-century version of the crack-house.

The novel idea touched on at the time of the *Women's Petition* and the closure of the coffee-houses in England was that an intoxicant could produce a consistent effect in its users, a consistent *moral* effect. Coffee would render the gallants unmanned, and the coffee-house make them into prattling gossips. Later on, smoked opium would be reported as making white women biddable in the clutches of Oriental predators, or cause Javanese men to run *amok* and kill all in their path. The object becomes lamentable.

There is a disconnection emphasized in these accounts between modernity and pre-modern societies. Drug and alcohol use in modern society is described as profane, in contrast to the sacred or semi-sacred use in past times, or currently among primitive cultures untainted by our ways. It is said that intoxication, and in particular hallucinogenic drug use, amongst ancient or primitive societies is a 'cultural practice', with some social, ritual or religious significance, as if intoxicant use in modern societies is not also a social practice. The examples we have that are uncovered by anthropologists are often of this nature, implying that in non-Western, non-modern societies intoxication has a symbolism missing from ours, and that the natives are or were incapable of conceiving intoxication as a pursuit for its own sake. This may be due to the attention paid in many ethnographic studies to ritual, rather than 'technique', and the difficulty of conceiving of intoxication for pleasure existing outside societies that have a concept of separate leisure time.

This duality is most often applied to the history of drinking. In the past, it seems that bucolic peasants quaffed their local brew, roistering merrily in Beer Street. Now, the office or factory worker downs a miserable pint to cope with the alienation of modern working life. This is the 'golden age' of drinking myth, with its narrative of the fall from grace, in which man discovered the nakedness of his artificial paradise; although the narrative runs in reverse (Roth, 2004). Rather than man being expelled from Eden into the outer darkness, it was paradise that changed. It was not man's knowledge of himself that caused God's wrath to fall upon him, but rather his knowledge of paradise, or what it had become, a fragmented, urbanized, alienated, anomic society in which men served the rhythms of machines and bureaucracies. This narrative of the fall serves as a counterpoint to the established Christian story of the fall from paradise. It was not we who failed God, but God who betrayed us, by failing to keep paradise up to trim. It is a secular tale of loss. The fall is hardest in those substances that were once cures for the ills of modern life, like opium, which promised much but became the source of a new drug scourge, that of overwhelming, all-consuming habit, or addiction as it came to be known.

Opium: the fall of the Flaunting Blossom

A certain surgeon always took some opium and gave of it likewise to his patient, when he had any considerable operation to perform, but I must

own, that a glass of generous wine had always a better effect upon me,
when I wanted to excite courage.

George Young, *A Treatise on Opium, Founded Upon Practical
Observations* (1753: 103)

Opium is derived from the resin of the opium poppy, *papaver som-
niferum*, which is refined and processed into, among other things,
morphine, codeine and heroin. Opium is the drug of the imagination
in Western eyes. Its name conjures up images of sultry opium dens,
English aristocratic outsiders puffing poetry and prose, and exotic
vices. These images of the drug are produced from the nineteenth
century onwards, and mostly occur in Western mythology and
demonology, which is both excited and repulsed by the images it
evokes. Before then it was largely known around the world as a medicinal drug. Opium is also so much *the* drug in historical accounts, the
first and only drug of choice. It easily passes from the agrarian world
to the chemical-industrial one, revealing its secret essence as it does
so. It can seem like other drugs are mere adjuncts to it, interesting
sidebars to the main course – and what a main course it is. From the
delights of de Quincey, to the tortures of Coleridge, philosophy and
poetry feed on it. Coca is too prosaic, cocaine came too late and alcohol
is too ubiquitous. Opium has obtained for itself the right mix of exoti-
cism and transgression, which covers up its mundane existence.

It has been in long-term use as a painkiller, ever since ancient
times. Accounts of the eighteenth-century use of opium place it fairly
and squarely as a tonic to help you throughout the day. The preface to
George Young's *A Treatise on Opium* scorns the use of opium by well-
meaning ladies and officious and ignorant nurses, 'pretending to
practice' and giving it out to any patient willy-nilly. The book notes
depression following use of opium giving a 'flow of spirits'. It also
notes a case of a patient resuming use of opium 'before the usual
time' to allay a depression brought on following an opium high, a
seeming case of withdrawal symptoms. However, there is no addiction narrative within which this would be placed by a modern writer.
This is seen purely as an attempt to ameliorate the lowness of spirits
following the previous high, rather than an addiction, a dependence
upon the substance itself. With reference to 'phthisis pulmonalis', a
fatal disease:

> Whereas the people of rank, who must have something prescribed for
> every ailment, and believe that we have a cure for every symptom, grow
> impatient if the physician does not abate their cough, and give them some

rest in the night. Opium, and nothing but opium, will do this; they take it in many different shapes, and find it of service in making them cough less and sleep more; therefore they continue it, become slaves to it. (Young 1753: 98)

Again, this is not presented as shameful addiction, but a somewhat unfortunate feature of social life. The poor, he goes on to say, cannot afford opium and die with their senses intact, although presumably without the benefit of a good night's sleep. There is no sense in the book of opium producing dependence in the patients. There is no sense of it being used outside medicine except as self-medication, and not as a recreational drug. Discussing habitual, apparently addict-like, use of opium, he largely sees this in a positive light as enhancing the efficacy of it as a medicine. He states that Turks are accustomed to take opium habitually, and that this is a good thing. They get the benefit but do not suffer from its soporific effects, because their habituation to it protects them.

Opium was queen of the healer's kit bag for centuries. In antiquity it was not universally used or referred to in medical texts. There was a long-running debate about its possible dangers and many were reluctant to prescribe it, which Pliny quotes from in his *Natural History*. Seventeenth-century doctor Thomas Sydenham promoted opium for use in smallpox cases, as well as laudanum, a tincture of opium in alcohol. Opium slipped out of the hands of medicine, though, in the nineteenth century coming into widespread use as an intoxicant, smoked or taken as laudanum, a favourite of Coleridge. Byron and Charles Dickens were also users. Laudanum was closely linked with the Romantic movement. Opium became an imaginative drug, which augmented and freed the imagination. It was fine for the upper-class dilettante, but not for the working classes (Berridge and Edwards, 1981).

There was a canary in the coal mine. Political conflict in Britain over the opium trade came before and in apparent contrast to later racialization. An article on opium dens, 'Opium Smoking at the East End of London', in the *Daily News* of 1864 contrasted the relative calm of a Chinese-run opium den with the 'white squalor' outside in the rest of the East End. Opium was preferable to alcohol. It portrays the clients as having a long relationship to the owner, who they pay on a regular basis. It is largely a positive portrayal, without the racist demonology of the corrupting Chinamen that is more apparent in US and Australian accounts from later in the nineteenth century.

Hartmann Henry Sultzberger (ed.) published *All About Opium* in 1884. The book is a collection of writings by a 'trader' in opium, intended as a riposte to the activities of the Society for the Suppression of the Opium Trade, which appears to have got the author rattled. The editor includes four articles on the opium pipe and smoking. Much of the objections to opium at the time were located around pipes, dens and smoking; these and the use of opium as a leisure habit associated with the Chinese. He also plays it off against the much more dangerous intravenous use of morphine.

> It is equally incontrovertible that thousands of hardworking people are indebted to opium smoking for the continuance of lives agreeable to themselves and useful to society. ('A Defence of Opium Smoking', *Pall Mall Gazette*, 13 November 1879)

Condemnation and defence of the opium habit itself centred around observations of opium smoking. The luxuriant practice of smoking – as opposed to dependence on the drug through eating or drinking – drew condemnation from Victorian commentators. Rev. James Johnston, commenting on the Chinese opium trade, represents smoking as being innately immoral and degrading as it is pursued purely for pleasure, and hence is a 'vicious vice' (Johnston, 1858).

Commentators were more ready to allow for the legitimacy of addiction arising through medical use, usually through drinking or eating; iatrogenic addiction drew sympathy because of who was addicted and how. In William Rosser Cobbe's memoir of his opium habit he also says that pipe smokers are a separate breed among opium habitués, because they choose the vice rather than having it thrust upon them by pain or being 'tied hand and foot by the physician'. Pipe smokers are morally depraved because they choose their vice (Cobbe, 1895). According to a Dr Little, Medical Superintendent in Singapore: 'Many drink, but do not abuse it; many smoke opium, but all abuse it', quoted in M'laren, 1860). Seeking to be intoxicated is abuse and, with opium smoking, the only purpose can be the seeking of insensate intoxication. This is repeated in Joshua Rowntree's *The Opium Habit in the East* (Rowntree, 1895). Sir George Birdwood, in a letter to *The Times* in 1881, argues in favour of smoking as a harmless indulgence, unlike eating and drinking of it.

> The Rajpoots are always taking these paregoric [camphorated tincture of opium] draughts from morning to night. But they are robust and active, constantly in the open air, and, as a rule, suffer no more from their immoderate potations of *kusoomba* than healthy country folk in England

from sound ale, or Tartars from *koumis*, certainly not so much as 'Glasgow bodies' from whisky, or Londoners from gin. (George Birdwood, letter to *The Times*, 26 December 1881)

One medical text praising the opium pipe as a good method of medicinal self-administration was that of Herbert Snow, but he seems to have been rare in making this judgement (Snow, 1890).

Discussions of the opium habit retained some separation from those of alcohol in the Victorian era. The opium smoker is distinguished from the alcohol drinker; the drinker commits crimes while intoxicated, and the intoxication itself is the cause of social disorder. Opium intoxication is quiescent, though – crime is committed to supply the means for obtaining more opium. They do not, in earlier works at least, seem to see a necessary connection between the two.

Opium came to be separated from alcohol because of its creeping racialization in Britain, the USA and Australia into the early twentieth century (Manderson, 1997). This description of an opium den, from 1850 precedes the establishment of opium as part of a racial threat:

> Nothing on earth can equal the apparent quiet enjoyment of the opium smokers. As he enters the miserable scene of his future ecstasy . . . he reclines on a board covered with a mat, and, with his head resting on a wooden or bamboo pillow, he commences filling his pipe. As he entered, his looks were the picture of misery, his eyes were sunk, his gait slouched, his step trembling, and his voice quivering, with a sallow cast of countenance and a dull, unimpressive eye . . . But now, with pipe in hand, opium by his side, and a lamp before him, his eye already glistens. . . (Robert Little, 1850: 5)

He goes on to describe the method of smoking, holding the smoke in the lungs, 'grudging the loss of each successive fume as he exhales' then he notes how the smoker lies in bliss at the prospect of his coming pleasure 'for not until a third or a fourth whiff do feelings of positive pleasure arise'. Little has begun to formulate a concept of addiction and withdrawal, saying that the opium smoker goes through the most horrendous pains if denied a fix.

> Scarcely a village or hamlet [in the USA] is to be excepted as unrepresented by its two classes of inebriates, the devotees to alcoholics and the more miserable slaves to opium. (Alonso Calkins, 1871)

Alonso Calkins attributes more deaths to opium than to alcohol. He is vehemently anti-'narcotic' and the 'morbid craving' for narcotic stimuli 'floated to our shores from the lands of the prolific orient' (Calkins, 1871: 20). He describes many cases of addiction, and notes the legendary longevity of the opium eater according to various sources which record no contraction in life expectancy from opium use. This was the beginning of a profound change in the way drunkards, laudanum drinkers and other opiate users saw themselves and others saw them. Opiate use came under the rubric of medicine as an addiction, and under that of insurance as a risk.

The trial of the insurances of the Earl of Mar revolved around the question of whether the opium habit shortens life. The Earl of Mar died in 1828, having consumed 3.2 grams of raw opium per day. The Edinburgh Life Assurance company refused to pay out on its policy as he was 'addicted to the vice of opium-eating in a degree calculated to shorten life'. Doctors were called by his estate to testify that opium use does not shorten life. Robert Christison, of the University of Edinburgh, was commissioned to investigate this and in 1832 reported in the *Edinburgh Medical and Surgical Journal*, using a small sample of opium users, that there is not enough evidence to convince him that opium use shortens life. He defended his position as having been called in support of the above argument. The object of the opium smoker is 'to make himself, not unfit, but fit, for society'. Opium came to be defined as a risky object through the calculations of insurance actuaries (Bull, 2002). In contemporary society we are used to defining everyday experiences through the lens of risk, but this was novel at the time. Dangers were no longer acts of God, but manageable, calculable, avoidable threats to life – which then became something to be managed and calculated, if not avoided. In spite of the failure of this attempt to pin the blame on opium, it and other drugs became population risks in insurance-like terms, thus legitimating government control of substances and population risk behaviour.

Apothecaries, medicine and medicalization

> A certain portion [of excitability] is assigned to every being.
> John Brown, *The Elements of Medicine* (1795 [1780]: 7)

Heroin injection appears like a nightmarish version of a medical procedure. The user pumps the arm to find a vein, injects a little of the contents of the syringe, pulls the plunger out to mix the blood in, then pushes it back into the vein. It appears this way because that is exactly what it is. Intravenous use is a technique derived from medicine, which was designed to deliver a drug as quickly and efficiently as possible. The science and technology of medicine intermeshes with drug use. Recreational drugs often began life in the medicine cabinet.

Several of today's illicit drugs were developed or popularized in the West as medicines – heroin, opium, cocaine and amphetamines, to take four – and medicine has been a powerful force for the control of drugs and alcohol, and for creating subject narratives such as those of addiction and risk, delineating the boundaries of the drug problem.

Opium was a gift from God for doctors, and was described as such. Here at last was something that would most definitely work in relieving all kinds of pain. Although mostly described in medicinal terms, for some it was valued for its ability to open the way for dreams and pleasures. It unlocked the senses, the box of delights. Many writers described how it altered perceptions and sensations.

Cocaine introduces us to the next stage in the life of intoxicants: those that were made and marketed as cures for modern life, as a medication for the soul. Most illicit drugs are entirely products of modern society, developed to deal with or address some of the problems of life in modern society, such as morphine and then heroin, both casualties of previous drug epidemics. In the case of cocaine, it was intended to alleviate enervation or enforced boredom that in the late nineteenth century were seen as the side effects of modern urban life.

Robert Christison's *Observations on the Effects of Coca or Cuca* was generally enthusiastic about coca as able to get rid of all fatigue.

> Nowhere does the author of the 'Royal Commentaries of the Yncas' [by Garcillaso de la Vega, 1609–17] say one word of any evil consequences actually resulting from the use of this vegetable becoming a habit. (Robert Christison, 1876: 5)

This was not a universal view. A later writer (Poppig, 1835) takes a different view, based on observation of indigenous South American life. The 'Indians' had to interrupt work several times a day for placid chewing. Those who were habituated abandoned society for a life in pursuit of the weed, becoming irredeemable *coqueros*. Coca, he implies, is like drinking for the Europeans or opium smoking for the Chinese – each race has its own vice. Christison himself did not consider it to be a vice, but rather a great potential aid to human endurance, which prejudice and ignorance has kept Europeans from adopting. Christison noted that specimens of coca leaf brought to Europe had been found to yield a 'crystalline principle, which physiologically possesses no mean activity as a narcotic' (p. 11). His pamphlet contains the common 'miracle description' found in the early writings of Sigmund Freud and in other accounts of the time, of the exertions made possible and the fatigues banished by the use of coca. He chews some leaves at the top of Ben Vorlich instead of having lunch, and finds his fatigue gone, the strength of youth reawakened.

Cocaine was synthesized in 1860 from the coca leaf. It sparked fascination amongst the middle class of Western society. Sigmund Freud, psychoanalyst, was an avid user and distributed it liberally to friends and patients. The medical profession was interested in it as a therapeutic drug, for drug addiction, alcoholism, depression, and as an anaesthetic. In the last decades of the nineteenth century, 'patent medicines' – over-the-counter remedies for anything that could be wrong with your life – were brought on the market as 'tonics' and 'stimulants' and contained cocaine as a vital ingredient. Coca-cola was originally marketed as a patent medicine and contained traces of cocaine (hence coca). Cocaine was one of the leading products of a rapidly growing pharmaceutical industry that would research, produce and market new drugs or new uses for drugs already in existence.

Why did cocaine become such a central drug of late nineteenth-century modernity, rather than, for instance, betel, the coca leaf or khat? It was a combination of the availability of the coca leaf, its sudden release from the social hierarchy of the Incas when that civilization was comprehensively smashed by the conquistadores, and its usefulness for the Spanish who found that Indians would work for days in the silver mines without other sustenance. It was inserted directly into the colonial economy, in a way that khat never was. Yet this only made its way back to Europe in the mid- to late nineteenth century, with the creation of Vin Mariani. Cocaine did not have the slovenly associations of betel or coca chewing, such as dribbled saliva. It might be argued that cocaine was a wholly colonized drug. It emerged out of a part of the globe where the indigenous civilization had been comprehensively smashed. It might have changed the way the plant is seen – as a crop to be exploited, rather than a habit of the natives not to be mimicked by the white man. It provided a fillip for the middle classes' newfound temperance and distaste for public drinking.

Temperance, Prohibition and the symbolic order of things

Eras of anti- and pro-alcohol sentiment alternate at intervals of about a lifetime.

David F. Musto, *Drugs in America: A Documentary History* (2002: 7)

Prohibition, the outlawing of most kinds of alcohol production in the USA between 1920 and 1933, is mainly remembered, and mostly misremembered, for its speakeasies, violent gangsters and their glamorous molls. Historically, drugs and alcohol control have run along three dimensions – regulatory categories, taxes and sanctions (Courtwright, 2003). In fact, few regimes are completely prohibition-ist. Even capital-P Prohibition in the USA allowed for the exception of communion wine and alcohol on prescription. Prohibition of all intox-icants is unusual, but not unheard of by any means.

The focus on Prohibition in the USA seems to have led us to think that the USA is somehow uniquely puritanical. In fact, Iceland had Prohibition from 1915 to 1922, and Finland from 1919 to 1932, without the romantic gangster culture of the USA. Tsar Nicholas II of Russia decreed Prohibition in 1914, just prior to the outbreak of the First World War. This destroyed a major source of government revenue, the consequences of which eventually contributed to the rev-olutionary overthrow of the regime (Schrad, 2006). Canada and Norway implemented partial Prohibition. Sweden came within a whisker in a 1922 referendum. The Nordic Socialist parties decried alcohol and a political ethic of socialist sobriety took hold here. Swedish Social Democrats still incline towards temperance in their party programme. Nordic temperance and alcohol control is much more of a live topic of political debate than in Britain. Saudi Arabia, Kuwait and Qatar cur-rently have alcohol bans in place.

The gradual regulation of drugs in Britain had begun with opium, the 1868 Pharmacy Act restricting its sale to pharmacists, although products with opium in them – patent medicines – were still available with no questions asked. Some substances, chiefly opium and cocaine, began to be defined as public problems on the grounds that they were making otherwise bright-eyed and productive upstanding young Britons and Americans into maddened fiends; that they threat-ened the purity of the race because cocaine-addicted white women were being fed into the clutches of black dealers.

Take cocaine at the start of the twentieth century: like other drugs, it was seen as a problem for some vulnerable people. Things began to change when it started to be viewed as a problem for society as well. It came to symbolize – as public anger and panic about drug use has ever since – the pains of social change, and the fear of a generation growing up without moral leadership or certainty. Opium and cocaine were the 'assassins of youth'. There was a racial element here: opium associ-ated with the Chinese; cocaine with black people. Drug problems were less and less viewed as problems of individual addiction, but as part of the public problem of immorality, vice and criminality.

Between 1909 and 1926 laissez-faire was brought to an end, and legislation was introduced to progressively control and restrict specific intoxicating substances. International controls on the opium trade were agreed in 1914. The Dangerous Drugs Act of 1920 and 1923, updated over the years, formed the groundwork, and has been amended at various times since to take into account new drugs. This long process was the construction of the worldwide drug problem.

Drug scenes

> They're selling hippy wigs in Woolworths man. The greatest decade in the history of mankind is over.
> 'Danny', *Withnail and I* (Bruce Robinson, Handmade Films, 1987)

The emergence of the 'drug problem' was reinforced by the appearance of drug scenes, consciously set apart from the leisure activities enjoyed by the rest of society. The existence of drug scenes – settings where drugs other than alcohol are used in a determinedly recreational manner – came about in the 1890s (Berridge, 1988). Here we can see both the origin of drugs subcultures and their form. There was a new aesthetics that emphasized sensation and inner consciousness. This was the ancestor of drugs as a 'youth problem' and also as a public problem. To some extent, then, the emergence of 'drugs' as a category was driven by these subcultures hungry for new sensations and forms of intoxication. It was already a youth problem by the 1910s, but perhaps without the specific concept of youth as something dangerous, rather than vulnerable, that emerged with the creation of the 'teenager'.

The 1960s brought increased drug use, with new or rediscovered drugs, and the emergence of youth movements promising to shake the foundations of Western society. The population of drug users and addicts changed – becoming younger, both middle and working class. Now drug users were criminalized rather than medically treated. Maintenance – prescribing heroin to registered addicts – was ended. Both 'problem' use – however defined – and recreational use among young people were on the increase. It was at this time that 'youth' began to be seen as a distinct period of life with its own habits and cultures – and became a market of ever-growing lucrativeness. New drugs became associated with youth, especially LSD, amphetamines and cannabis. LSD gave birth to a style, psychedelia, which was supposedly representative of its effect. Illicit drugs and their cultural associations again became influential in mainstream culture, with psychedelia influencing art and film imagery.

Youth culture spawned whole new industries based around serving the tastes and desires of the affluent generation. This new taste for experience became mainstream in the late 1980s, when it generated a new drugwise club culture, that of rave, which fed into the drug-normalized youth culture of the late twentieth and early twenty-first centuries (Measham et al., 1994; Measham et al., 1998; Parker et al., 2002). The existence of drug scenes, or a drug scene, are less relevant to understanding illicit drug use, given how widespread illicit drug use is now across classes, contexts and, within limits, age groups. It is more illuminating to examine the way in which drugs are used and what they are used for. Caitlin Notley identifies archetypal users, realists, searchers, and traders among adult non-problem users (Notley, 2005). Archetypal users take mainly cannabis, stemming from a past life as members of drug-using subcultures. Realists mainly use cannabis but are more likely than archetypal users to take dance drugs as well. They use drugs in a normalized, rationalist way, weighing up costs and benefits, and emphasize controlled use. Searchers are more like the idealists of the 1960s and the upper-class opium smokers of the late Victorian period, seeing drug use as part of an experiential journey. Traders see themselves as players, immersed in the illicit operations of the drug market, vaunting their independence and disdain for other drug users.

Conclusion

What is the link between the Chinese mandarin reclining on a couch with his opium pipe and the user lying on a mattress in a cold flat injecting a toxic mixture of heroin and a variety of adulterants into a vein? That they are using a substance originating from the same plant? That they are reviled by some as representing the depths to which humanity and dignity will be abandoned in the pursuit of intoxication? Maybe there is no link and perhaps we are wrong-headed to seek one. Although there are tempting parallels between past eras and the present, they often seem trite or limiting. It can be said, however, that the heroin addict in a council flat in Manchester is the inheritor of nineteenth-century tracts decrying the Oriental opium habit, and the long march towards international prohibition. In every substance we can taste the traces of history; the long, careful breeding of intoxicating plants through selection; the tipping point that was the development of distillation; the trading empires that grew from a few ships bearing cargoes of exotic spices and plants over thousands of miles of ocean swell; the advances in human control over chemistry at a molecular level, driven by the hothouse industries of a young country demanding its place in the sun. At each period an observer might think that humanity has scaled the heights of intoxication, but then we find ourselves to be in the foothills.

3 Customs, Cultures and the Experience of Intoxication

I walk down the main street on the way to the Ballroom. Town is full of groups of drunks trying to pick fights, students trying to avoid them, and taxis strangely absent of passengers but intent on running down anyone who strays into the road. I deftly dodge the small puddles of vomit that had begun to accumulate on the pavement, and head down the small side street off the main road in which stood the Ballroom, formerly Club Paradiso, formerly the Torture Garden, formerly Venus, all the way back to 1930 when it was the Crystal Ballroom, its slogan, 'freaks, perverts and weirdos'. There's a certain edge to tonight. I feel a bit weird going to a club on my own, like one of those old guys who sits in the same place in my local bar every night, talking to no one. I wonder what they come in for. They don't appear to be waiting for someone to make conversation, they seem quite happy just to sit there. Occasionally they say something to the barman, or watch the TV if there's football on. Maybe they are listening for the sound of one hand clapping. Zen masters of the ancient art of balancing on a bar stool and ignoring everyone else.

The Ballroom nightclub sits in a part of town slowly returning to swampland, its presence signalled by the thumping bass soaked up in the humid night. Sweat builds under my shirt. I slip two E's in the queue before nodding at the bouncer and going into the club's dim entrance. The humidity, drunken lairiness and gloaming outside are like a crisp day in an Arctic summer compared with the wet gloom inside, steam rising from the sweat of a thousand pulsating bodies. I feel a sudden, sharp change of perspective, as I start to come up. My body tenses as I hold the feeling in check. Pushing forward, I melt into the crowd. People move out of my way as I go towards the stage. Light, heat and noise orchestrate my mind and body. I let the dam burst. Every sensation is a good one now. I touch hands with others, men and women, hugging, smiling, one moment of being that excludes all others.

Remote control for the soul

> [. . .] I was once walking in the broad daylight of a summer afternoon in the full possession of hasheesh delirium. For an hour the tremendous expansion of all visible things had been growing toward its height; it now reached it, and to the fullest extent I realized the infinity of space. Vistas no longer converged, sight met no barrier; the world was horizonless, for earth and sky stretched endlessly onward in parallel planes.
>
> Fitz Hugh Ludlow, 'The Apocalypse of Hasheesh', *Putnam's Monthly* (1856, 8: 48)

A few famous attempts have been made to describe the effect of opiates and – less frequently, cannabis – in print, for instance, in Thomas de Quincey's *Confessions of an Opium-Eater*, and Fitz Hugh Ludlow's *Apocalypse of Hasheesh*, quoted above. There is a rather larger body of literature that was created by writers who wrote from their experiences with opium and cocaine in one way or another, such as Samuel Taylor Coleridge's *Kublai Khan* or Sir Walter Scott's *Bride of Lammermoor*. Perhaps reflecting its more mundane status, alcohol has tended to produce reflections on its external effects and changes in behaviour towards others, rather than on internal states, as well as longer, often autobiographical, pieces reflecting on its ills, maudlin sentiment, and the rest of the less flattering end of the range of alcohol-induced emotions. There are two difficulties in constructing some idea of what various intoxications are like, and what makes them like that. One is that so many illicit drug experiences are represented as being exotic, out of this world, as in Ludlow's account, and that alcohol attracts a better class of writer. The other is that alcohol-influenced experiences have the appearance, to a Westerner at least, of being wholly mundane or trivial. Western societies lack a language for drunken intoxication, although they have many words for it, mainly reflecting the supposed disinhibiting nature of alcohol.

A positive language for drug-induced intoxication has been confined to rather outré literary reflections by unreliable interlocutors on opium and cannabis. There is an extensive scientific and policy discourse about problems and damaging side effects of intoxication, which revisits descriptions of states of intoxication, except negatively (in terms of loss of control, inhibition, judgement, coordination and so on). It is mainly in anthropology and symbolic interactionist sociology that we find accounts examining the positive uses of intoxication and the positive steps taken towards achieving states of intoxication. This body of work includes research into how the experience of intoxication is shaped and learnt in local contexts, that looks at, for instance, the cultural shaping of drunkenness, and the learnt effects of cannabis highs. War stories and travellers' tales from the land of opium are beguiling in their outlandishness but detract from our understanding of the more widespread everyday experiences and uses of intoxication. A privileged Victorian gentleman throwing himself towards the extremities of mental experience in opium or cannabis, and returning with tales of the dark side of the moon, will have a very different attitude to his drug of choice than a prostitute using the same drug to numb herself to the cold hours she spends with clients like him. Celebrity dope fiends and abject yet articulate addicts make good copy. They are familiar narratives, endlessly regurgitated in political and media commentary, and in film and literature. Most experiences with psychoactive substances are nothing like that, however. What these images do is to reproduce the idea that illicit drugs, and tobacco and alcohol, are devices that consistently produce the same effects, be they good or bad, in different individuals.

Were you drunk at the weekend? Did you get a bit tipsy, queasy, roaring or catatonic drunk? Or all of them in sequence? If so, how did you get drunk? The answer most people would give, is 'By drinking a lot', or 'By drinking more than I should have'. This is black box pharmacology, in the technological sense of a system whose workings are hidden and in which certain inputs produce predictable outputs. In this case, humans are the black box. The chemicals go in, and the effects come out, like winding up a clockwork toy and setting it to run across the floor, banging into furniture as it goes. The folk knowledge among users about what substances 'do' is in practice a lot more sophisticated than this. LSD users, for instance, recognize the subtle effects of environment and mood that can produce radically different hallucinogenic experiences. It is the simpler version that is reproduced in policy and scientific understandings. Their central conceit is that the effects of psychoactive substances are contained within their chemical structure, and that includes not just physical but also behavioural, social and moral effects. This is reflected in academic and policy terminology where, for example, alcohol consumption is said to have 'caused' such ills as poverty, murder and robbery (Williams and Brake, 1980: 3), and, more recently, terrorism and sexual violence.

This is the biopharmacological self. Many of the mechanisms through which substances work to induce changes in behaviour have been discovered and described. In different instances, smoking tobacco introduces nicotine into the blood, which rapidly crosses the blood–brain barrier and activates the nicotine receptors there and in other parts of the nervous system, raising levels of the neurotransmitter dopamine. It increases heart rate, blood pressure, alertness and memory. The MDMA or similar chemical in an ecstasy pill releases serotonin into the brain's synapses, which has the effect of creating a sense of elation and exhilaration. Heroin, like other opiates, mimics the action of the body's endorphins, and binds to the opioid receptors, tissue to which chemicals bind and thus change brain activity, such chemicals being present in the brain, and also in the gastrointestinal tract and spinal cord. In non-habituated, but not first-time, users it induces a rush of intense euphoria. Cocaine, like nicotine, increases dopamine levels, and hugely stimulates the central nervous system. The user experiences a rush of energy and a sense of self-confidence. Cannabis contains delta^9-tetrahydrocannabinol (THC), the most psychoactive of the sixty or so cannabinoids present in the cannabis plant. Like opiates, it is an agonist for particular receptors, in this case, cannabinoid receptors. The user feels a sense of relaxation and well-being. The biopharmacological view of how drugs and alcohol function and what makes them pleasurable is that the active chemicals they contain alter brain functions, and that these register in the mind as being tipsy, loved-up, aggressive, and so on.

In chapter 2, I mentioned the historical narrative of an ever more finely tuned understanding of what drugs do. That is it. These findings are illustrated by the very popular presentations of 'brain slice' graphics that show sections of the brain lighting up or going dark under the influence of drugs (see chapter 4). However, the implications of these processes are much fuzzier than the mechanical representation of them would imply.

It appears at first to be eminently commonsensical, not least to those canny souls who can be seen in off-licences and liquor stores carefully weighing up the comparative price/alcohol ratio of various wines, beers and spirits before making their purchase, as if the other constituents of the drinks were just by-products or pollutants in an alcohol delivery mechanism. Following on from that, drug and alcohol problems are seen to result from overindulgence, or surrendering the self to the substance. Everyone has a limit, which is zero for some people and some substances; everyone should know their limits, and problems begin when that limit is breached. The hangover, the overdose, and the white-out, are the payback for having had too much of a good thing.

Those same systems that deliver the drug and push our mental buttons also ensure we pay a physical and mental price for our fun.

Some of these substances generate dependence and withdrawal symptoms when the user is denied them or chooses to relinquish the chemical crutch. A payback is also demanded following excess use. The moral economy of intoxication is at work, and every pleasure has its price. Some readers will be familiar with the exquisite torture of an alcohol hangover. Ecstasy users often experience a midweek comedown following weekend use of the drug, which leaves them feeling drained and emotionally vulnerable. Cocaine users undergo rapid onset of depression and the slough of despond, which can last for days after heavy ingestion. Heroin withdrawal has its own well-documented horrors, although it takes some time to build up dependence and so generate withdrawal symptoms, contrary to accepted wisdom.

In essence, the drug carries the user on a trip, which they cannot control. They buy their ticket, but after that the drug decides on the ride. This black-box perspective is limiting, not only in the sense of its workings being opaque to human control, but also in the assumption that inputs produce expected outputs, which have little to do with the actions of the people involved. This chapter will examine the evidence that suggests psychoactive drugs are not black boxes of the soul, looking at the social factors shaping intoxication. Two common themes are that most psychoactive substances cause disinhibition and/or sensual and perceptual distortion. Alcohol is the particular stock-in-trade of many of these narratives because a strong folk narrative has built up around it, that of disinhibition.

Alcoholic disinhibition and status transition

The culturally loaded definition of alcohol as a substance that disinhibits is reflected in common English language phrases like being 'out of one's tree' when drunk, and the ever-repeated stories of drunken antics passed around by friends and dined out on by acquaintances that make up part of a good night out for many. This is more scientifically presented as impairment of the 'higher brain functions', the ego, or the reasoning self. It is as if the brain possesses a governor circuit which ethyl alcohol interferes with, reducing the individual to a set of uncontrolled impulses. Alcohol is a substance with the power to cut away the bonds of civilization that hold baser, animal desires in check, rendering individuals myopic towards the consequences of their actions.

Disinhibition may involve disregarding of restraints around sexuality, of norms keeping apart distinct categories of people, situations or objects, or the use of violence. In the case of the biblical story of Lot and his daughters in Genesis, alcohol allows for the violation of the incest taboo. Thinking themselves the only human beings left alive following the divine devastation of Sodom and Gomorrah, Lot's two daughters get their father drunk and have sex with him. The next day, he has forgotten what has happened. They then bear his children. Common regulations on drinking in Western societies reflect these assumptions about what it does. Alcohol in public spaces is monitored and governed. Some United States jurisdictions ban the possession of an open container with alcohol in it in a public place. In many states it is a crime to be or appear to be intoxicated in public. Public drinking is in some circumstances associated with public disorder. Yet the association is oddly inconsistent. Drinking in a beer garden, or a permitted street festival, or a Catholic church service, renders the practice acceptable.

That suggests that there is no such thing as a blanket disinhibition caused by alcohol, which we might expect to happen from this vision of alcohol as gumming up the brain's brake fluid. The form that disinhibitions take is always specific to the situation, if the situation allows for it at all. Anthropological evidence indicates that many taboos – the incest taboo being one, unlike Lot's story – usually remain in place whatever the supposed disinhibiting properties of alcohol may be, as will be seen later on. Those taboos that are broken tend to be broken in a socially acceptable, carefully defined manner. Drinking and collective raucousness commonly go together in the USA, Britain and Finland, but this is not a case of too much fuel in the fire. Alcoholic disinhibition can be used deliberately and creatively to facilitate the fulfilment of a social role, as when young men demonstrate the ability to engage in violent, confrontational masculinity. In other cultures, the associations and uses of drinking and drunkenness run in very different directions.

Despite its limitations, the notion of alcoholized disinhibition is useful because it indicates that being intoxicated often involves a transition between social roles, or a modification of social status. One of the attractions of drinking in Western cultures is its appearance of flattening status hierarchies, for instance, by rendering ugly people attractive, dull people witty and shy people gregarious, even if only in their own eyes. More importantly, drinking situations are supposed to temporarily suspend social hierarchies, such as those of boss and employee. Behaviour that is not endorsable when sober will be excused or celebrated when drunk. Like the Shakespearean jester, the drunk may take advantage of his or her temporary role-suspension to make statements that are normally unsayable, and will be forgiven this transgression. Disinhibition therefore implies a surprising clarity – of purpose, desire, and intent – from which the shackles are taken. Distortion is also an effect of intoxication, yet it implies the opposite – a lack of clarity, a sensual and psychic befuddlement.

Sensual distortion and monstrous enhancement

> It has also been conjectured that Van Gogh abused digitalis (which was used at this time in the treatment of epilepsy); toxic levels of this drug cause a disturbance of colour vision, which might account for the artist's preference for yellow, beige and ochre.
>
> J.-C. Sournia, *A History of Alcoholism* (1990: 86)

Jean-Charles Sournia drops the hypothesis into *A History of Alcoholism* that Van Gogh's unique use of colour might have been due to the effect of his heavy use of digitalis. Digitalis was used at the time to treat mania and epilepsy. Van Gogh's doctor may have prescribed it to him in heavy quantities. Its use could have led to the condition of xanthopsia, which gives a yellow tinge to vision, and coronas, which cause the sufferer to perceive halos around light sources (Lee, 1981). Given his use of blue in his work, which should not be common in a painter with xanthopsia, this retrospective diagnosis is far from certain. The list of possible disorders Van Gogh could have suffered from is a long one, including sexually transmitted diseases, temporal lobe epilepsy, Meniere's disease, alcohol poisoning, and various mental illnesses, in which xanthopsia must fight for a place. Some analysts of the painter's work and life ascribe aspects of his work to these other conditions (Blumer, 2002). Eagerness to impute Van Gogh's possible digitalis use to abuse, and his use of colour in some paintings to the consequences of that, reflects another dominant conception of intoxication in Western societies, as consisting of distortion, as well as our contemporary lens for viewing eccentric or abnormal behaviour as symptoms of pathology. Presumably, a healthy Van Gogh would have been a figurative realist painter.

Drinkers in Anglo-Saxon societies in particular are familiar with the notion that the experience of intoxication means encountering various perceptual distortions. 'Beer goggles' is a slang term for the common experience in which potential intimates become more attractive the drunker the observer is, often inviting rueful reflections on the morning after by both parties. Beer goggles are now more than a metaphor. A

United States company, Drunkbusters, produces 'Impairment Goggles' to simulate the effects of alcohol intoxication. The goggles create powerful distortions of visual perception. The wearer experiences double vision, false-depth perception, and blurring of small details such as letters, so that the wearer is required to approach objects and other people slowly to be sure as to their identity and exact location. The goggles are used to demonstrate the effects of alcohol consumption on driving ability, and in sex education. The intention is to demonstrate how badly a primary perceptual faculty is affected by alcohol, and how this impairs one's other abilities. For instance, putting on a condom while drunk becomes very difficult. The drunk person expends time and effort in (over)compensation for their impaired abilities, while insisting that everything is fine.

The beer goggles, in both literal and metaphorical form, encapsulate the understanding that intoxication, especially alcoholic intoxication, equals sensual distortion leading to impairment. It distorts perception, memory, reason and judgement. There is a distinction between distortion and disinhibition. The former relies on an idea of the self as a driver in the body. Alcohol throws oil on the tyres and mud on the windscreen. The latter suggest that the self is a balance of forces in the mind which intoxication throws off, allowing some that are normally controlled to come to the fore.

A commonly experienced distortion is alcohol-induced myopia, as it is called, in which alcohol intoxication reduces the effect of factors outside the drinker's immediate environment, past, present and future, whether relationships, anxieties, work worries and other influences. For instance, the future prospect of a hangover in the morning tends to diminish the more one drinks, as does the memory of past hangovers. The moment is made all. There is a double meaning to this, though. 'Myopia' meant in this sense can be an enhancement. In other contexts we are expected to strive for this. Focusing the self on the present moment to the exclusion of all else is an ability that is highly valued and desired in athletes and college lecturers with deadlines. One of the effects of cannabis, to encourage a focus on tiny and previously unnoticed details of the environment, could be highly valued by artists. This becomes a problem in terms of the social valuation of the outcome, a night of regretted sexual intercourse not being comparable to a win at tennis. The difference between impairment and enhancement is then a value judgement made outside the experience itself.

The difference between an effect being positively or negatively valued is one of contextual spin. A perceptual distortion may involve finding things funny that aren't. 'Aren't' is a localized definition, meaning finding things funny that sober people do not, or that, on sober reflection, do not seem so hilarious. Its brief, pleasant oblivion is paid for by the litany of broken hearts, promises and noses counted the following day, and the slow dripfeed of fragmented returning memories of things said and done that, alas, seemed like a good idea at the time. The issue here is partly that this is not an accurate picture, as we shall see, but also that it is wholly negative. Even the pleasures of intoxication are put down to temporary madness, a madness which in other contexts is highly valued. The conclusion then reached is that the only way to control these negative effects societally is to control the substance itself, either by restricting its availability through taxation and regulation or through banning it altogether, restoring through the state the impairment of judgement presumably lost to the individual.

Illicit drugs also come under the distortion narrative, although here the distortion is not only perceptual, but consists of distortion of the self. In drug mythology, they make you do things you would not otherwise do, and feel what you would not otherwise feel. You can be taken out of your self (heroin), trust people you would not otherwise (ecstasy), or lose the will to resist rape (GHB). They can be monstrous enhancers, such as PCP allegedly gifting the user with superhuman strength. Illicit drugs are thought of as being more specific and precise in their effects than alcohol. They are given various specific classifications that are meant to reflect the effects embodied in them, as stimulants, depressants, psychedelics, deliriants, dissociatives or empathogens. They seem then to be very different from alcohol in the way they act and the effects they have, although the effects of some can be nearly as varied. Their specificity might in fact lie in the culture surrounding their use rather than in their chemical nature. Alcohol has its status as multiple disinhibitor and distorter because it is in such widespread use. We can see every time we go out for a drink how alcohol affects people in wildly different ways; we have some lay understanding of this. As illicit drugs are the habit of a minority, many do not appreciate that the same possibilities apply.

The above disinhibition and distortion explanations of how drugs and alcohol intoxicate tend to treat the individual under the influence of intoxicants as like a car to which the wrong type of fuel has been added. Knowledge of the mechanisms through which intoxicants interact with the body is important, of course, but intoxication cannot be reduced to these mechanisms. In fact, most would recognize that there is a subjective element involved in drug and alcohol experiences, which although subjectively experienced is socially structured. To continue with the same metaphor, the operation of a car depends on its own internal workings, but also on the weather, the layout of the highway, the rules of the road, the behaviour of other drivers, and the experience and skills of whoever is behind the wheel. Intoxication experiences are always individual and specific to the time and place where they happen, but this is not purely a personal reaction to circumstance. It involves a socialized subjectivity that responds to cultural norms and ideological values, along with the sensual elements of its setting.

Cross-cultural chemistry

> Specificity of drug action is to a considerable extent a fiction that has served to promote the neglect of the range or multiplicity of drug effects.
> Henry L. Lennard et al., 'The Methadone Illusion' (1972: 882)

The effects of alcohol are enumerated with some precision in folk and popular culture. In one episode of *The Simpsons,* the long-running satirical cartoon series, 'Selma's Choice', Homer Simpson's sister-in-law Selma takes two of his children, Bart and Lisa, to visit 'Duff Gardens'. It is a theme park run by the Duff Corporation, who make Duff, Homer's favourite, or only, beer. Duff Gardens is a Disneyland built by the Soviet Commissar for Beer Production. Attractions include the Beerquarium, with the 'happiest fish in the world'. It also has the 'Seven Duffs', characters in beer-bottle costumes who represent various states of drunkenness. Their names are Tipsy, Dizzy, Sleazy, Edgy, Surly, Queasy and Remorseful. They represent some well-recognized stages of drunkenness and effects of drinking in the Anglo-Saxon world. Alcohol has the power to make men by turns angry, violent, lustful and maudlin. This liquid has the notable quality of being gender-specific in some of its effects, not causing women to become loud or boastful, but lowering their sexual inhibitions. This is a clue that there is a lot more at work than pharmacology on its own.

Alcohol is viewed and treated differently between cultures. Across European societies, there is no relationship between the population's propensity for drinking and for getting drunk (ESPAD, 2007). Ireland has a high rate of abstinence and a high level of alcohol problems. Comparative cultural research indicates that the effects of alcohol on behaviour are not related to levels of consumption in the population or to the chemical effect of ethanol, but to social and cultural expectations and beliefs about the effect of alcohol. There is a long-established distinction between the wine-drinking 'wet' cultures of Mediterranean Europe – where drinking is part of daily life and mealtimes in partic-ular, and, although heavy and frequent, does not lead to public drunk-enness – and the beer- and spirit-drinking 'dry' cultures of Northern Europe, where drinking is separate from normal life, and where becoming visibly and publicly drunk is the aim of drinking. Recently, this distinction appears to be losing its force, with drinking behaviour in the Southern wet cultures converging with the Northern dry cul-tures, in what appears to be a case of cultural diffusion (Allaman et al., 2000).

In some cultural settings inebriation is expected to quickly descend into drunken violence. In others, individuals will be merrily drunk until they pass out. Craig MacAndrew and Robert Edgerton, in their classic *Drunken Comportment* (1969), draw on a wealth of anthropo-logical evidence showing that in different societies people learn not only how to drink – the rules governing who can drink what, when and where – but also how to 'do' drunk. In the main, they are concerned with the prevailing assumption in Anglo-Saxon countries that alcohol is a disinhibitor, and that many of its damaging social effects can be put down to its tendency to befuddle the higher brain functions, leaving those circuits of the brain concerned with lust, wrath and gluttony to have their moment.

They collect many examples of continued 'inhibition', meaning cul-tural proprieties being maintained, in states of heavy intoxication, and of disinhibition that takes place within clearly defined limits. There are cultures in which drinking does not lead to clowning around, sexualization, aggression and maudlin remorse. For example, being involved in fighting alongside impeccable maintenance of sexual pro-priety; or rampant promiscuity alongside the maintenance of complex incest taboos. One people, the Aritama of Colombia, drink themselves into a state of unobtrusive gloom. For them, intoxication is not seen as a state of enjoyment and they seem to seek to challenge themselves through drinking. They work hard, drink hard, but do not play hard. In all, there is no generalized, consistent loss of restraint around alcohol across cultures.

There are forms of drinking that have at best limited analogies with drinking practices in Anglo-Saxon cultures: for instance, ritual drink-ing 'to pull down the clouds' (bring rain); the inducement of drunken visions (holy/religious experiences) and 'fiesta' drinking, involving a carnivalesque inversion of social hierarchy. Some of these drinking systems can exist side by side. MacAndrew and Edgerton describe a historical example from Colonial America of the Papago, Native Americans who got drunk on wine in a fiesta fashion, and on white man's whiskey, which was reported as having a violent/chaotic effect on them, absorbing the form of intoxication associated with the drink of the dominant culture. Disinhibition is socially and culturally powerful as much as it is chemically potent. It provides a time out, a script for behaviour that might not be accepted in sobriety. Drunken intoxication is the cultural enactment of alcohol-influenced behaviour. More simply, in any society people quickly learn what drunken behaviour is and how to 'do' being drunk. Getting drunk in the wrong way – which might be too often, too much or violating the unspoken rules of drunken comportment – is sanctioned, and the drinker quickly learns to keep himself or less usually herself in check.

For instance, in an Oaxacan village (Dennis, 1975) the drunk has a clearly defined social role, like the savant, seeking out social gatherings and saying what cannot be said by the sober without sanction. This might range from a political critique of official lackadaisical indolence to village gossip. Although formally embarrassing, this is informally welcomed and accepted. The drunk allows information to be transmitted against the strong privacy norms of Oaxacan society. He does not have to conform to the everyday deceptions of polite society, although when sober the same person will be full of apologies for his behaviour.

There are some suggestions as to what aspects of a culture contribute to a particular kind of drunken comportment being the norm. In the society of the Bolivian Camba, the men drink a very high-strength spirit to rapidly attain a drunken state. Dwight Heath notes the fluid and uncertain social bonds of Camba society, suggesting that drinking allows them to engage in 'sociable isolation' (Heath, 1962). Ambivalence is common, especially in indigenous Central and South American cultures where there is an ambivalent relationship with the society of the colonizers. In a Brazilian cult, drinking enables a deity to possess the cult member (Leacock, 1964). The *encantados* – the possessing spirits – like to dance and sing, and many also like to smoke and drink, and they enter the body of the cult member to do this. The *encantados* may drink themselves silly, but the cult members claim to never suffer a hangover as a result of the *encantado* drinking. Transgressive behaviour when drunk is explained by the nature of the particular *encantado* possessing them. They are not the ones who are drinking, so they do not experience the ill effects afterwards.

There are limitations in putting cultural variation in drunken comportment down to socialization of drinking norms, without much scope for interactional reflection or agency, or conflict and resistance. This kind of approach can fall into cultural determinism, in which individuals enact society's drunken knowledge. Change comes about only by cultural contamination, such as with Native Americans and the white man's liquor. Yet there is creative, dynamic cultural work being done in intoxication, for instance, reaffirming mythically egalitarian bonds (Paton-Simpson, 2001), or as symbolic resistance (Mitchell, 2004), for instance, the enacting of resistance to class and gender expectations (Friedman and Alicea, 1995), which is especially relevant with the creation and affirmation of group values (Young, 1971) through ritual.

Ritual intoxication and socially obligatory drinking

Drugs and alcohol have socially active characteristics in addition to their pharmacologically active ones. Ritual is one way through which an object's characteristics become socially active, or activated. Rituals consist of symbolic rule-bound behaviour. Rituals are culturally embedded. They are specific to a locale and society in their form, although some are universal in nature such as the existence of rituals around birth, marriage and death. One near universal is that many societies have some ritual that involves intoxication, either through using a psychoactive substance or invoking 'ritual ecstasy'. Rituals suspend normal life, generally being a time out from the day to day. Hence, they are restricted in some way, not open to all. They are often a time out from some other people who occupy the everyday, whether family or the laity. Rituals are coded into expected behaviour. Unexpected and especially rule-breaking behaviour will often be questioned, if not causing complete outrage. Missing out on buying your round, or buying the wrong drink, in the wrong glass, can all be socially sanctioned by peers. Finally, rituals have social functions. These may involve the expression of normative values, binding group or personal relationships, or marking a transition from one stage in life to another. Rituals distinguish the sacred from the profane. In modern Western societies, nothing is sacred except the self, so in our societies many rituals are generated to elevate and affirm self.

Intoxication rituals form an operative part of the relationship between 'culture' and 'intoxication'. There are some broad conventions shared in many intoxication rituals, such as hospitality and sociability. Some drug-using subcultures place an emphasis on mutuality. Dutch heroin users share their heroin with partners, friends, acquaintances, or with someone who is 'sick', and exchange drugs for services such as a place to shoot up or to curry favour with a dealer (Grund, 1993). Rituals, when collective, have an obligatory, enforceable element to them. There are many situations where intoxication is socially obligatory, such as some business lunches, office parties and academic conferences. There are varying degrees of obligation, from the requirement or otherwise to drink at all, to drinking pace, technique, style, alcohol strength, taste and type of drink. Obligations can be set on the amount consumed or degree of intoxication. In the Falkland Islands 'Camp', the area outside Port Stanley, a certain level of drunkenness is manly and may be simulated. The norm of obligatory drinking is powerful, and is maintained by gestures of disapproval such as being asked several times if 'you really only want lemonade', with questioning of motives, attacks on masculinity if the refusenik is male, accusations of anti-social tendencies, drink spiking and occasional violence (Paton-Simpson, 2001).

Why is it drinking that is obligatory in this way, rather than having a cup of coffee together, which is not normatively enforced? It could be that mutual intoxication makes people feel trusting, safe and relaxed, although the descriptions of enforced drinking do not give the impression of a relaxing, carefree environment. It may be that sobriety undermines collective jollity, gives the lie to it and shows it up for being false egalitarianism. The ghost at the feast, non-drinkers are interactional deviants – increasing the load on others to be drunkenly sociable. Non-drinkers are identified as faulty socializers. A participant who does not drink or does not drink in rounds fails to keep the interaction going, and others have to do the work for him. This is encapsulated in the term 'social drinker', meaning someone who drinks enough to qualify as sociable, as functional. Ethnographic evidence seems to suggest this is less the case with illicit drugs use; indeed, some groups of users will value having one person staying 'straight'.

Drinking and social exclusion

'Don't you *ever* go drinking with your buddies?' I asked in some exasperation. 'Hell!' he replied, 'I didn't think you counted drinking! *Everyone* always drinks with their buddies!'

Gerald Mars, 'Longshore Drinking, Economic Security and Union Politics in Newfoundland', (1987: 93)

Drinking can be examined in terms of its functions for the group of which the drinker is part. The practice of buying rounds of drinks, common in Britain, Ireland, Australia, New Zealand and elsewhere, establishes a temporary, internally united community, presumably unlike the atomized tea and coffee drinkers. Yet acts of internal solidification are also boundary-making and exclusionary. Gerald Mars (Mars, 1987) examines drinking functions in terms of the way that drinking practices amongst Newfoundland longshoremen (dock workers) involve setting the boundaries of the in-group, maintaining its internal coherence, and excluding those who are not considered to be reliable or desirable members of the work gang. The primary divide in the men he studied is between union 'regular' men, who obtain regular work, and non-union 'outside' men who work sporadically.

Longshore work seems at first glance highly unreliable. Men are picked each day for the work gangs by the foreman in the 'shape up'. There are always more men available for work than can be taken on. It would seem this is a recipe for job insecurity, with the foreman having a high level of power over the men, and no worker being able to rely on having a job from one day to the next. In fact, the 'gang' can effectively control hiring of men, and can decide who is 'in' and who is 'out' through a combination of social bonding, group formation and closure. They will effectively trade with the foreman a reliable pace and quality of work, in exchange for regular hiring of the same men. This gives those on the inside job security and some measure of control over their work. Such collective action requires a fairly high level of group cohesion, which is maintained in the dense network of work relationships replicated in the taverns, which exclude the outside men.

Regular men drink beer in the taverns on the wharf, always in the same groups. Men did not think drinking was part of 'leisure time' but an unremarkable although necessary activity that came with the job. Drinking rituals reflect differences but also reinforce them. What Mars's informants refer to as 'loners', meaning non-drinkers, are always outside men. The only exceptions are teetotal union activists who have the wherewithal to speak up against the foremen. They remain regular men. Outside men have no stable social relationships with other workers. They never know where or with whom they will work that day, if they will work at all.

Men arrange themselves in the taverns according to their job hierarchy and functions. They work as a team, and drink as a team, and will often sit in the tavern according to the arrangement that they work in. Drink buying does not follow the round system common in many other communal drinking settings. Individuals 'gift' drinks from the more marginal workers to the less so. Only very high-status men are able to opt out of this obligation. This is not a casual after-work drink with one's workmates, but a vital part of group maintenance, and of maintaining one's inside membership. Reflecting the basic insecurity of formal job tenure, men who are too ill to work will still limp in to drink with their usual workmates, maintaining their work presence and ensuring they are kept informed of developments on the dock. Drink is very much an extension of work and, for regular men, there is little distinction as to where work stops and drinking time starts. Although not without pleasure, it is very far from unencumbered leisure.

Outside men do not have the reliable work or drinking routines that the regular men enjoy. They still drink near the docks, but never in the taverns. Like American teenagers or British youngsters, their drinking spaces are parked cars or the open air. The latter is illegal and means that they must keep a weather eye out for the vigilance of the police, and they drink furtively. The bottle of cheap wine or rum is preferred to multiple bottles of beer because it can be shared. The host doles out drink in a single cup to his guests. Rather than being a down payment on future obligations, as with the regular men, sharing drink is a return for favours done or anticipated – alerting a man to work available, information about the arrival times of boats, or the hope that this will be forthcoming in future. Each drinking group is temporary and lasts as long as the host feels he wants to continue with the largesse.

In addition to the internal functions of group cohesion and solidarity performed in drinking rituals, there are performative aspects of taste, distinction and display, embodied in what one drinks and how one drinks, whether sipping, gulping, drinking from a bottle or a glass. There are subtle residues of ritual conventions embedded in utensils and paraphernalia. For instance, the exquisite porcelain teacups that you can only get a fingertip into are leftovers from the Rococo tea-drinking style that involved sticking one finger out while sipping to show delicacy (Schivelbusch, 1992). Arabian coffee cups did not have either handle or saucer. The handle was introduced to allow the consumption of a hot liquid, now replaced in many modern coffee shops by a cardboard girdle and a notice saying 'contents are hot'. The 'mug' displays its functionality in form and size, and, in the supersize tea mugs that are increasingly common, it displays its excess. The 'Bordeaux' glass, the snifter glass, and the pint glass, all encode some norms and values around what intoxication is for and about. The demonstrative masculinity of the pint of beer contrasts with the demonstratively delicate and refined masculinity of the whisky snifter.

There are many elaborate practices around alcohol that exhibit one's femininity or masculinity, social status, class identification and drinking competence. Male drinking subcultures – such as, in the USA, fraternity-house parties and drinking among US Navy personnel – are sites for the negotiation of subordinate/dominant masculinities, and boundaries of gender, class, ethnicity and status (West, 2001). The subculture might reinforce itself and its status hierarchy through the retelling of stories of drunken feats or drunken disgrace, drinking games and competitive drinking (Peralta, 2007). Masculinities, femininities, sexualities and other identities, are performed in the drinking environment. The drinker can in some circumstances challenge, transgress or subvert those same associations, such as the man who disguises his avoidance of drinking from his buddies by purchasing a 'rum and coke' without the rum.

Pierre Bourdieu (Bourdieu, 1984) identified the relationship between cultural taste and social stratification, a society-wide division between regular and outside men and women maintained through the production and distribution of cultural capital. A key element of cultural capital is the ability to make the right distinctions, to exhibit the right kind of taste or, more exactly, the right kind of taste about tastes. This latter quality, the way in which some individuals appear to embody the right qualities and can move seamlessly from judging the concert season to the output of avante-garde shock-artists, distinguishes the effortlessly confident aristocrat from the hesitant, culturally deferential autodidact (the self-taught).

Taste is encoded in objects, and distinction in how the individual relates to those objects. Consumption of food and drink forms part of the taste structure. The middle class constantly use their eating habits to distinguish themselves from the vulgar, the unhealthy and the tasteless, casting a penumbra of moral superiority over the metropolitan dinner plate. Well-established displays of taste are to be found in the language of the wine list, the popping of champagne corks and the enjoyment of 'real' ale. Taste involves the demonstration of competence and skill. It is always practical, involving not just having the object but also knowing what to do with it. So, in addition to there being feminine drinks, usually sweeter and slighter than men's drinks (Social Issues Research Centre, 1998), feminine *drinking* is as much part of the display as what the drink is. When in public, this involves sipping rather than gulping and being slower to finish than men in the group.

Taste rituals reinforce status, strengthen relationships and affirm identities. Yet this is a rather glum picture and does not consider too much what is in it for those who partake. What engages them in the ritual, what commits them to it? One purpose served by drug and alcohol rituals is the generation of collective emotional experience, in which each participant has a stake, especially when it comes to seeing the ritual sequence through to the end.

Collective emotionality

Ritual is in some ways an appropriate term for the generation of intoxication experiences because in its anthropological sense rituals are meant to bring about uncommon states of being or consciousness, outside the everyday. A common feature of drinking and drug use is the maintenance of a collective level of consumption, as in the examples of rounds and sharing used above, and the existence of a sequence, which has to be gone through for the experience to be complete. Sharing drugs and alcohol involves sharing a common mood, thus enhancing it.

The emphasis on sequence may be relevant to one of the primary purposes of collective intoxication rituals, which is the production of collective emotionality. Repetition is required because it involves practices and learnt experience. Getting drunk once doesn't count. A ritual sequence requires the full chain of acts and events to be completed satisfactorily. Chasing the dragon refers to smoking the fumes from burning heroin, by putting the heroin in kitchen foil and heating it from beneath with a lighter. When heroin smokers 'chase the dragon', the heroin has to be 'free running' and not leave a trace, as evidence of its quality (Grund, 1993). For a satisfactory experience, the ritual has to be complete, the heroin burnt away and consumed.

As in the leading vignette, the simple act of taking an ecstasy pill in a nightclub is usually the outcome of a much longer sequence, which would have started hours or days previously, and will end many hours or even days afterwards. It is not usually a one-off decision made by an individual clubber when proffered ecstasy by a dealer or the 'pusher' of drug-war demonology. The preparation for a night out might begin with a group of young friends meeting at someone's house, where one of them will have done the job of 'sorting' everyone with a pill. A cannabis joint may be passed round and a mixture of vodka and high-energy drinks consumed as glittery make-up is applied, fingernails are painted with fluorescent nail varnish and outfits are compared. A sense of anticipation will pervade the party as they get ready to leave, discussing previous nights at that club, comparing it to others in terms of music and atmosphere, and speculating as to what might happen during the night.

On arriving at the club there will often be a queue. While waiting to enter, our group will hear the heavy bass thump sounding from inside the club, a mouth-watering sound. Friends will be spotted and greeted. Steam escapes from the nightclub door, telling of the heavy, humid atmosphere inside, generated from hundreds of pulsating bodies. At this point anticipation will be at its most intense, and members of the party may 'drop' their pills to avoid them being discovered in a search by the door staff, and to allow time for the effects to kick in. A female member of the party might secrete some in her bra for use later on, where a search will not reveal it.

Inside, the music will be much more intense. The party will leave coats and bags at the cloakroom and head straight for the dance floor. Here the music will be so loud as to be a physical experience, with bass lines thudding through their bodies, nearly rattling jewellery as the air moves back and forth. The party will go on to the dance floor, among packed bodies that nonetheless part in a friendly manner to let them pass. Feelings of exhilaration and excitement are enhanced by the ecstasy, but also by the music, light and crowds, and waves of a warm, empathic euphoria will sweep users. Hugs and pledges of admiration and love will be exchanged. In the collective oceanic experience (Malbon, 1999) egos will be submerged, and selves will soften into each other. They will dance not in the inward-facing formation of the student disco, nor the women on the dance floor with watching men around the edge, but all facing the DJ, who orchestrates their communal sensations.

Later, after the first rush has passed, the evening will enter a familiar rhythm. Some of the more overheated party members will seek out water. Others will pause for intense discussions and observations about the music, their relationships and other clubbers, or look for familiar faces, heading for familiar spots around the club. Nothing from the workaday week will be allowed to disturb this extended moment. Some will top up on further pills, perhaps later on trying the newly fashionable Ketamine, or will fuel themselves with more high-energy drinks and alcohol. Later, some will seek a break from the heat and intensity in the club's chill-out room, resting on beanbags amid candles, perhaps discussing their next move, before rejoining the throng on the dance floor.

Finally, at 4, 5 or 6 a.m., after a last hurrah the music will stop and the lights will come up, bathing our friends in white light. Someone, usually female, will have had the foresight to go to the cloakroom before the final rush and collect everyone's belongings. If an after-club party has not already been arranged, now will be the time for shouted arrangements, hurriedly exchanged addresses and vague directions. Few will wish to return home to bed, even if they could sleep, all feeling that the evening has more life left in it. The best nightcap is a relaxing chat on somebody's sofa with a joint or perhaps a Valium. Some of the more hardcore party people will seek to continue the celebrations well into the following day.

Extended rituals like this are repeated across the world every weekend. In this example, each element in the sequence contributes to the whole experience. Entering late, or dropping out early, will diminish it, something the participants are tacitly aware of. All become committed to generating the collective emotional experience through ensuring the sequence is followed. Members who drop out or who miss the evening altogether may be gently chided with accounts of what they will be missing, are missing or have missed. What the group is doing is generating an amenable setting for their drug use that involves other members of the group, the pre-club, clubbing and after-club settings, and the combined sequence of all. They are also generating and affirming commonly held values, such as a certain open sociability, with an asexual eroticism.

Learning, set and setting

> Western society is remarkable for the importance it assigns to differences in the precipitating conditions of hallucination.
>
> Anthony Wallace, 'Cultural Determinants of Response to Hallucinatory Experience' (1959: 62)

Alcohol is almost a human universal and has many different guises, so perhaps the existence of cultural differences in drunken comportment is not a surprising phenomenon. Illicit drugs are different, surely – they are chemicals that are profoundly disturbing to mind and soul. We hear so much about instant addiction at the first sniff of an illicit drug that it is commonsensically assumed that they are a class of chemicals by themselves with their power over humanity, fierce substances that will send users spinning out of control. However, when we use the research evidence to look at how drug users experience intoxication, we find that it is intricately linked to past experience, expectations and setting.

In a laboratory cannabis experiment with experienced and naive subjects, the experienced subjects became observably high on smoking it. Of the nine naive subjects, only one had a clear reaction, becoming euphoric. He was the only one of the nine with an expressed wish to do so (Weil et al., 1968). The others reported noticing little effects, mainly mentioning perceptions of time distortion. How do we explain this absence of giggling or obsession with flecks on the wallpaper and the munchies? Perhaps cannabis only affects certain people, and others are in some way physiologically or psychologically predisposed to seek out and appreciate the effects of being high.

The result of these experiments hinted at what has become a well-known formula – that psychoactive substances only have observable effects in conjunction with set and setting. Norman Zinberg originally put forward this formulation, suggesting that the subjective effect of a drug was a combination of the substance, set – the mental frame which the user brings to their drug use, including expectations about its effects – and setting, the societal and local context in which the drug is taken (Zinberg, 1984). Elements of set include expectations and past experiences. Alcohol placebo studies indicated that 'set' has a role in drunken impairment. Experimental subjects who were given a non-alcoholic drink that they thought contained alcohol showed signs of impairment. Expectations of how much the alcohol would affect them impaired experimental subjects' coordination under both alcohol and placebo (Fillmore and Vogel-Sprott, 1995).

As is the case with anthropological studies of drunken behaviour, it is necessary to understand the creative processes through which individuals come to acquire a sense for intoxication, the dynamics of the intoxication experience itself, and the particular historical and social factors involved in shaping it. We learn what intoxicants are through our encounters with their physical effects, themselves filtered by our culturally learnt experiences and the reflections of others. Whether a cup of coffee or something 'stronger', almost all people employ some kind of practice that has developed out of reflecting on those initial sensations and expectations. Processes of collective and individual learning are at work, in which set and setting are created and controlled, and the latter is the key to understanding intoxication experiences. Most drug and alcohol use is controlled, and the cultures that surround them help to maintain control.

Here the touchstone is Howard Becker's research with marijuana users in 1950s America (Becker, 1953). At the time, Becker was writing against the prevailing orthodoxy that certain individuals were psychologically predisposed to deviant behaviours like cannabis use. For Becker, the process of acquiring a cannabis habit, of using a certain drug for pleasure, is not in principle different from normative processes whereby initial confusion or disdain for the perceived benefits of an object or experience is overcome, such as learning to like the taste of caviar, the music of Arnold Schoenberg or English 'bitter'. The process of learning 'appreciation' of salted fish roe, atonal music or warm beer involves the user changing their relationship to the object. This process of seeing what others see in an object or experience is the acquisition of a culturally validated sense of taste, the ability to distinguish between novel objects and experiences and to evaluate them positively or negatively. According to Becker, this happens with subculturally validated taste as well, such as that for drug-induced experiences.

On its own, smoking marijuana, puffing on a joint, was not enough to get high. Smoking alone was not the way in which the users Becker interviewed learnt to be cannabis smokers. Users had to learn how to smoke, and to interpret their internal feelings as being high. He defined three stages to using cannabis for pleasure. The first is the physical act of learning to smoke, for the user to ingest the smoke into their lungs and hold it there long enough so it can have a physiological effect. The second involves learning to recognize those effects as being high, rather than just feeling a bit odd and slightly unwell. Finally, the user has to learn to enjoy being high, or come to the conclusion that being high is an enjoyable state of being. Part of this was smoking with others, observing them getting high, knowing what getting high is. One try was not generally enough. With Becker's sample, people had to try a few times, usually because they had to learn to smoke 'right', to inhale and to hold it in their lungs. When politicians are confronted with evidence that they smoked cannabis in their youth, a common response is to insist that they 'puffed but did not inhale'. It seems this is not merely a rhetorical device to get them off the hook, but in fact it is a common experience for the novice user who does not know how to smoke properly (i.e. effectively, producing the right sensual effects).

Experienced smokers would teach the tricks of the trade, such as not to smoke a joint in the same way one smokes a cigarette, to take in a lot of air, to hold the smoke in for as long as possible. If they do not do this, the novice never takes in enough cannabis to have any effect, and to boot has to be with people who are stoned when they are not. Like starting out to smoke cigarettes or drink alcohol, learning to get high often involved initial unpleasantness, such as feelings of panic and paranoia as the drug took hold. Some forced habituation was necessary to obtain the full benefits, although this in part involved reinterpreting initially frightening symptoms as pleasurable – learning to control the experience and to like these feelings, to enjoy the different perspective that it gives. Not everyone who started out trying cannabis completed this process. For those who did, what was important was not their personal qualities, but the way in which what they felt about what they were doing changed as they progressed further into the cannabis experience.

More recently, Michael Hallstone (2002) identifies some changes to the process Becker identified in learning to smoke and get high. Because cannabis use is so widespread in Western societies, there are many more opportunities for the novice to observe other smokers, learn what getting high is and so on, such that a large proportion of users in Hallstone's study do in fact report getting high the first time they smoke. Hallstone touches on something else new, the replacement of reflection in others with self-reflection in the experience of smoking cannabis. His respondents do not report that they have had to have anyone else tell them that they were high at all. They describe it as a solitary experience, although often one undertaken in company. What his respondents might be identifying is a change in the process of getting high. It is now less a communal subcultural experience than that observed by Becker, and is more individualized, atomic hedonism. As more people now 'know' what getting high consists of, they are able to draw on many other sources of information – the mass media, popular culture, parents, older siblings and so on – rather than having to rely on a local subculture separated from those networks to know what is expected. We are simply a much more drug-aware society.

There is a possibility that cannabis is unique among drugs in that so many of its effects appear to be learnt or, more precisely, place specific. Cannabis is classified as a psychodysleptic, as consciousness altering. It changes mood, but seldom the same way twice, and not for the same person in the same way. This is part of its attraction. It is a highly *specific* drug. Users are capable of talking for long periods about what they are feeling, broadcasting their current state of mind and sensory perception to those in the vicinity. Talking about the experience as you are having it is not merely an annoying habit; for those who do this it is a part of the experience itself, a kind of playing off the self and setting against the drug experience. The specifics of setting are heavily enacted with cannabis use in company, and perhaps alone also. So-called 'hard' drugs such as heroin are thought of as being far less open to this process, the injection method in particular meaning the user takes a much more immediate and direct 'hit'. However, recent studies of controlled heroin users have indicated that users can find in heroin a variety of mental effects beyond numb detachment, including stimulation, the precise opposite of what heroin is supposed to provide (Warburton et al., 2005). It is not only alcohol experiences that are culturally constructed and variable.

Second nature and appetite

There are some more 'congealed' or sticky elements of intoxication experience that last beyond immediate set and setting. The strong habitual element to drug and alcohol use is well noted. There are aspects of drug and alcohol experiences that have meaning and significance only in repetition. Intoxication is never a one-off. It takes on meaning through action. Pleasures and pains form part of the practical action of intoxication. This allows it to be located in the specific local, cultural, social and economic contexts that shape it and to see how it is deeply structured without being culturally (or otherwise) deterministic. Pierre Bourdieu's concept of habitus (Bourdieu, 1980) comes in useful here. Habitus is the the set of practical logics and often unreflexive predispositions that govern day-to-day life and which appear to us as 'second nature'.

The 'set and setting' approach could be seen to employ a mind–body dualism. Drug effects are ingrained in the organism, and addiction and intoxication are the symbolic appropriation of physical feelings in the mind of the user. There is a sense in the above accounts that physiological reactions happen and then the conscious mind interprets or does not interpret them. If they interpret them 'correctly' then the person becomes a regular user. This perspective does not contain the non-reflective actioned characteristics of everyday life, in which compulsion and desire are experienced as forces existing outside the self, tending to ignore the visceral aspects of experience, all sorts of desire that are physically felt. More credence needs to be given to the deep structures at work in shaping intoxication experiences.

Darin Weinberg calls this a praxocological approach (Weinberg, 1997), meaning engaging with drug use in terms of practical action within a habitus of being. Symbolic appropriation is only part of human experience and human understanding. We understand with and through our bodies. What we have to do, then, is look at how these visceral experiences are constituted, what they are constituted from in practice, and how they derive from the historically specific, cultural, local context in which drugs are used. The drive towards intoxication is learnt and instinctual, felt and symbolic.

It is not voluntary. Medieval peasants who ate bread made from grain infected with lysergic bacteria thought that they were witnessing devilish beings (Camporesi, 1989). Their religious world-view held that, in their world, there existed witches and demons who could cast spells. This is hard to grasp for secular Westerners who are used to the contemporary sense in which every mention of evil and the devil is taken to be either metaphorical or simply embarrassing. The visions they experienced would have been understood as every bit as real as what they saw in their non-intoxicated state. Those undergoing convulsive ergotism were seen as bewitched or possessed. The episode would not have been interpreted as a distinct episodic experience related to a specific substance; nor would it be acquired within biomedicine as a case of poisoning. For moderns, who have a very different understanding of their selves in relation to the world, intoxication is experienced as an internal affair. For modern men and women whose consciousness is placed at the centre of their state of being, drug use often constitutes an internal journey, a travelling within the self. Cannabis and ecstasy open the doors of perception – inwards.

Habitus is something that presents itself to us as instinct, as second nature. This is frequently lost in the accounts created by social and natural scientific experts of drug and alcohol use. They tend to generate objective schemas that describe human action in black-box terms, of drug or alcohol inputs creating outputs of addiction, crime, misbehaviour and so on. This form of knowledge leads to self-fulfilling outcomes. Users in general, but addicts or delinquent users caught within the systems supported by social and natural science knowledge, learn what is expected of them and perform accordingly. Gymnastics can be described in terms of geometry, but the gymnast is not a geometer. Likewise, intoxication can be described in terms of the interaction of agonists and receptors, purity of the substance or the delivery mechanism, yet the person experiencing intoxication is not a chemist or a neurologist or a biochemist. It is much more fruitful to explore the experience of intoxication in terms of set and setting, and the embodiment of socially structured subjectivity.

Consciousness and enlightenment

The evident variations in intoxication as a state of altered conscious-ness show how we learn to expect and want consciousness to be altered. That also makes an assumption about the state of sobriety. It assumes that our sober, unintoxicated, selves are in a state of static equilibrium, which intoxication then pushes over. This perspective divides and walls off intoxication from consciousness. It disconnects them, as if there was no relationship between the two, and reinforces the subordinate status of intoxication as disinhibition and distortion – a departure from the norm. This means that we treat intoxication as an ambivalent state to be in, like the sane mind desiring and at the same time not-desiring to experience madness. In practice, this treat-ment of intoxication as absent consciousness allows us to use it to excuse ourselves. Phrases like 'I was very drunk at the time, darling' cause amusement through recognition of the cynical knowingness involved in appealing to drunken disinhibition. This *is* very much how we act. So perhaps I do treat my drunken self as the Hyde to my sober Jekyll, and most of my friends manage to forgive me in the morning.

Our sober and intoxicated states could in fact be akin to the dynamic equilibrium that comes from a constant movement of forces. When we walk we are in state of constant dynamic equilibrium, a dis-equilibrium where balance is maintained through constant imbal-ance. Intoxication is then perhaps not a *particular* state of mind or internal balance of forces, but a dynamic between self and place that is enacted under the influence of psychoactive substances. This means that a consideration of the way that intoxication is constructed in society must take into account how consciousness is defined also.

The placing of consciousness at the heart of self represented a sig-nificant historical development, and something very modern. This was the Enlightenment legacy, the self as an aware, acting, individual mind, the rational, untroubled self. In the nineteenth century, some members of Europe's middle classes began to use drugs in order to change and explore their consciousness (Davenport-Hines, 2004). This was partly driven by speculative curiosity as to what conscious-ness was. Cocaine was one of the vehicles for this exploration.

Examining what it is about consciousness that is being changed when intoxicated can illuminate what sober consciousness is meant to consist of. Alcohol is associated with loss of inhibition; cocaine, with confidence, euphoria, alertness, and ecstasy, with pleasure, empathy, stimulation, and a misguided faith in one's dancing talent. These statements imply that we must think that we are inhibited, lacking confidence, dull, unhappy, cold and withdrawn and so on. In spite of this, it is common to treat intoxication as not real, reflecting the privileging of uninhibited consciousness, which is why indiscretions committed under the influence are mostly treated less severely than those practiced under cover of sobriety. Yet many people feel much better when they are intoxicated, as if they wish they were like that all the time, while being aware that such a state of affairs is neither possible nor desirable.

There is extensive anthropological work on the cultural shaping of intoxication, with rather less numerous literature on its historical position within modernity, its social shaping, along with a small number of works that pay attention to the micro-social processes by which intoxication is acquired. Intoxication is useful. It is part of the constitution of social worlds and selves. It is generative of values, selves and places.

Drugs and alcohol are a social presence in society. They come to stand in for social problems, such as urban blight, crime, disease, deviance and disorder. They are seen as being generative of types of people, usually pathological – the crack-mother, the heroin junkie or the alcoholic. In the next chapter we will see how they are generative of social problems that go beyond their context to become significant narratives of human experience, like addiction.

We construct social worlds visually, and through other sense-forms as well. Intoxication has a slippery relationship to the senses, appearing to heighten some and dull others, creating audio, visual and perceptual hallucinations. It is perhaps best understood as forming its own relationship to the senses. Partly because of this quality, intoxication is always approached as localized. There seems to be no general intoxication, but a myriad of specific experiences that have little in common except that they are different from sobriety. It is fundamentally an experience of the individual, and although the mechanisms of this experience can be described through pharmacology and neurology they cannot capture what it is, only why it is.

The language of neurotransmitters, agonists and antagonists is one part of the story, but in abstracting intoxication this decouples the experience of it from consciousness. It would appear to fit in well with a society which creates social worlds that are even better than the real thing – the real thing being no longer worth its salt, unobtainable, or risky and dangerous.

Conclusion

The blissful cloud of summer-indolence
  Benumb'd my eyes; my pulse grew less and less;
Pain had no sting, and pleasure's wreath no flower.
O, why did ye not melt, and leave my sense
Unhaunted quite of all but - nothingness?
       Keats, 'Ode on Indolence' (1816, II: 6–10)

When you smile, your brain releases opioids. They bind with mu-opioid receptors to fire off little neurons telling you that you are happy. This is good. When you inject heroin, exactly the same thing happens, except a lot, lot more of it, more than you can have ever experienced before, like a million smiles all at once. The argument in this chapter is that this is not, in fact, exactly what happens. Those opioids do not just make you happy. If you take heroin a lot the rush goes. If you make yourself smile a lot, like an air stewardess engaged in emotional labour (Hochschild, 1983), that smile means nothing, it becomes a game face. That is why when you drink you can be happy drunk, sad drunk, maudlin drunk, violent drunk, sober drunk and all the other kinds of drunk you get. There is an ambivalence to intoxication, the desire to 'get out of oneself', while claiming that one is not oneself when under the influence. There is ambivalence also with regard to the scientific knowledge of intoxication mentioned earlier, that if mood and state of mind are merely the results of chemicals swirling around the brain, the question arises of how we can trust our minds and our perceptions. It is almost disappointing to learn that feelings and sensations can be so easily subverted by the right intoxicant. The conscious self slips away from us into the pharmacist's cupboard. I hope to have shown how this is not entirely the case. Intoxication is creative of selves, and created by them, mediated through culture, ritual, expectations, set and setting.

4 Drug Problems, Abuses and Addiction

A series of photos showing heroin and methamphetamine users slowly fading away over time has been used to illustrate the effects of drug-induced damage. One sequence involving an American methamphetamine user, taken over a number of years, is particularly striking. As it progresses, her eyes shrink into their sockets; lines appear on her face, then lengthen and deepen; her mouth turns downward; her face assumes a skeletal air. Her entire demeanour becomes sunken. They are a powerful and disturbing set of images. Yet the one comment I can make with a high degree of certainty is that the wasting of the human organism presented there for public consumption is not an effect of methamphetamine itself, in a straightforward sense. Her drug use is the catalysing factor, but if she was, for instance, an otherwise healthy, successful professional who engaged in controlled use of methamphetamine, then the likelihood is that she would resemble any other woman of her age and status in looks and bearing. If you learnt that the woman in question was homeless, had to rely on street prostitution for her income, suffered from a poor diet and highly disrupted access to health care, or did not have a safe environment in which to smoke, the attribution of her very real suffering to the drug as a substance with harmful properties would be called into question. We cannot know either way for sure, as the images are presented without context. What the pictures do is to fetishize. They disguise the conditions of their production. We see the problems associated with methamphetamine and heroin use, but have no information as to what has created them. There is no way of telling whether any of the factors mentioned above are true for the subject or not. The viewer is invited to assume that it is the drug itself that has painted the picture, when it is more likely only one of the brushes on the canvas.

Functional problems

ORDELL: I'm serious, you smoke too much of that shit. That shit robs you of your ambition.

MELANIE: Not if your ambition is to get high and watch TV.

Jackie Brown (Quentin Tarantino, Miramax Films 1997)

Sociologists often display what appears to be a morbid interest in the pathological, in mangled minds and damaged bodies. It is to be hoped that this does not indicate the existence of a serious character flaw shared by the profession. This trait has its uses. The pathological, as disturbing of the peace, illuminates the normal. It demonstrates how the normal is produced, is created and has life breathed into it; what codes of behaviour attach to what situations and which people, and what systems exist to channel mental and physical energy in one direction or another. That goes for society's members as well, for what is displayed as reprehensible, punishable behaviour tells each individual exactly where the boundary between the acceptable and the unacceptable lies, not to cross it, and what awaits them if they do. The morbid appetites and dangerous intoxications lurking in the shadows of socially obligatory drinking and normalized recreational drug use serve their purposes. The shadows cast by drug and alcohol problems put our fears into mortal form. The problems and pitfalls of intoxication – addiction, bingeing, violence – are not only the dark side of the happy-go-lucky, likes-a-drink, jack-the-lad or lively lass images that attach to normalized forms of intoxication. Both are part of a whole – a symbolic economy of actions and stillness, words and silences – that inscribe some kinds of intoxication, some substances and some users as morbid, destructive and wanton.

A general survey of the problems associated with drugs and alcohol is beyond the scope of this chapter, as is an exploration of what social and personal factors shape particular substance-use problems. What I intend to do is examine smoking, drug addiction, alcoholism and other dangerous intoxications as phenomena that are created and given significance in socially meaningful terms. In order that these problems can be ameliorated or avoided, we need to take an informed look at how they are produced and defined, and not be guided by the kind of dogma and prejudice that makes them intractable. The prevailing view of substance-use problems is that they inhere either in the malignant properties of the substance, with illicit drugs, or the weak and inadequate body and mind of the user, with alcohol and smoking, or, in the case of medicinal drugs, they are ignored altogether. The predominant ways in which these problems are defined and dealt with constitute major barriers to an effective and sympathetic approach to those who suffer from substance-related harms. The reason that substance-use problems continue to be defined in this way, frequently in the teeth of the evidence, is that they are 'useful problems', they serve the purpose of directing our attention away from difficulties created by the prevailing social order and on to the temporary solutions people find for them.

The uses of abuses

> HOMER SIMPSON: To alcohol! The cause of . . . and solution to . . . all of life's problems.
> *The Simpsons*, 'Homer vs. The Eighteenth Amendment' (Bob Anderson, Fox Broadcasting Company, 1997)

In the previous chapter I looked at how drug and alcohol use could be socially functional. Drug and alcohol problems also have their uses. Illicit drugs in particular frequently come to stand in for social problems and social conflict. In doing so, they handily resolve seemingly baffling puzzles about human behaviour, providing a portable explanation for all sorts of woe. The use of khat by Somalis is used to explain both the tenacity of poorly equipped irregular fighters against well-armed combat troops in Mogadishu, Somalia, and poverty, social disruption and isolation among Somalis at home and abroad.

Khat is a plant with stimulating properties used by people of Somali, Ethiopian, Kenyan and Yemeni origin. It is illegal in the USA, Canada and much of Europe, though not in the UK. It contains the stimulant cathinone (a Schedule I controlled substance in the USA). Forty-eight hours after picking, the cathinone degrades to cathine, which is not restricted. Somalia had, since 1991, been without a stable, functioning government or state. Outside the northern Republic of Somaliland, the country has been riven by violent struggles between warlords. The United Nations launched a humanitarian relief effort in 1993. In October 1993, US forces led a combat operation in the capital, Mogadishu, to secure humanitarian efforts against the forces of the warlord Mohamed Farrah Aidid. After a bloody two-day urban battle, the US troops were forced to withdraw, the battle having cost the lives of hundreds of Somalis and eighteen US servicemen. US military commanders put the apparently superhuman fighting efforts of militiamen down to their use of khat.

That the militiamen were highly skilled and experienced fighters and perhaps were boosted by their fierce opposition to having, as they saw it, their turf invaded was not enough to explain their tenacity. Also irrelevant was the previous blunder in which a US-led attack managed to kill most of the elders of Aidid's Habar Gedir clan, cementing local opposition to UN intervention. In the eyes of their Western enemies, they had to draw their inhuman strength from somewhere external to them, and external to military, ideological and political concerns, in this case a substance which is most often consumed as a mild stimulant.

Khat causes Somali gunmen to be reckless and relentless in battle, but apparently has the opposite effect on Somali men when they are in the UK. Commentators are as concerned about Somali men who use khat all day and appear to do little else (Advisory Council on the Misuse of Drugs, 2005). Mike Gapes, the Member of Parliament for Ilford South, London, said: 'The Somali community has high levels of unemployment and non-engagement with the rest of society. Although there are many successful Somalis, it is a community which is under-achieving and I believe khat is partly to blame.'

It is the use of khat rather than, for instance, government policies, linguistic or structural barriers that explains high unemployment and other social problems. The problems of an ethnic group are frequently attributed to its internal characteristics or habits, when these identifiably differ from those of the majority. Positive characteristics are attributed to the drug rather than to their own abilities, and negative experiences or behaviour are attributed to use of the drug rather than problems of culture, material deprivation or family structure.

Reducing social effects to the use of particular substances is not always done negatively. The upsurge in ecstasy use, and a decline in alcohol consumption among British youth in the early 1990s, has been claimed to contribute directly to the Northern Ireland peace settlement and the decline of English football hooliganism. While the loved-up image of the Cardiff City Soul Crew and Millwall Bushwackers is a pleasing one, the decline of in-ground violence might be more closely related to changes in policing and, in the latter case, to the introduction of seating, increased costs of attendance, the marginalization of some sections of the fanbase and the intensification of crowd surveillance that occurred in the same period. There is a complex interplay between what surrounds and shapes the use of a drug, and its internal, chemical, characteristics, as explored in chapter 3. Drugs themselves seldom if ever drive social problems or social change, whether positive or negative. They frequently come to be shorthand for either, as do other potentially transgressive activities, such as sex, but they can cohere and solidify experience. They become part of the spiral of social transformation and re-establishment of the status quo.

Framing the drug problem

> Stop believing that your drugs are morally superior to my drugs because you get yours at a store . . . The Beatles took LSD and wrote 'Sgt. Pepper'. Anna Nicole Smith [minor celebrity who died of a prescription drug overdose] took legal drugs and couldn't remember the number for 911.
>
> Bill Maher, *Real Time with Bill Maher*, 13 April 2007

Most academic texts on drugs and/or alcohol devote a large part, or all, of their analysis to personal problems associated with drug and alcohol use: addiction, crime, overdose and longer-term health problems. Yet a history of the motor car could be written (and many are written) without any obligation felt on the part of the author to mention the many people killed or maimed in car accidents, even as unfortunate 'side effects'. Death, injury and suffering can result from illicit drug use, alcohol use, paracetamol and aspirin (Pirmohamed et al., 2004), driving, sport, being admitted to hospital, and cheerleading (Davis, 2006). In only one of these instances does a personal harm become a social problem, and it does not appear to correlate very well to the aggregate extent of that harm over other sources of harm. With drugs, it is the ones that are used by or associated with people of low social status, ethnic minorities and youth that are most reviled. Society seems well able to reconcile itself to extreme intoxication behaviour among its more privileged echelons. With drug problems and pleasures, it is what surrounds and shapes the substance and the user as much as the internal characteristics of either that is key.

The constellation of events and experiences that become defined as the drug problem are not a factor of the natural properties of particular drugs, or the harms they cause, but are constructed in the process of selecting some harms as representative of general properties of the drug and its users. Harms that can be associated with many types of illicit drugs and many users of them are all gathered together as evidence for the drug problem, whereas harms caused by alcohol are attributed to biology, individual failings or bad luck, and those caused by prescription and over-the-counter pharmaceutical medicines are ignored altogether. A personal difficulty stemming from the use of a psychoactive substance is coded differently depending on the social status of the substance and the user. Human beings do not like to think about too many problems at once, and casting one set of events and circumstances as a public problem handily hides others from view, especially those closest to home. It means that drinking alcohol does not automatically make one complicit in the 'alcohol problem', but using illicit drugs makes the user legally and morally complicit in the drug problem.

This is apparent from the way in which drug debates are constructed, in the terms in which debates are set, the generation and interpretation of accepted, socially powerful facts about drug use, and what the 'crucial issues' are defined as being (Dingelstad et al., 1996). The terms of the debates around drugs are shaped by particular interests – professional, institutional, corporate and governmental – that have the power to negotiate their terms and limits. For example, professional discussion of medicinal anti-depressant drugs might frame the problem in terms of their side effects and how these can be managed. Patient groups might emphasize misdiagnosis and under-medication. Some patients suffering from mental illness may be concerned with forced treatment, which they can be subject to in the UK under the terms of the 1983 Mental Health Act. Calling them 'medicinal' already frames how the other issues involved will be spoken of – as issues of technical competence, patient compliance and treatment outcomes.

A certain amount of problem displacement is apparent. For instance, major funding for the Partnership for a Drug-Free America comes from pharmaceutical corporations, including the Nonprescription Drug Manufacturers Association. There are, in contrast, no powerful and legitimate interest groups speaking up for the illicit drugs 'industry'. As an example of how the debate could be framed differently, therapeutic users of street cannabis might view the drug problem as largely consisting of their being forced into an illegal activity in order to obtain effective treatment, and the continual fear that treatment may be suddenly cut off, but this is not accepted as a legitimate framing of the drug problem in most debates.

In the case of illicit drugs, the differential power of the user is an important factor in how their problem is framed and dealt with. This duality can be seen in the very different way use of crack-cocaine among affluent whites in the late 1970s and poor blacks in the 1980s was 'treated': in the first instance, with sympathy and support; in the second, with punitive sanctions (Reinarman and Levine, 2004). Well-off illicit drug users rarely end up in jail. Rush Limbaugh, the American media personality, included illicit drugs among his many turbocharged rants about what was destroying the USA. Users should be sent to jail, and the way to deal with the sentencing imbalance between blacks and whites for drug offences was to imprison more whites.

He passed up the opportunity to put this into practice in 2003 when he himself was investigated by the Florida Palm Beach State Attorney for illicit use of Hydrocodone and OxyContin, the latter known as 'hill-billy heroin' for its popularity in poor, rural areas of New England and Appalachia. Charges were dropped on condition he paid $30,000 dollars to cover the cost of the investigation and entered an eighteen-month course of therapy, to be delivered by his own doctor. Those who have the resources – financial and social – to keep their drug use man-ageable can do so. Those who have their lives disrupted by the violence of the illicit drug economy and the interventions of law enforcement agencies are in an altogether more precarious position, as more policed than protected.

Another way in which the drug problem is created from whole cloth is by dividing alcohol from illicit drugs and narrating the problems of alcohol as largely belonging to the flaws of individual users. The alcohol problem is held to be largely the responsibility of alcoholics and binge drinkers, rather than, for instance, the brewery companies that produce the drug (the drug barons) or the pubs that sell it (the pushers). There is little of the vertical integration of guilt and stigma associated with the illicit drugs trade. In the case of illicit drugs, every-one complicit in the production, supply and consumption of the sub-stance is part of the drug problem. In the USA, 'complicity' can include shop assistants selling the equipment needed to make methampheta-mine, which consists of cold medicine, butane and matches (Balko, 2006b). In 2006, Georgia shop owners and shop assistants were on the receiving end of Operation Meth Merchant, a sting in which infor-mants bought the ingredients for a 'meth kit', items commonly used in the home production of methamphetamine, consisting of over-the-counter cold remedies, camping gas and matches. The shopkeepers were arrested and prosecuted for supplying drug-making equipment, rather than selling camping gear to a festival-goer with flu. Their know-ingness and complicity was read back from doing what their job involved, a particularly harsh form of entrapment that is required when the crime is one of a transaction between willing partners.

The best trick the devil ever pulled was convincing the world that he did not exist. The most effective trick of the trade in constructing debates around drug problems is that of hiding the fact of their construction, making it appear that problems have occurred naturally, and doing so in terms that are amenable to some interests over others. The way drug debates are constructed hides the problems caused by prohibition of illicit drugs. Drug policy reformers have an uphill struggle to draw attention to this. Most books and articles critical of the drug war point to the often evidence-free processes by which illicit drugs came to be made illegal, and in particular the nefarious scheming of Harry J. Anslinger, Commissioner of the Federal Bureau of Narcotics during 1930–62, who relied on racist and invented accounts of the effect of cannabis on 'Mexicans and Negroes'. The repetition of this part of drug-war history is not intended as an interesting aside in the authors' main story. In relating it, they are attempting to make visible what is hidden behind drug prohibition, and to call the terms of the drug problem into question.

Deconstructing the drug problem is not some clever-clever piece of academic showboating. The distorted way in which these problems are set up is damaging, often to the most vulnerable in society. At best, it limits the support that can be given to people who have suffered various substance-use related harms, by rendering some invisible and others stigmatized. At worst, it actively contributes to the generation of harm. For instance, magic mushrooms (*psilocybe*) are used as a popular recreational drug in the UK. They carry very low risks of social and psychical harm and dependence. Users do not become dependent, overdose, or exhibit aggressive or harmful behaviour. Their popularity was until recently encouraged by an anomaly in British law, by which dried or otherwise processed *psylocibe* mushrooms were defined as a Class A controlled substance, whereas the fresh kind could be sold legally, usually in 'head' shops. In 2005, the UK government closed this loophole, so that all forms of *psylocibe* mushrooms became classified along with heroin and crack-cocaine as Class A substances. Now that magic mushrooms are no longer easily available, many users have turned to other illicit substances, such as LSD and Ketamine, which are more risky, and the purchase of which involves the user in criminal activity. The actions of prohibition agents change the political economy of risk, frequently damaging the people they are supposed to help. For instance, aggressive policing of street-level heroin users makes unsafe injecting practices and violence more likely (Fitzgerald, 2005). Drug-related deaths correlate positively with rises in the budget of the US Drug Enforcement Administration (Duncan, 1994). These side effects of the war on drugs are rarely written up as 'prohibition-related harms'.

Fried eggs and Swiss cheese: your brain on drugs

The drug problem is illustrated by images of what drugs do – to the body, the mind, and the self. These have the quality of being apparently unarguable. A picture at first sight is not a contestable text. The mechanisms of the brain have come to predominate in scientific and popular understandings of how drugs work, and the damage that they cause. One way of framing the damaging effects of illicit drug use is in terms of the brain and in imagery suggesting that severe, permanent damage is being done to it by 'drugs'. A well-known advert was released by the Partnership for a Drug-Free America in 1987. A man holds up an egg and says: 'This is your brain.' He holds a frying pan and says: 'This is drugs.' He cracks the egg into the frying pan and, with it bubbling away, declares: 'This is your brain on drugs. Any questions?' It was a powerful image, being frequently repeated and parodied in the media. A batty 1998 reprise features a pretty young woman destroying her kitchen with a frying pan as a metaphor for snorting heroin, while ranting about the consequences of it for friends, family, bank balance and self-respect.

The tagline for the 'Fried egg advert' appears to have dreadful grammar. 'This *is* drugs'? Surely, it should have been, 'This is *a* drug'? In fact, this apparent grammatical slip was, in the terms set by the construction of the drug problem, entirely correct. The phrase constructs 'drugs' as a single, unified category, including all illegal substances and excluding all legal ones. Cannabis, ecstasy, heroin, cocaine and amphetamines are lumped together as a catch-all 'drugs'. The worst effects of some are attributed to all. Righteous people are 'anti-drugs'. Deviant, morally reprehensible people are 'pro-drugs' and, by extension, pro-frying of brains and demolishing of kitchens.

The food theme continues in a powerful set of images purporting to show the effects of ecstasy use on brain chemistry, produced using scans of the brain of ecstasy users with neuro-imaging technology (positron emission tomography, PET). There is extensive use of this kind of imagery that produces a picture of the drug-affected brain as faulty. It is a very effective technique when communicating to the public the effects of drugs. They show parts of the brain lighting up as different substances are taken. Some compare the 'drugged brain' to the healthy brain, showing the drugged brain to be duller, darker or less colourful. The ecstasy users' brains were shown as dimmer than those of the controls, their neurotransmitters having been depleted (McCann et al., 1998). In one study they appeared like a Swiss cheese, full of holes. They were used by the US National Institute on Drug Abuse (NIDA) to show another 'brain on drugs', this time more of an analogy than a metaphor.

These images are very powerful as they appear to offer a window on to the brain. In reproductions of PET scans, we see what looks like a photograph. We are used to thinking that a camera photograph represents 'what's there' in front of the camera lens. So these brain scans must also show what's there. Yet these apparently neutral snapshots are highly partial and misleading. A camera filters light and shadow. A PET scan image is a representation of signal strength. Both are constructed and then 'read'. In some instances, they have been selected to exclude cases where users' brains appear to be much the same as those of controls (Ainsworth, 2002). Many studies do not exclude polydrug users so cannot establish with any certainty whether the observed differences can be traced to the particular substance under investigation or not (Kish, 2002).

There is also an implied commonsensical link between the Swiss cheese images of bright and dark splodges and users' actual mental functioning that is not demonstrated in reality. The images are chosen and in some cases combined to exaggerate very subtle differences that may have little or no relationship to actual behaviour or performance. It is rather like turning the contrast up on a monochrome television monitor to make shades of grey into stark black and white. However, because journalists, politicians and the public do not know how to 'read' brain scans these images are seared very powerfully into their minds as 'the brain on drugs'. Yet they have very little to say about the actual effects of specific substances on human behaviour and mental and physical development. They do have a lot to say about the shaping of the terms of discourse around drugs. A more appropriate tag would be: 'This is your brain on the war on drugs.'

Drug deaths, damage and side effects

[Our most destructive habits] commonly begin as pleasures of which we have no need and end as necessities in which we have no pleasure.
Thomas McKeown, *The Role of Medicine: Dream, Mirage or Nemesis?* (1976)

The 'drugs problem' may be a construction of the way illicit drugs are classed as a single category, and harms associated with them are all placed in that category, but those harms are real enough, apparent in the number of drug-related deaths every year. Yet, even here, the constructs of the drug problem are apparent. A drug-related death appears to be a stark fact, not a social construction. A death is singular, but not final, however. Attributing one death to a drug or another cause is not straightforward. It is a social process. For instance, is a death in a car accident in which the driver was drunk a drug-related death? Would you have to show conclusively that it was the drug that caused the accident, or would finding traces of the drug in the driver's body be enough? A woman dies from water intoxication due to overconsumption after taking ecstasy. Is that a drug-related death? It is not directly caused by the drug, but a combination of anxiety and one of the side effects of ecstasy, which is to limit the body's ability to process water. Would it be better to describe it as an ignorance-related death? This debate may be of little comfort to grieving loved ones, but it is necessary in order to understand the parameters of the drug problem.

Illicit drug-related deaths are special deaths, and are never allowed to be ordinary, routine deaths. In advanced, developed societies with ageing populations the 'routine' and the 'special' deaths are becoming ever more distinct (Guy and Holloway, 2007). Routine deaths, mainly those from old age, are the most prevalent, are often closely managed, and hence are the least visible. Routine deaths take place in segregated institutions like the hospice or hospital, or in the home. They are to some extent predictable and fit into the predominating societal and medical death narratives. Special deaths are uncommon and are shockingly visible. They are bizarre, outlandish, and deviant, but also close to home.

Drug-related deaths challenge the script of worthy deaths. There is no grief script, no palliative/death management process, and the response by others can make suffering worse, for instance, stigmatizing and blaming relatives. Death is often blameless, but these deaths certainly are not. Someone is at fault, whether a drug dealer, neglectful parents, or the user themselves. Death is usually private, but these often become public. The media specialize in making a death into a tragedy, and in the cases of poster-child deaths like that of Leah Betts, they become highly politicized. Leah Betts, who died in 1995 after taking ecstasy, became (literally) a poster child for the dangers of illicit drugs. She was an eighteen-year-old from an ordinary family who died, it was claimed, after trying the drug for the first time. The narrative – of an innocent young life taken by an evil drug – was complicated when it emerged that the cause of death was swelling of the brain, as a result of her drinking 7 litres of water in ninety minutes. It later became known that she had taken the drug in the past, which rendered her no longer 'innocent'. These deaths are a matter of public record (literally) as 'special deaths', deaths that are in some way threatening or that need a public investigation and dissection. However, most drug deaths do not fit the narrative either. The victims are too poor, too involved in drugs, too old, too knowing – and the stigma of a drug death leeches on to them and those close to them, as it is discovered that they were not children sacrificed to Baal, but complex, aware individuals.

The General Register Office for Scotland records 336 drug-related deaths for 2005 (General Register Office for Scotland, 2006). Looking at the statistics, it is notable how they overturn some assumptions about the danger zone for drugs deaths, which is presumed to lie in wait for the young and naive or damaged. The highest number of deaths, 126, occurs between the ages of thirty-five and forty-four, not among the younger, presumably less experienced users. One would expect naive users to be more at risk rather than these experienced users. Some socially generated effects are excluded from this figure, such as the risks of needle-sharing, and deaths due to the use of legitimate medications. The definition of a drug-related death in Scotland excludes deaths resulting from mental and behavioural disorders that arise from the use of alcohol, tobacco and volatile substances, those caused by secondary infections and complications, those from AIDS where the infection vector was shared needles, where the drug was part of a painkiller or cold remedy, such as paracetamol, and deaths from road traffic accidents that happened under the influence of drugs. In the USA, the Drug Abuse Warning Network uses a far broader definition, including causes of deaths related to alcohol use if the deceased is under twenty-one years of age, the legal drinking age in the USA. The National Minimum Drinking Age Act in 1984 deprived US states of Federal government revenue under the Federal Highway Aid Act unless they prohibited the purchase of alcohol by under-twenty-ones. Some drug-related deaths are therefore contingent on the age of the deceased.

Any categorical definition is in some way contingent and will perhaps include or exclude borderline cases in ways that may seem arbitrary to an uninvolved observer. The intention here is not to nitpick – there are of course reasons for each of these decisions – but to explore what goes into allocating a death to the category of a drug-related death and another not, which underscores what is and is not a dangerous substance. This figure then appears as an accomplished fact, and takes on a life of its own. For example, an increase in the numbers of deaths will be reported as indicative of a worsening drug problem, but may be due to other facts, such as a rise in the average

age of users, more polydrug use, and increased risk behaviour, which may itself be a product of drug-war myths.

> People rarely die from heroin overdoses – meaning pure concentrations of the drug which simply overwhelm the body's responses. What, then, are we to make of frequent reports of heroin overdoses from Plano, Texas and Strathclyde, Scotland? People do die while consuming heroin – but the overdose myth may actually make such deaths more, rather than less, likely. (Stanton Peele, 1999)

Before the Second World War, street heroin was very pure, at around forty times the purity of today's heroin. Overdoses became much more common in the 1970s, after the start of the drug war, meaning that deaths from heroin overdose became more likely as heroin purity decreased, the opposite effect from what we would expect if heroin was the cause of overdose deaths. Many so-called heroin overdoses result from the use of drug cocktails, such as alcohol and cocaine, alongside heroin. In Stanton Peele's view, users who think they are reducing the risk of overdose by limiting their heroin use often aim for the same effect by taking other drugs alongside heroin, which in combination are far more risky.

Side effects, problems associated with the use of some illicit drugs, are folded into the drug problem as hazards of the drug itself. In the Advisory Council on the Misuse of Drugs Report, *Pathways to Problems*, on the 'hazardous' use of drugs, alcohol and tobacco by young people, one of the indirect harms listed for heroin use is prostitution (Advisory Council on the Misuse of Drugs, 2006). The Report's authors were, of course, not intending to suggest that heroin use will turn a user's thoughts towards employment in the sex industry. Rather, the vulnerabilities of heroin use and prostitution intersect because of the difference between the financial demands of a heroin habit, the paucity of legitimate earning opportunities for many who have this habit, and the fact that both industries operate at the legal and social margins. The fact that some heroin users engage in prostitution to fund their habit could as easily be seen as resulting from the lack of legitimate opportunities available to them, a function of the marginalization of heroin and its users.

The spread of addiction

> 'Aren't you worried about becoming a cokehead?' Hugo enquired.
> 'No danger of that. The secret is to keep moving around. Be a moving target. A bit of sensi here, a snort of gianluca there, some vintage French

wines, then some Scotch, a chase of the dragon, a tab of acid, some mushrooms, that way you don't end up being dependent on anything.'
                              Tibor Fischer, 'We Ate the Chef' (Fischer, 2000: 57)

The construction of drug problems is most evident in the long historical process by which addiction emerged as the dominant narrative
through which drug and alcohol use is understood, a process which is
by no means finished. In 1716, Duncan Forbes, future President of the
Scottish Court of Session, and his brother had been so drunk on their
way to their mother's funeral in Edinburgh that they arrived at the kirk
(Church) to realize they had left her body behind (Buchan, 2003).
Instances such as these speak of a time when one was not so much
out of oneself when drunk, but drunk much of the time, as far as possible. Early eighteenth-century Edinburgh was a time and place when
drunkenness was not exculpated from daily life, any more than violence or throwing one's slops into the street were (Cockayne, 2007).

The reforming doctor and scientist Thomas Beddoes, writing in
1795, refers to the habit of drinking spirits of a Highland chieftain,
which was apparently cured by a slow reduction of dose (Brown, 1795
[1780]). 'Cured' is probably too strong a word. It appears to have been
a habit that the chieftain found not to his liking, but no reference is
made to it being a disease, a condition that could be generalized to
other bodies and minds. There is no sense of a disease entity being
present, or an experience that could be applied to other populations
and substances. The Western medical science of addiction, as it came
to be known, has changed over the two hundred-odd years since, from
recognizing unfortunate habits in some people, from which the right
treatment would dispose them, to conceiving of a dominating appetite
as a – and for some substances, the – prime mode of relating to them.
Society is currently undergoing another change, to taking up addiction
as a paradigm for the individual's relationship to the world.

Some drugs are problems because they motivate too much. Others
take away motivation. To some observers, cannabis use systematically
alters the users' personality traits, producing a drift towards apathy,
diminished attention, and less ability to plan and carry out complex
tasks (McGlothlin and West, 1968), a constellation of symptoms
referred to as amotivational syndrome. The use of the concept has
declined in psychiatry, the evidence for it now being considered to
consist of simply ongoing intoxication, rather than a profound shift in
personality structure (Johns, 2001). Addiction is the opposite problem
from amotivational syndrome. It is a state that motivates people
entirely towards finding and using more of the drug. It is more than

just a descriptive metaphor. The concept of addiction as a metabolic disease came to dominate understanding of drug and alcohol problems from the early twentieth century, and continues to exercise a hold over the imagination of users and society.

The rise of addiction presaged a new focus on the self-control demanded of individuals in modern society. Addiction is a threat to self-willed agency. It takes away self-control, and gives it to an object. The roots of this vision of addiction go back to the early modern period. The concept gained prominence in the USA during the early nineteenth century, although its origins can be traced back to the late eighteenth century. It was first developed in reference to alcohol, before it was applied to use of other drugs and eventually to all sorts of apparently compulsive behaviour. It was part of a process in which sins became sicknesses, and deviant individuals were ascribed to types. The drunkard became the alcoholic (Levine, 1978). What was before a regrettable sin became an individual type who was sick, who was unable to help his deviance but who could be cured of it.

Addiction has been created as a unified field from disparate elements – withdrawal, relapse, habit and so on – a combination of physical processes, personal practices, psychological attachments and individual and professional narratives. The World Health Organisation's ICD-10 classification of diseases uses five dimensions to evaluate addiction or dependence, which is now the preferred medical term. These are: withdrawal, reinforcement, tolerance, dependence and intoxication (World Health Organisation, 2007). Withdrawal refers to the reaction when the habituated user no longer has access to, or denies themselves access to, the substance. Reinforcement is 'a measure of the substance's ability, in human and animal tests, to get users to take it again and again, and in preference to other substances'. Tolerance is a progression over time whereby more and more of the substance is needed to satisfy the user. Dependence is a measure of the difficulty users have in quitting, the rate of relapse, at which users who have stopped return to using the substance, the self-rated 'need' for the substance, and continued use of the substance despite evidence of harm. Finally, intoxication is included for, 'though not usually counted as a measure of addiction in itself, the level of intoxication is associated with addiction and increases the personal and social damage a substance may do', so intoxication becomes guilty by association.

These elements are constructed and defined in very different ways. For instance, 'dependence' is partly reliant on subjective reports of the user, and partly on an aggregated measure of how successfully users give up the substance, which then depends on other factors, such as the user's desire to quit. Addiction only becomes apparent when the user tries to stop, and in the case of socially sanctioned habits like coffee- and tea-drinking, this may be never. Continued use 'despite evidence of harm' is also malleable, since evidence of harm is taken to include legal problems arising from use of the substance. A smoker will encounter fewer legal problems from their use of cigarettes than will a user of a controlled substance like cocaine, so the harm is in fact generated within the legal and institutional context, rather than the relationship between the individual and the substance. Intoxication is also highly localized and reliant on such things as the state of mind of the user, their expectations, their context and the dose and form in which the substance is taken. It seems to have no intrinsic relevance to the other dimensions of addiction chosen. Tobacco has the highest 'capture rate' (the proportion of users who become addicted) of all substances, but in the forms most commonly consumed is only mildly intoxicating. To some extent, then, the definition of addiction is self-referring and highly culture-bound.

Addiction seems to be both a challenge to autonomous self-identity, and a narrative that can reassert ontological security by retelling many aspects of experience as a disease – a 'hook' – which means that the individual's autonomy is destroyed and rebuilt. Until fairly recently, addiction applied to harmful use of drugs and alcohol. A recent development is that addiction has become a paradigm for behaviour in many other spheres of life, and not only in joking references to chocoholicism. One study (Knight, 2005) was reported as finding that email was addictive and had similar confusing effects on the mind to illicit drugs. It was directly compared with cannabis. Gambling was formerly seen as a vice, but it is now described in terms of addiction. Use of the Internet, exercise, eating, sex, all carry addiction potential and there are more and more people who describe their behaviour in these terms. This development speaks of a loss of faith in human progress, and a questioning of the terms of that progress. The idea that major public problems would be defined in terms of the general population having too much food, or chocolate, would appear ludicrous to people who had experienced the deprivations of wartime rationing or the Great Depression. There is a widespread sense, particularly in Anglo-Saxon countries, that we have created a runaway juggernaut that cannot be controlled but only clung on to for dear life.

Environmentalists try and find the brakes. Anti-capitalists attempt to take the wheels off.

As so often in this field, developments are paradoxical. Western society emphasizes choice and agency, expressed through consumption; at the same time, a growing range of consumption practices are pathologized as addictive (Reith, 2004). Addiction, however, is less and less located in a dangerous object, or the habits of specific social groups, but lies in the interpretation of the individual as having lost control over his or her consumption practices, whether it be gambling, sex, shopping or chocolate. Addiction is the revenge of the object on those who will (literally) consume it. There was a contradiction in the nineteenth-century notion of the addict identity, though. Something lost in modern accounts, but still relevant, is that addiction was a disease of the will, but it was also too much will, a will to consumption, a will to forgo every other need – for food, respectability, sleep – in order to pursue its object. Addiction requires an effort to maintain, and represents a triumph of the self over all else.

Consuming hunger: addiction as a disease

Drugs and alcohol are very dangerous, we are told. So why would people, knowing the risks, take drugs that have the potential to harm them? A commentary for the journal *Science* from 8 January 1886 notes the widespread addiction to opium, for which is blamed the deaths of patients and soldiers due to sudden opium deprivation (Anon., 1886). It reflects on a pamphlet by Dr Meylert, *Notes on the Opium Habit*. Amongst the recommended remedies listed for opium habituation are coca and avena sativa, noted as not being of much use; cannabis indica, hydrocyanic acid (hydrogen cyanide), hyoscyamus (henbane), stychnia (strychnine), chloroform and quinine. Moral treatment is also mentioned, but this is in the form of the patient's trust in the physician, not the sense which would later become commonplace, the restoration of moral rectitude to the patient. The addict is in potential physical, rather than psychosocial, danger. A cure will allow him or her to be weaned off opium with as little suffering as possible. The concept of addiction and its treatment that came to dominate science and lay understanding in the following century was very different. It became a disease of the soul rather than the body.

Alan Leshner was Director of the US National Institute on Drug Abuse (NIDA) from 1994 to 2001. He published two articles with the assertive title 'Addiction is a Brain Disease' (Leshner, 1997, 2001). His argument, one that is widespread among addiction scientists, is that the addicted brain is physically different from the non-addicted brain. He draws on an extensive swathe of research that breaks apart the previous distinction between physiological and psychological addictions. This distinction had been used to separate substances thought to be habituating, such as cocaine and cigarettes, from those that were addicting, like the opiates. In fact, all psychological events have some kind of physiological basis. According to the addiction-as-disease perspective, changes wrought by drugs in the brain's reward system – for most drugs, the mesolimbic dopaminergic system – have left them permanently altered in ways that promote further substance seeking. In these terms, drugs change how we want – they alter incentive salience, to use the technical term, and embed harmful social behaviours.

From this perspective, addicts are simply not in control of their behaviour, and cannot be judged for it. Addicts are not seeking the euphoric reward from drug use. They are simply seeking. The brain is altered and remains altered after the drug has been removed, so that the addict is never cured, but is always in chronic danger of relapse. Therefore, moderate or safe use of drugs for the recovering addict is not a possibility. For decades, post-modernist sociologists and philosophers criticized what they called Cartesian mind–body dualism, which envisages humans as disembodied pilots of the machinery of the body. Many a text would declare its purpose as deconstructing mind–body duality. Here at last is what they called for. It is a scientific acceptance of the end of mind–body dualism, in favour of the dominance of the body – really, the brain – over the mind.

Leshner's confidence seems misplaced. It is known that drugs and alcohol are addictive substances, because . . . people are addicted to them. That amounts to a tautology, a self-proving but meaningless statement. It tells us nothing about what addiction is and why some people define their actions in relation to a psychoactive substance as being 'addictive'. Not everyone who *tries* cigarettes, drugs or alcohol continues to use them, and not everyone who regularly takes them conforms to expected dependent behaviour patterns. In fact, most do not. This would suggest that drugs are not wholly addictive, or that the origins of the features of behaviour called 'addiction' lie elsewhere. To explain this anomaly, drug users and alcoholics are spoken of in terms of 'addictive personalities', meaning that some people have the mental and physiological propensities to develop reliance on regular doses, while others have the mental strength, or the brain equivalent of a thick hide, with which they can consume drugs or drink heavily without becoming ensnared. Addiction and alcoholism are terms for particular patterns of behaviour by some people.

There is a physical basis for any psychological process or observed human behaviour. It could not be otherwise, the brain being a physical organ. Yet this explains little. Most regular users of psychoactive substances do not develop addictive or harmful patterns of behaviour. Most of those who do, will stop without outside intervention. These are not the patterns of behaviour that characterize a chronic relapsing disease. Furthermore, the set of changes in reward pathways that Leshner identifies are not specific to drug use, but are generalizable to many other forms of behaviour. Most recently, the brain reward system held accountable for drug addiction has been implicated in overeating (Wang et al., 2006), predictably publicized as food being an addiction. In that sense, any repetitive, habitual or desired behaviour which has the possibility of being excessive could be described in this way – sex, masturbation, driving, watching television, and playing the lottery – and are.

Addiction, within the scientific literature and in popular terms, is usually understood as the adaptation of the mind and body to the drug, such that when the drug is withdrawn the user experiences withdrawal symptoms – mental or physical sickness, which the drug can cure. The user wishing to stop must fight these symptoms with willpower, otherwise he or she will give in and relapse into the dark night of drug dependence. We miss a vital sociological element that makes addiction a meaningful experience, and that tells some people they are addicted, causing some to embrace their self-diagnosis as addicts. Addiction is appetite that has acquired a particular status and meaning. It is the appetite speaking to itself. This applies to the route into addiction and the perception of an individual that they are addicted. Addiction is the specification of appetite in the mind of the individual. They come to experience what they are feeling as a hunger for a specific substance. The state of addiction is an identity that is embraced by some drug and alcohol users and not others. It provides a sick role, a way in which a deviant can accept their deviant status yet remain connected with the rest of society. Addiction has to be experienced to become real, and spoken back to, articulated in terms like Leshner's and that of many other addiction specialists.

The experience of addiction

Cocaine isn't addictive; it's just very moreish.
Overheard

Impairment is a primary narrative of intoxication. Addiction is an impairment of the self, a disease of the will (Ribot, 1896; Valverde, 1998). It may not be a disease, but it is a powerful script for action and reflection on personal experiences with drugs of all sorts, and other forms of behaviour. Addiction and pleasure are properties presumed to inhere in the chemical composition of the substance itself and its interaction with receptors in the brain, and are held to be the two ends of pincer movement in which the human mind is caught as it begins its slow journey towards chemical servitude. The statement 'I control the drug, it doesn't control me' is often quoted ironically, as a sign of the self-delusion of the drug user, detached from reality and no longer able to see the effect of intoxication and withdrawal on him- or herself and on others he or she has contact with. Animal experiments have been used to back up this perspective. Laboratory rats able to push a button to deliver cocaine will do so until completely exhausted, ignoring food and water to do so. This is used as evidence that addictive drug use results from a very basic neurophysiological compulsion, and that if currently illicit drugs were freely available, many or most would be addicts.

> If heroin were easily available to everyone, and if there were no social pressure of any kind to discourage heroin use, a very large number of people would become heroin addicts. (Goldstein, 1979)

> Availability is the mother of use. (Califano, 2007)

Despite apparent similarities with human behaviour, there is a limited extent to which we can generalize from these experiments. The neurophysiological compulsion perspective is based on partial evidence, composed of laboratory experiments on animals, which are notoriously difficult to generalize from, and self-selecting testimony from addicts who blame the substance for subordinating their selves to it. This discourse is constructed as illicit drug addicts are encouraged and often required to seek treatment. They have a direct inducement to perform as addicts.

The existing animal experiments had frequently used rats isolated in cages. Bruce K. Alexander conducted his series of Rat Park experiments in the 1970s. He worked on the knowledge that rats are social animals. Isolation would produce great distress in them. Hence he thought the excessive drug use was the result of that distress, not the drug's effects. In those circumstances, the compulsive use of a drug like cocaine or morphine is a self-fulfilling hypothesis. Distressed animals and humans will use drugs to self-medicate their distress when they can. The Rat Park was designed to mimic the rat's natural environment. It contained a large, mixed group of rats, with space to play or have sex. The experimenters tried everything they could to get the rats to behave in an addictive manner. One set of rats was force-fed morphine for fifty-seven days and then introduced to the Rat Park. Despite this, they did not demonstrate a preference for morphine solution over water. The morphine was sweetened in order to induce sugar-loving rats to try it in preference to water. Again, they would try the morphine and reject it. The implications of the experiment, that addiction is not a natural process, were largely ignored.

Further evidence that Goldstein's theory is incorrect comes in the form of a natural experiment involving American soldiers during the Vietnam War. The use of heroin and other opiates by American servicemen during the war was common. They were easily available, especially relative to the more common drugs in use in the USA at the time. This caused considerable consternation, as it was expected under the prevailing theories that if the men had used heroin they would most likely be addicted, and would then form a large problematic and generally incurable addict population on their return to the USA, which would require massive expenditure on treatment. Concern became particularly acute during 1971 when the number of US troops in Vietnam was being reduced, with thousands returning to the USA and to civilian lives.

The US administration tasked a team led by Lee Robins to identify which men needed services and of what kind (Robins et al., 1974). Her study set out to identify the range and extent of drug use in Vietnam by US Army enlisted men, how many had used drugs on returning to the USA, what proportion remained drug-dependent, and their treatment needs. She confirmed that a large proportion had used opiates – 45 per cent of enlisted men returning in 1971. Further, one fifth had used them sufficiently to become physiologically habituated, displaying withdrawal symptoms if the drug was denied them. Her findings would have been enough to set the panic alarms off, had she not looked at their drug use since returning to the USA. Most who had used drugs in Vietnam, including those who said they were addicted, had simply stopped using them on their return. Of those who had reported addiction in Vietnam, 2 per cent reported continuing addiction when back in the USA. When out of the context in which their heroin use had begun, without the easy and cheap availability of opiates they stopped using them, without treatment or reported extensive difficulties.

Her study indicated that the most demonic of demon drugs, heroin – which we are assured will result in instantaneous addiction – can be used almost casually and without dangers of long-term addiction, given the circumstances. Her findings do not mean we have no need to worry about the problems of heroin users, or other drug-dependent individuals. It should alert us to the need to identify those features of users' environments that *can* lead them to long-term and harmful dependence (Robins and Slobodyan, 2003), in order that these risks be effectively ameliorated. The study's findings indicate that one of these risks may be the expectation of addiction itself. In constructing some substances as having the ability to invoke demonic possession we can create a cage for the user, who is encouraged to interpret his or her experiences as evidence of being powerless before addiction. That element of the experience of addiction can become self-confirming. It lies at the heart of the construction of a related, but distinct, addiction paradigm, that of alcoholism.

Alcoholism: familiar dependence

It is easy to deny one's self festivity; it is difficult to deny one's self normality.

G. K. Chesterton, *Heretics* (1905: 103)

In Howard Hawks' *Rio Bravo* (Warner Bros., 1959), Dude (Dean Martin) is a washed-up alcoholic. In the long, wordless opening scene, we see him in a bar. Too poor to afford another drink, he implores a man for money. The man taunts him with a dollar. He throws the dollar into a spittoon for the pleasure of humiliating Dude into abasing himself by picking it out, plainly something that has happened before. Dude bends down to pick it out of the spittoon, when his former partner, Sheriff John T. Chance (John Wayne), intervenes by kicking the spittoon away. Dude reacts by punching his old friend.

Setting alcoholism apart from addiction may seem like reproducing the division between acceptable and/or named and stigmatized and/or invisible substance-use problems. However, alcoholism does stand apart from illicit drug addictions, in its nature as a social metaphor and cultural trope that is much more powerful in its relative ordinariness than the wretched image of the drug addict. Alcoholism is partly a subset of drug addiction, but also resists being included in its rubric, and stands partially outside and independent of it. In part, this independence reflects the autonomy and independence of alcoholics themselves, and the unusual combination of treatment and social movement that is Alcoholics Anonymous (AA).

Illicit drug addicts are relatively powerless, socially speaking. Those caught in the net of surveillance and punishment or coercive treatment have relatively little power or control over the institutional process they enter into, although they are not entirely without autonomous choice. Those addicted to prescription medications lack even the acknowledgement of their existence, with no kind of accepted narrative for their experience. Alcoholics, in the classic mould set out by AA in the first step of its twelve-step programme, declare themselves to be powerless over their illness. Within the declaration that, 'we were powerless over alcohol, that our lives had become unmanageable', is paradoxically a statement of power. Alcoholics have far greater scope than other addicts to define their condition, and to organize their own treatment. To some extent, alcoholism gives them greater personal and social power. They can claim their condition as an identity, define its parameters and the course of its aetiology. Indeed, doctors often report alcoholic patients to be difficult for precisely the reason that they challenge professional wisdom and demonstrate persistent autonomy from professional medical control.

Their power is partly due to the class and social status of many declared alcoholics, but also the work that declaring oneself an alcoholic can do in terms of cohering one's own identity. Alcoholics have a higher social status than other addicts, partly because of the criminalization of illicit drug users, but also because of the development of a distinct alcoholic identity autonomous from medical narratives. The recovered alcoholic in American society has a special social standing, as a person who has relinquished something that was more dear to them than anything, who has struggled and overcome (Room, 2000a). This partly explains the emphasis in AA on abstinence and the rejection of moderate drinking as a possibility for the alcoholic. Making moderate drinking a goal degrades the achievement of alcoholic sobriety to something like the status of a reckless driver learning to drive slower. Alcoholism tips the neat ordering of the 'problem of the drug problem' over. Alcoholism in the West is perceived as a middle-class illness, one that affects more men than women, more the middle-aged than the young. The stereotype of the alcoholic is often seen as a quite successful person, an Anglo-Saxon, middle-aged, businessman, married with children. Although alcoholics come in all shapes and sizes, this remains the predominating stereotype. The contrast with illicit drug addicts is sharp. It is not the alcohol habit's propensity to interfere with work and family life that makes it so problematic, although it does of course interfere. Rather, it is the fact that alcoholics are visibly good at getting on with things in spite of the 'alcohol challenge', the danger of alcoholism. Their clever strategies for maintaining a facade of sobriety, their wily manipulations of colleagues and family members are legendary, being woven into the mythology of the alcoholic. Alcoholism is very different from drug problems in placing the individual centre-stage as an active player in their suffering, rather than a victim of the drug *deus ex machina*.

Alcoholism emerged historically from the wreckage of Prohibition. Temperance and addiction-as-disease perspectives located addiction in the substance, first of alcohol and then of other drugs. In the 1930s USA, the locus of alcohol addiction transferred from the drug itself to the individual, partly under the influence of the early AA movement. It was claimed that some people were prone to alcohol addiction, allowing alcoholism to be recognized as a disease while normal drinking remained a socially acceptable pastime. The 'individual vulnerability' perspective allowed a society recently abandoning prohibition of alcohol to take the sting out of legalization. The problem was held to be not in fact liquor itself, but rather that certain individuals were metabolically prone to fall into a self-destructive dependency on it. The existence of illicit drug addictions are employed as evidence to delegitimize those drugs, and to exclude the possibility of controlled use with minimal harm. Alcohol addiction, in contrast, was used to legitimate alcohol and to delegitimize temperance, a once powerfully progressive ideology that became a topic of fun following the repeal of Prohibition.

Who then speaks for alcoholism? Again, in contrast to illicit drug addictions, it is frequently the alcoholic. Illicit drug addictions are usually explained by experts, enforcers and policymakers. Alcoholics more often speak for themselves, actively contributing to the discourse on alcoholism. One might study Alcoholics Anonymous by looking at the distinctions, both explicit and implicit, drawn by members between different kinds of alcoholics. An addiction specialist might study them in terms of the DSM-IV or ICD-10 criteria of dependence in observed behaviour, levels of alcohol consumption, liver damage, persistence in spite of harm and so on. In practice, AA members would also draw on expert criteria, while maintaining alcoholism as something only the AA insider can 'know'. This insider perspective means that the representation of alcoholism in literature is very different from accounts of drug addiction, as it is often the alcoholic who is writing.

Alcoholism is the solution to the problem of alcohol, the problem of having a drug whose recreational use is almost universal, in a society that prohibits the use of most recreational drugs. The alcoholic is a socially meaningful category in a way that, for instance, the heroin addict is not. In terms of intoxication with alcohol, often we drink to be able to break social boundaries with, if not impunity, then with abandon. The alcoholic (as opposed to the drunk) is in contrast something of a conformist deviant. He or she drinks not to break boundaries, but drinks within them – in the morning, at work and so on – but mostly closely observes the proprieties by concealing drink from family members, only drinking when alone and so on. So the alcoholic is not demonstrative of those who drink wrongly, such as the permanent drunk, the drink driver, or the violent drunk. The alcoholics because of their apparent success demonstrate how one may drink with impunity, whenever one feels the need to.

Illicit drug users are often implicitly required to 'perform' addiction in order to access services, whereas the real problems they encounter are deprivation, poor mental health and domestic violence. The terms within which they perform are set by the institutions and services they engage with. What alcoholism does for normal drinking is not what heroin addiction does for recreational heroin users. With heroin, there is a world to be entered, but with alcoholism the world of alcohol is one that the individual is already a part of, by dint of being a member of an alcoholized society. For alcoholics, it is the world of recovery they join. AA does not express the interests of alcoholics to the outside world, in the way that Rotterdam's *Junkiebond* (Junkie Union) expresses collective demands. They do not see themselves as having common social and political demands, for instance, for social inclusion. The AA narrative specifically rejects the adoption of any public 'line'. Again, paradoxically, for alcoholics the problem is often stated in terms not of rejection and stigma but of inclusion and collusion, of being supported in their drinking by family, friends and colleagues. There is a renewed emphasis on drinking pathologies in the UK, Europe and the USA, making alcohol part of the problem of consumption in modern life.

Vulnerable selves

[Our drinking] started getting out of control . . . it would be like 'I cannot believe I was with that guy the other night.' Sometimes you just wake up next to him or something, and you don't know what happened.

Female freshman, 'Alcohol and Acquaintance Rape: Strategies to Protect Yourself and Each Other', US Higher Education Center for Alcohol and Other Drug Prevention, 1999

A recent development in public health policy has drawn alcohol, cigarettes, food and some illicit drugs together into the 'problem of consumption', whereby more and more public policy is targeted towards regulating and getting individuals to regulate their consumption. This change has been driven by a number of factors – the generalization of addiction and risk as tropes for the relationship between individuals and objects in their environment, including other people, the fragmentation of rave culture from the mid-1990s, and, in Britain, the nightclub/pub-driven regeneration of town centres, which has fundamentally altered many drinking spaces.

> The intoxicating draught . . . removes all sense of fear and shame, and emboldens them to commit every wicked and desperate enterprise. (Henry Fielding, 1824 [1751]: 375)

A story from *Time* magazine's Europe edition on binge drinking by young people is headlined 'The British Disease' and is illustrated with a photograph of a classic British Friday-night fight. The tableau is familiar. One, presumably well-oiled, young man attempts rather cackhandedly to punch another, while a woman, presumably girlfriend to one of the pair, tries gamely to hold the two men apart (McAllister, *Time Europe*, 11 December 2005). There has been a change in the grouping of alcohol and drug intoxication as social problems from the mid-1990s on. The UK government has focused on the management of intoxication as a phenomenon, alongside the control of specific substances. This has not displaced long-term health risks, but has shifted the problem category of alcohol users from middle-aged, middle-class male alcoholics to younger, female, binge drinkers.

Binge drinking means drinking without apparent limits. In the developed world, where material abundance exists alongside psychological insecurity, we currently hear a lot about limits – the limits to growth, the predicted demise of all we hold dear. Binge consumption demonstrates a scorn for limits, so is fundamentally at odds with the zeitgeist. Bingeing is appetite without satiation. To do this requires overcoming the appetite (in the biological sense). Continual gorging demonstrates a victory over the body. In this way, it is the inversion of addiction. If addiction is slavery of the will to appetite, binge drinking is the victory of the will over appetite. In that sense, it has a little in common with carnivalism, the periods of gorging and excess that were part of folk culture in the Middle Ages. Fiona Measham (2004) writes of carnival time and the pursuit of pleasure in British leisure culture. From the early 1990s, there had been a shift from the 'ecstasy plus Lucozade' purity of the rave scene to a cocktail of various illicit drugs and alcohol used by young people in Britain. Their drug and alcohol use defies the limits of consumption and the boundaries between different substances. This new intoxication practice has reconfigured the drug problem to some extent, as one of risk and vulnerability, not from the substance, or one's own possible proneness to addiction, but from others.

> If you fall over or pass out, remember your skirt or dress may ride up . . . for all our sakes, please make sure you're wearing nice pants and that you've recently had a wax. (Suffolk Constabulary, *Safe!*, 2006)

An advert produced by the Portman Group, the British alcohol industry body that aims to promote responsible drinking, called 'Who's Looking Out for You?', plays on fears of sexual assault resulting from intoxication-induced vulnerablity. It shows a young woman in the foreground, a look of fear on her face. In the background, a shady, predatory young man stares at her. Suffolk Police produced a tongue-in-cheek women's lifestyle magazine, *Safe!*, proffering sisterly advice to young women about the risks of excessive drinking (Suffolk Constabulary, 2006). These risks are mainly to their appearance, dignity, and also implied vulnerability to rape. Some North American college websites advise students that one of the risks of a night out is having their drinks or food poisoned with 'date rape' drugs. These messages address the recreational user, rather than the problem user, and suggest that the dangers of drug and alcohol use lie less in their propensity for addiction than in their exposing the user to risk from others.

Unsafe others

> Robberies by the aid of chloroform are becoming of almost daily occurrence . . . If this new species of crime, already so alarmingly prevalent, be not met by stern and fearful retribution, robberies will be multiplied tenfold, for the use of chloroform involves little risk to the rogue, unless it be the risk of the halter.
>
> *New York Times* (15 May 1855)

Chloroform was first used as an anaesthetic in 1847. Reports soon began to circulate of men and women being robbed under the influence of chloroform. The attacker would, it seems, wave a chloro-form-impregnated handkerchief under their noses and they would wake up hours later, naked and stripped of all their possessions. These – usually unconfirmed – accounts continued to appear in the press into the twentieth century. A provision in the 1861 Offences Against the Person Act created a specific offence of assault by stupefaction, specifically naming chloroform and laudanum. At the end of the twen-tieth century and the start of the twenty-first, the fear of drugged assault resurfaced in the form of drug-facilitated sexual assault.

The Drug Enforcement Administration (DEA) defines GHB, Rohypnol and Ketamine as 'predatory drugs', a category of drugs that it claims are deliberately used to facilitate sexual attacks by men on women. In its website, it presents the dangers not as being the nine-teenth-century racialized fears of the white slaver using opium – that the victim is sedated and then raped – but that the victim has her will sucked away from her by the action of the drug. The drug, like the clever rapist, leaves no evidence on or in the victim's body that she has been assaulted. It is metabolized quickly and no trace is left with which to provide evidence of a drug-facilitated assault. The DEA also claims that the victim's memory is impaired and this 'eliminates evidence about the attack'. It states that:

> The tasteless and odorless depressants Rohypnol and GHB are often used in the commission of sexual assaults due to their ability to sedate and intoxicate unsuspecting victims. (Office of National Drug Control Policy, 2005)

One would expect the statement that Rohypnol and GHB are often used to commit sexual assault has some serious research to back it up. Similar statements appear on police and student union websites around the world. However, there seems little in the way of hard evi-dence. Data-free reporting and policy are the norm here. In response to the apparent threat of drug-facilitated rape, various measures have been implemented, mainly in the form of risk-screening advice that is supposed to make the drinker safer.

One is the drug-test coaster – which seems to be little more than a gimmick offering false reassurance, as they are unreliable tests (Meyers and Almirall, 2004). Police in Peterborough gave 900 drug-testing kits to drinkers in the Christmas period of 2005 (*Evening Telegraph*, 31 January 2006). They now provide bars and clubs with testing kits, so that people who have left their drink alone or have had one bought for them can have them tested. The community safety office for Peterborough police noted that none of the tests had been positive, but thought that the existence of the kits brought reassurance, although it seems they would have been as likely to generate anxiety. Similarly, a previous push to give out drug-testing kits had been labelled 'a success' by the police, although there was no mention of positive tests being reported or any spiker being caught.

One of the few studies to investigate this scientifically analysed 2,003 specimens from victims of sexual assault where drugs were thought to be a factor – usually in that the victim was thought to have taken them (Slaughter, 2000). Two thirds of samples were positive, mostly related to alcohol and cannabis, of which less than 3 per cent were GHB and Rohypnol (a benzodiazepine). The study lasted two years and incidences of GHB/rohypnol appeared to be declining. There was no suggestion that these drugs had been involuntarily administered to the victim. A US study employed a nationwide system of testing urine taken from victims of claimed sexual assault where drugs were thought to be involved (Elsohly and Salamone, 1999). From a twenty-six-month period, 1,179 samples were analysed: 39.7 per cent were negative for any psychoactive substance tested for. Of those that tested positive, 40.8 per cent were positive for alcohol, then cannabis at 18.5 per cent. Benzodiazepines came in at 8.2 per cent (not necessarily all Rohynpnol) and GHB at 4.1 per cent. Plenty of benzodiazepine and GHB samples were positive for other controlled substances and for alcohol. The prevalence of the term 'date-rape drug' as the dominant narrative to describe GHB is shown by the fact that medical personnel use the term, even when administering it as an anaesthetic. A report on a death caused by GHB is put primarily in the context of it being a date-rape drug, despite most recorded deaths caused by it being due to voluntary ingestion (Jones, 2001). The drug has become understood in these terms, as a date-rape drug rather than a recreational (albeit risky) drug.

The rape-drug phenomenon speaks of a myth that women need to be protected from men, but also from themselves. These drugs are particularly scary because they apparently allow rapists to rape with impunity. The fact that the criminal justice system has been allowing many to do just that for years, without any chemical assistance, has been skated over. The public problem perspective is apparent again, creating a largely fictional problem in place of the very real problem of widespread sexual violence. The failings of society to tackle sexual violence are transferred to the 'rape drug'. The damsels-in-distress approach is reactionary in two ways. First, it endorses the innocent maiden picture of the rape victim, young and naive and slightly stupid for drinking the potion given to her by the evil sorcerer. Rape victims who don't fit this picture are then given short shrift. Second, it emphasizes women's need for protection. It not only constructs the perfect crime, but it also constructs the perfect victim. A woman who is unconscious cannot have her actions argued over in court, or have a defence lawyer imply that she in fact consented. In constructing the drug-rape victim as the perfect victim of rape, the drug-rape lobby are devaluing the women who do not correspond to this image, which most do not.

The panic fed into a new set of rules of behaviour for women to follow, reproduced by countless newspaper and magazine articles. The rules are that a woman should never go alone to a bar, club or party; she should never accept a drink from a man she does not know well or trust; she should observe her own and her friends' drinks at all times and never leave a drink unattended; and she should not leave a bar, club or party with someone (a man or anyone) she has just met.

Three of these four rules are the kind of evidence a defence lawyer would use to draw doubt on a victim's testimony in any case of stranger rape. The complainant went to a club on her own (she is sexually loose and available). She accepted a drink from a strange man (she is unable to say 'no' and mean it – she led him on). She left with a strange man (she had consented to sex). They are effectively playing the rapist's game and accepting the narrative that there are some things that good girls don't do. Furthermore, they chime with a widespread sense that what ends up in a woman's glass is her responsibility, whether she is involuntarily spiked or voluntarily intoxicated (Finch and Munro, 2005). They also construct a world in which men are innately dangerous to women. Women have to be on their guard at all times. Intoxication spaces like pubs, clubs and parties become places of fear and anxiety.

There are rapists who use drugs to assist rape, but like most other forms of sexual assault the reality is very different from the myth. Medical staff have been known to drug patients in order to rape them. One Canadian nurse used a legal tranquillizer, Halcion, to rape hundreds of women (Moore and Valverde, 2000). Yet these cases are not included in the date-rape drug narrative because they do not tie into the illicit leisure of carnivalistic youth culture, or of women drinking in public.

In the early 1990s, an anti-drugs advert shown in Scottish cinemas implied, without daring to state plainly, that the drug ecstasy made men rape women. The substance was at the time called a 'rape drug' in the press, supposedly either making women unable to say no, or men incapable of accepting a refusal. This claim was in the realm of 'not even wrong'. It was the inversion of the truth. One of the pleasures of acid-house clubs and raves was that sense of safety for women, the non-predatory aspects of it, which were directly associated with ecstasy use, or rather the absence of alcohol use (Henderson, 1993). The drug-rape panic seems to throw this backward, so that public spaces are once again areas of fear and trepidation for women. It could be argued that risk has become constitutive of social intercourse. Risk constitutes the social world. The drug-rape panic is making environments that are relatively safe into felt unsafe environments. Risk goes along with blame. Women victims of violence get more blame when they have been drinking, male aggressors less (Richardson and Campbell, 1980). The focus on impaired victims is easily renarrated into one of intoxicated victims responsible for the situation they have got themselves into.

Nicotine bodies

Nicotine withdrawal symptoms include irritability, craving, cognitive and attentional deficits, sleep disturbances, and increased appetite. These symptoms may begin within a few hours after the last cigarette, quickly driving people back to tobacco use.

National Institute on Drug Abuse, 'NIDA Research Report – Tobacco Addiction' (1998)

Addiction is a way of rationalizing the apparently irrational. Smoking is one drug that is given no rational explanation. Alcohol, heroin, cannabis and cocaine, each have a public health narrative that acknowledges there are locally rational reasons for partaking even in abusive use, in terms of life stressors, hopelessness and other pleasure-deficit explanations. Smoking does not easily fit in with alcoholism, binge drinking and drug addiction because it is such an ordinary, mundane habit. However, it is increasingly being explained in terms of a physical adaptation, in which there is a systematic priming of the body through exposure to nicotine, both voluntary and involuntary through the neurochemical processes of nicotine dependence (Fagerström and Sawe, 1996; Fagerström et al., 1993; Groman and Fagerström, 2003), conceiving of smokers as patients with a disease or chronic disorder (Blazic-Cop et al., 2001; Boyle et al., 2000; Hughes, 1999; Khurana et al., 2003). Smoking has come to be increasingly defined in terms of a bodily disorder of nicotine addiction. A

2006 series of British Department of Health adverts, 'Hooked', shows rather violent images of smokers with large fishhooks in their mouths, with the tagline, 'The average smoker needs over 5,000 cigarettes a year'. The advert would have a very different meaning were it to state that 'The average smoker *wants* over 5,000 cigarettes a year', or 'likes', or 'enjoys'.

This has supported and been supported by the development and popularization of pharmaceutical smoking-cessation therapies, principally nicotine replacement therapy (NRT) and also buproprion, a development underscored by recent attempts to develop a nicotine vaccine (Fagerström and Balfour, 2006) and neurotransmitter antagonists (George and O'Malley, 2004; Jarvik and Henningfield, 1988) that will rework the body to make it nicotine resistant, although this conception may itself be challenged or augmented by an understanding of nicotine dependence as a mental disorder (Campion et al., 2006), which would define most smokers as being mentally ill.

Smoking lacks the involved, bordering on romantic, intensity of alcoholism and opiate addictions. It is problematic for the disease concept of addiction. Addiction is constructed as a kind of bondage of the soul, which is trapped in the physical matrix of the body. This has proved very hard to apply to smoking because, although the long-term health risks are not in doubt, smoking causes very little personal or social disruption. It does not interfere with smokers' ability to work or fulfil social obligations. It does not cause legal problems, and only limited financial difficulties. Alcoholics famously run up debts but smokers appear not to. Conversely, there is no concept of controlled use either, as there is with alcohol, for instance (Schaler, 2000), and heroin (Warburton et al., 2005). Any use is dangerous. So smoking addiction is accepted universally as a phenomenon in policy and public health circles and is largely uncontested by social-constructionist critiques that have applied to other forms of addiction (Cohen, 2000; Keane, 2002; Levine, 1978; Lindesmith, 1938).

Of the UK population, 23 per cent smoke and a further 27 per cent are former smokers (Lader and Goddard, 2005). In the USA, 29 per cent use tobacco products, (Office of Applied Studies, 2005). In the UK, levels of smoking among the population fell steadily from the mid-1970s to the 1980s, the rate of decline slowing during the 1990s. Smoking has become concentrated among less well-off groups. The majority of smokers say they would like to stop, although this frequently is a case of 'give me chastity and continence, but not yet'. Encouraging successful quit attempts is a key part of the public health strategies in Europe and North America (Secretary of State for Health, 1998). These changes in smoking patterns and norms have altered the social acceptablity of smoking. There has been a generalization of smoking risk, beginning with the construction of passive or involuntary smoking (Berridge, 1999), that shifts the focus on to smokers as risky to others. Any contact with a smoker – rather than their smoke – is risky for exposure (Matt et al., 2004). The smoker is also risky in terms of producing vulnerability to smoking in others, to their immediate family and to subsequent generations. Smokers themselves are considered to be so socially and economically damaging that employers are justified in refusing smokers employment, whether they smoke at work or not (Gray, 2005).

This damage is also organic. The brain is constructed as vulnerable in that a single cigarette can 'prime' it for future smoking (Fidler et al., 2006) and addiction (Gervais et al., 2006). To some extent, then, all members of the population are potential nicotine bodies, to be protected from involuntary exposure and priming. Quite unusually in comparison to every other chemical substance, there is deemed to be no safe level of exposure (Surgeon General, 2006), signalling that it belongs to an almost uniquely dangerous category of chemicals. Scientific and policy discourses have increasingly emphasized the physically addictive nature of smoking, in terms of nicotine dependence (Tobacco Advisory Group, 2000) and in the use of terminology such as 'tobacco epidemic' (The World Bank, 1999; World Health Organisation, 2006). Smoking is also unusual in that addiction is generalized to almost the whole population of users: 95 per cent of smokers are supposed to be nicotine dependent, although in fact only about 40 per cent of medium to heavy smokers exhibit signs of being nicotine dependent. Again, this contrasts with alcohol and most illicit drugs where it is acknowledged that dependence only threatens a minority. While not attempting to play down the extensive health and therefore social costs of tobacco use, this does place smoking in a problem category all its own in terms of other psychoactive substances.

It should be said that the establishment of tobacco as an addictive substance involved a by no means trivial struggle against a powerful industry determined to claim it as merely a habit (Sharfstein, 1999). However, since this was achieved, the debate has shifted fundamentally to change smoking from being a combined habit and addiction, to something entirely different. We are all, smokers, ex-smokers and never smokers, potentially nicotine bodies, through smoking itself or exposure to environmental tobacco smoke. This is fairly novel in that addiction here is not a progressive, incurably metabolic brain disease affecting the afflicted, but something more like an environmental hazard, whereby some people are contaminated and contaminating with nicotine. It is becoming a paradigm for alcohol as well. This focus on the body of the smoker as nicotine adapted has been supported by the development of Nicotine Replacement Therapies (NRT) which address the physiological element of addiction by directly providing what the smoker's body is presumed to need. It rejects abstinence by giving the addict what they want, good nicotine.

Commodifying addiction and selling good nicotine

> Nicotine is addictive. We are, then, in the business of selling nicotine, an addictive drug.
>
> Brown and Williamson (1963), in Action on Smoking and Health,
> *Tobacco Explained: The Truth About the Tobacco Industry in its Own Words*
> (1998: 16)

The existence of addiction medications has raised particularly interesting questions. Most are effectively medicalized versions of the drug itself. Methadone and buprenorphine are synthetic opiates used to treat heroin addiction; and both are used illicitly as recreational drugs. This fact highlights the artificiality of the distinction between legitimate medicines and illicit recreational substances. The boundary between the two is always potentially porous and blurred, and requires some effort to maintain. The same substance in one context becomes a different drug in another, an object that shares none of the characteristics of its medicinal form. Methadone has the curious quality of, when used as a recreational drug, being imbued with the opposite characteristics of its medicinal self (Lovell, 2006). A new generation of addiction medicines are designed to act directly on the brain, altering its incentive structure.

The first NRT product was Nicorette gum, introduced in 1984. It now comes in several forms, chewing gum, patches and inhaler. Patches are intended to give a steady dose of nicotine. Inhalers are supposed to mimic the action of smoking and the user-regulated intake of nicotine. Of successful quitters in 2004, 26 per cent used NRT, and 56 per cent did not seek any formal help or advice (Lader and Goddard, 2005). NRT is modestly effective. There need to be between eight and seventeen instances of treatment to produce one successful outcome. The relapse rate is 70 per cent within a year. Not all quitters want to use NRT and many smokers and ex-smokers have negative attitudes about its perceived lack of effectiveness and risks of dependence and side effects (Etter and Perneger, 2001).

Recent work puts failures of NRT down to genetic differences in the ability to metabolize nicotine in the liver, leading to either too strong a dose, producing side effects, or too weak a dose, failing to satisfy cravings, and suggests pharmacogenetically tailored NRT would be much more effective (Association of Crown Research Institutes, 2006). Despite this, only 9 per cent of smokers who had failed quit attempts stated that cravings were the main reason for restarting (Lader and Goddard, 2005). NRT has been made available over the counter (OTC), without prescription, and has been detached from the behavioural support offered when it was prescription only.

Smoking is one addiction where the addict is mostly expected to arrange their own treatment, and to some degree their own diagnosis. The Fagerström scale of nicotine dependence is used in quitter's self-help guides, and websites run by NRT manufacturers. Both the experience of addiction and recovery are highly individualized. Over-the-counter provision of NRT takes place within a context of neo-liberalization, marketization and globalization of health-care provision (Lewis and Dixon, 2005), and the political focus on healthy lifestyles and the management of productive selves (Fitzpatrick, 2001). It presages a shift of treatment from clinics and consultations to pharmacies and phone calls (Baines and Whynes, 1997; Department of Health, 2000). There is a dual privatization, of providers and patients (Pollock, 2004), and attempts to limit health service cost growth and/or transfer costs to consumers, of which the generation of non-smoking healthy selves is one element.

Around the world there are ever stronger restrictions, legal, financial and normative, placed around smoking tobacco. Smoking in all workplaces and public places has been banned in many jurisdictions of the USA, Canada and in Europe. Smoking restrictions are encouraging smokers to think in this nicotinized way, which is one of their stated intentions. So explanations of smoking that 'it helps me concentrate when I work', or 'I enjoy it with a drink', are no longer viable, as one can no longer smoke in the workplace or a pub. The sensescape, the material setting of smoking, is changed. Smokers *have to* start thinking in terms of nicotine bodies, and of smoking as the practice of managing nicotine intake.

NRT is increasingly marketed as a consumer device. Companies manufacturing some forms of NRT sell it heavily as a consumer product. For instance, the website for Nicorette gum emphasizes its minty flavour and chewiness, and links to its new Fruit Chill version, which promises 'a delicious blast of fruit with a hint of mint' (GlaxoSmithKline, 2006). In Britain, marketing for NRT products is regulated by the Advertising Standards Authority. The ASA requires proof to be presented if the seller is to suggest that the smoker does not need to make any effort beyond buying the product in order to stop smoking. It is proof the ASA states it has never seen (Committee of Advertising Practice, 2006). This insists on having some role for the smoker's agency, although it often ends up being a marginalized one, reduced to a two-word declaration that the product 'requires willpower' or 'commitment'. Presumably, those who fail to quit using the product simply lack the necessary willpower. It is a rather under-mining statement, as willpower is precisely what smokers claim to need to quit and not to have, and this is the one thing the product specifically will not give them. Health professionals and pharmaceutical companies reimagine smoking as a personal physical pathology.

However, these are not the only representatives of morbid appetites, nor the most pervasive. Roche's product information sheet on Valium gives the advice that 'Addiction-prone individuals (such as drug addicts or alcoholics) should be under careful surveillance when receiving diazepam or other psychotropic agents because of the pre-disposition of such patients to habituation and dependence' ('Valium (brand of diazepam) tablets', Roche Pharmaceuticals 1999). It is notable how upfront the company is about placing addiction as a quality of the individual rather than the product, rather as if British American Tobacco blamed heavy tobacco dependence on the 'addiction-prone' personalities of smokers. In a sense, this chapter is making the same point – that addiction may begin, but does not end, with the qualities of the substance in question. Human behaviour is always rich and complex. What the rhetoric of addiction does is reduce that to a series of closed, self-referential and judgemental statements about the quality of a particular act, taking drugs (Booth Davies, 1997).

Conclusion

It is most absurdly said, in popular language, of any man, that he is disguised in liquor; for, on the contrary, most men are disguised by sobriety.
Thomas de Quincey, *Confessions of an English Opium-Eater* (1886 [1822])

The heroin junkie, the crack-mother, the lagered-up lads blazing with aggression on a Friday night, are the ugly faces of intoxication. They are not folk devils – living examples of who we should not be – but folk nightmares, subterranean reminders of our intoxicated alter egos welling up from beneath the surface of the admissible dinner-party line of cocaine and bottle of Chardonnay. Like the aggressive drunk who latches on to you at a party, they corner you and rant in your face, defy all politeness or cajoling, slip from maudlin sentiment to feral hatred with no apparent reason, before collapsing sorrily on your lap. As well as outlining the boundaries that separate recreational and problem use, it is necessary to delve into modes of intoxication, the practices and discourses that closely connect the pathologized forms of intoxication to those that are normal and accepted; to understand that the pathological is an extension of normal practice. There are two elements to hold in balance here: first, the way in which some forms of substance use come to be defined as problems, and others do not; and, second, the fact that the problem behaviours are themselves products of normal intoxication, consciousness and practice. What this means is that we do not just shut drug and alcohol addiction or abuse away like the madwoman in the attic. The problems associated with drugs and alcohol – the terms these problems are couched in, the treatments made for them – are applied to other social problems. It becomes a common, easily applied framing for social problems. Drug and alcohol problems are sites for the production of metaphors and discourses which resonate beyond these substances, in the general-ization of addiction as a form of life, the construction of the alcoholic self, of risky subjects and subjects at risk, and helpless, drugged bodies.

5 Governing Drugs and Their Users

At the end of 2005 I was visiting one of my research students, who was working in Ecuador. I flew out of Quito in the very early morning at the end of a very pleasant stay. The plane was scheduled to land in Guayaquil (Ecuador) before going on to Mexico City and then Houston, Texas. I'd had very little sleep the previous night and had celebrated my departure with a meal of chicken vindaloo – a fearsomely hot curry. At Guayaquil we were all herded off the plane and made to wait in the departure lounge. The previous night's vindaloo was playing havoc with my guts so I hurried off to the toilet, where I was intercepted by the airport drug squad, who started talking urgently at me in Spanish. My command of the language is hopeless but I gathered that they were excited to have spotted an unshaven, scruffy, sweaty gringo making a run for the toilet, having doubtless lost his nerve and wanting to get rid of the cocaine in his stomach.

I tried to explain in my best Spanglish that I 'really did need the toilet' which was probably the worst thing to say in these circumstances. Unimpressed, they searched my backpack and then took me off for a full body X-ray, and yanked my luggage off the plane and searched that. I was a bit worried given what I had heard about corruption and the planting of drugs, and that Ecuador gets money from the USA the more gringos it arrests for drug trafficking on flights to the USA. In my agitated state of mind I interpreted this as constituting something of an incentive to 'find' cocaine. In contrast to the image projected by drug warriors of the 'drugs war' as a hot war fought by sexy agents in combat gear, the drug agents who searched me became politely bored when they realized that they were not about to discover anything to write home about. Eventually I was able to board the flight, to the suspicious stares of passengers. The man in the seat next to me gave me a sleeping pill to calm me down, and I woke up on the ground in Mexico City airport.

Drug controls: legislating intoxication

Every psychoactive substance in common use has its control regime, the intricate lattice of formal and informal controls and sanctions structuring its use. This chapter explores how some drug-control regimes work and the terms in which they operate. The control of psychoactive substances is concerned with the control and management of people and populations, users *and* non-users. The late twentieth and early twenty-first centuries have seen the emergence of regimes that rely less on prohibition and the deployment of space–time restrictions, the dominant mode of drug and alcohol control for much of the twentieth century. At the start of this century the distinction between licit and illicit drugs had started to lose some of its importance, compared to the distinction between managed and unmanageable intoxications. There has been a change from morality to risk as the primary mode of drug and alcohol governance, moving to surveillance technologies and multiple self-monitoring to produce managed intoxications. However, this should not be overdone. There are signs of a recriminalization of illicit drug use following the more libertarian cultural currents that emerged in Europe and the USA during the mid- to late 1990s (Measham, 2007). Whatever happens in future, it will be another episode in the long human story of attempts to legislate intoxication.

> Let us then discourse a little more at length about intoxication, which is a very important subject, and will seriously task the discrimination of the legislator. I am not speaking of drinking, or not drinking, wine at all, but of intoxication. Are we to follow the custom of the Scythians, and Persians, and Carthaginians, and Celts, and Iberians, and Thracians, who are all warlike nations, or that of your countrymen, for they, as you say, altogether abstain? But the Scythians and Thracians, both men and women, drink unmixed wine, which they pour on their garments, and this they think a happy and glorious institution. (Plato, *The Laws*, Book I, *c*.360 BC)

Every act of providing or consuming a psychoactive substance takes place within a regime of regulation and control. The act of smoking a cigarette puts the smoker at the last stage of a long, globalized chain of agricultural production, industrial processing and manufacturing, transportation, marketing and commodification. A cigarette is regulated by taxation, and rules on the way in which it is sold and to whom. In the UK, cigarettes may not be sold singly, supposedly to reduce sales to minors. The content is relatively untouched. A manufacturer may add six hundred additives, many of which are intended to optimize the function of the cigarette as a nicotine delivery device (Bates et al., 1999). The act of snorting a line of cocaine puts the user at one point in a network constituted in similar terms, although with only involuntary marketing involved, and which is free of formal controls on the product. In contrast, the drinker of Scotch whisky consumes a closely monitored product, with the requirement that it is produced by a specified method in order to retail by that name. The regulation of licit products is much more effective than the control of illicit products.

The US-led enforcement of the international legal framework known as the 'War on Drugs' is one regime, a small element of which, the interdiction of suspected drug mules, I encountered in the above narrative. It is also made up of economic forces, institutional power, cultural dynamics and status hierarchies, definition of the problem, acceptance of some kinds of evidence over others and so on. The regulation and control of every psychoactive substance is organized along a number of different planes or dimensions, according to its legal status, medicinal uses, availability, form, effect, and the social status of the user. These underscore and reproduce their social acceptability or otherwise, the location and form of their use, and knowledge about them. In this, drugs are like any other product, as they have regimes of control applied to them. Even those in which there could be said to be a complete free market, such as coffee, are subjects of political economy, laws and agreements covering international trade that reflect the power of different parties, labour law, taxation and ideologies of health and well-being. In fact, there are far more explicit regulations on coffee than on cocaine.

Legal does not mean safe and illegal does not mean anarchic. It is not very difficult for most young people in North America, most countries in Europe and elsewhere to obtain illicit drugs relatively cheaply. As the illicit drug trade is invisible, myths about the trade flourish. Drug dealers are represented as fat, bling Hispanic males, cutting cocaine or heroin with Vim (cleaning powder), rat poison and powdered glass, before pushing it on to unwitting schoolchildren. Even drug dealers and users believe many of these myths. Yet they do not conform to this stereotype. Some are female, some are part-time, and none attempt to 'push' drugs on to unknowing schoolchildren, an unreliable clientele who cannot be relied on to keep quiet. Most prefer to sell to reliable clients that they know (Coomber, 2003, 2006). Illicit drugs are adulterated far less frequently than is assumed. Not wanting to kill their clientele, dealers do not adulterate their product with dangerous substances. When additives are put into illicit drugs it is likely to be to increase their psychoactive effect, for instance, by allowing more rapid absorption, or to pad out profits at an early stage of the process, like a supermarket injecting water into its sausages (Coomber, 1997a, 1997b). Indeed, although there can in theory be no controls on the content or form of a prohibited substance, except what the provider thinks they can get away with, many of the same pressures apply in the illicit as licit markets: the need for a reliable customer base, a reputation for a quality product, and a constant worry about the competition.

As chapter 2 indicated, what are first thought of in terms of legal regulation, direct restrictions on possession of various substances – making just having a particular chemical about one's person or one's property a crime – is a historically novel form of control. The framework of drug prohibition, which puts each substance under a different level of control is not the only way in which drugs and alcohol can be regulated and in our society is not the sole way, although many other elements of substance-use control cohere around the legal system. Historically, the regulation of drugs in the modern world begins not with restrictions on sale or possession, but in the nineteenth-century regulation of ungovernable and dangerous populations of drinkers, women and the working class, through controls on public houses (Kneale, 1999).

Another source of regulation lay in the rules governing the adulteration of drugs, alcohol and food, a serious problem in nineteenth-century Britain (Harding, 1986). The Pharmacy Act 1868 restricted the provision of opium, along with other medicines and poisons, to pharmacists. It helped establish the pharmaceutical profession's control of distribution and access to medicines (Berridge and Edwards, 1981). However, this merely meant that the supply was put into professionally qualified hands. It did not restrict the availability of opium as such. In the UK, the free market continued to dominate until the twentieth century. With these measures, and later measures to regulate the contents of over-the-counter nostrums containing cocaine, concerns were directed towards the effect on middle-class Anglo-Saxons.

Prohibition of opium, and later cocaine and cannabis, was on the other hand driven by concerns about race (Manderson, 1993; Woodiwiss, 1998). In 1887, the USA outlawed the importing and smoking of opium by Chinese, but not white, people. South Australia outlawed all non-medical use and supply of opium to native (aboriginal) Australians in 1895 (Manderson, 1997). Smoked opium and the opium den symbolized white fears of the Chinese, and action against opium was symbolic (and real) action against the threat of the Chinaman (sic). The Australian and US legislation left largely white use of patent medicines containing opium alone. The dangers of the drug were not the object of these laws. Their object was the Chinese immigrant, who threatened contamination of the white race, particularly white women, and, in the Australian case, also degeneration of the aborigine. Opium stood in for the racial, sexual and cultural threat represented by the Chinese.

In Britain, prohibitive measures, though not absent, came rather later, with a 1916 amendment (Regulation 40b) to the 1914 Defence of the Realm Act (DORA). Regulation 40b outlawed any possession of cocaine by any other than 'authorized' persons. The debate around this embodied the same fears of sexual and racial mixing and threats to the life of the nation that were present in the earlier Australian and US legislation. DORA was supposed to be a temporary interruption in cherished British liberties necessitated by a national emergency. However, governments rarely relinquish powers they abrogate to themselves, and the provisions of Regulation 40b, and other aspects of the Act, remained in force in the post-war era. The case of actress Billie Carleton, who died after attending a Victory Ball in 1918, was quoted in support of this. Cocaine was supposedly the cause of death, and in the aftermath there were demands for 40b to become permanent law, although not without occasional adverse comment:

> It may be admitted that matters appertaining to the organisation, equipment, supply and operation of His Majesty's forces and ships . . . are essential necessities in war-time; but it is not easy to see, for example, how an amendment of the Dogs Act, 1906, or the prohibition of dogs shows come within that category, or how the sale or gift of cocaine or opium to an actress would endanger the successful prosecution of the war.
>
> (Sidney W. Clarke, 'The Rule of DORA' (1919: 38))

The UK Dangerous Drugs Act of 1920 did just that, prohibiting the production, supply and possession of cocaine, heroin and morphine except under licence.

It was one of several confirmations of the internationalization of Prohibition, along with, for instance, the 1914 Harrison Narcotic Tax Act in the USA. The Hague Opium Convention of 1912, in spite of its title, aimed to control and limit for medical purposes only the production and distribution of opium, morphine and cocaine. It particularly aimed for the suppression of opium smoking. The convention was signed by the governments of Germany, the USA, the UK, China, France, Italy, Japan, the Netherlands, Persia, Portugal, Russia and Siam. Subsequent laws in signatory countries implemented elements of the convention. These developments represented a change from the regulation of psychoactive substances as poisons, to their regulation and control as drugs. They were the first steps towards establishing illicit drugs as a category separate from alcohol and tobacco, and the founding of international drug control.

Three international conventions now govern global drug prohibition: the 1961 Single Convention on Narcotic Drugs; the 1971 Convention on Psychotropic Substances; and the 1988 Convention Against the Illicit Traffic in Narcotic Drugs and Psychotropic Substances. The United Nations International Narcotics Control Board (INCB) monitors the implementation of the various UN Conventions on 'narcotic drugs and psychotropic substances' in member countries. Operating like a World Trade Organisation in reverse, it ensures that signatories may not permit narcotic drugs to be produced, traded or sold. In the UK, there are regular questions asked about the extent to which sovereignty is ceded to the European Union. A vocal conservative lobby in the USA sees the United Nations as a sinister world government in waiting, shackling legitimate American aspirations. Radical governments and popular political movements throughout Latin America look on the USA in a similar light. Yet very few politicians or political movements question, or even acknowledge, the fact that all nation-states have signed away the basic question of legislating drug control to the INCB.

Although there is an unusual level of international agreement embodied in the UN Conventions, which require all signatory governments to adhere to prohibition, there is a range of interpretations of how prohibition is implemented practically. They range from the unremitting policies of some South-East Asian and Middle Eastern countries, to the decriminalization and decoupling of cannabis from 'harder' drugs practised in the Netherlands (Roberts et al., 2004). No country has abrogated from the Conventions or proposes doing so. However there are very different aims proclaimed in drug control. The US government states its aim in drug policy is to reduce the numbers of drug users; the Netherlands, to reduce harm caused by drug use; and Sweden, to 'create a drug-free society'. The UK's aims of reduction in supply and crime levels, prevention of uptake and increase in treatment seem modest beside Sweden's stated ambitions. They echo the UN drug-control strategy proclaimed in 1998, which aims for a 'drug-free world' by 2008 (Arlacchi, 1998), an achievement that would make this book redundant. Thankfully for my publisher and me, what can be called at best very limited progress has been made towards that goal. In a realpolitik world, drugs policy is one of the few utopian social agendas around.

Illicit drug classifications

The UN Conventions set out a scheduling process which classifies each substance, theoretically balancing risks against any potential benefits to public health. Schedule I covers drugs that are a serious threat to public health, and with little or no medicinal value; Schedule II, drugs of limited therapeutic scope, such as amphetamines; Schedule III, drugs useful therapeutically, but which have abuse potential, such as barbiturates; and Schedule IV, drugs which are mainly used medicinally, but which may cause dependence, such as tranquillizers and some analgesics. The process of allocating each drug to a particular Schedule is controversial. For instance, cannabis and LSD, both Schedule I drugs, do potentially have therapeutic value. Scientific knowledge of the extent of their therapeutic uses, however, has been limited by their scheduling as the most risky drugs, which has restricted the research that can be carried out. In a circular process, knowledge of the beneficial effects of illicit drugs, and indeed of their harms, is limited and distorted by the fact that they are illicit.

On a national level, similar classifications are found, which grade substances in order of seriousness on the same basis of potential for abuse versus medicinal use. The US classifies drugs into five schedules under the Controlled Substances Act (Title II of the Comprehensive Drug Abuse Prevention and Control Act 1970). Schedule I drugs are defined as having a high potential for abuse and no accepted use for medical treatment, Schedule II as high abuse potential but having limited medical use, Schedule III as lesser abuse potential and accepted medical use, and so on. The UK similarly classifies illicit drugs under the 1971 Misuse of Drugs Act into three classes, A, B and C. Some countries are more restrictive than the Conventions require. For instance, the Conventions permit limited medicinal use of Schedule I substances, whereas the USA does not.

The scheduling systems, like most systems of categorization, are messy, ad-hoc classifications (Levitt et al., 2006), and there is at best a limited correlation between the class of drug and the harms associated with it (Nutt et al., 2007). In the UK and the USA, ecstasy and LSD are classed along with heroin as Class A/Schedule I, although their risks are far lower – arguably much lower than many drugs given a less restrictive classification. Cocaine and coca leaf are also both in Class A, although coca leaf is more akin to coffee. With reference to UK drug classification, the chair of the UK Advisory Council on the Misuse of Drugs, Professor Sir Michael Rawlins, said in testimony to the House of Commons Select Committee on Science and Technology that the system had a symbolic element (House of Commons, 2006).

The UK House of Commons Select Committee on Science and Technology examined the classification system in its 2006 report, *Drug Classification: Making a Hash of it*. The Committee had found some merit in separating the classification of penalties for possession and trafficking of illicit drugs from an agreed scientific classification of harm, which would by necessity cover the substances with most harms associated with them, alcohol and tobacco. The UK Home Office response was largely to concede that there was no consistent principle at work. Below is an excerpt from the Home Office reply to the House of Commons report:

> The distinction between legal and illegal substances is not unequivocally based on pharmacology, economic or risk benefit analysis. It is also based in large part on historical and cultural precedents. A classification system that applies to legal as well as illegal substances would be unacceptable to the vast majority of people who use, for example alcohol, responsibly and would conflict with deeply embedded historical tradition and tolerance of consumption of a number of substances that alter mental functioning (ranging from caffeine to alcohol and tobacco). (Secretary of State for the Home Department, 2006: 24)

The government wholly rejected the suggestion that alcohol and tobacco be included in a harm-based classification system, while acknowledging, 'that alcohol and tobacco account for more health problems and deaths than illicit drugs'. Handily summarizing two of the main points of this chapter, it acknowledged that some substances were illegal effectively because they are illegal. Some substances that 'alter mental functioning' happen to be historically embedded in British society and tolerated, while others are not. In an example of the tortured logic that becomes necessary when there is such a glaring mismatch between policy and reality, the very irrationality of the system of drug classification is used to support its continuation, on the grounds that a system of classification that included licit drugs would offend those who use them responsibly. The UK government effectively acknowledges that the current drug classification system performs the function of legitimating the use of alcohol and tobacco, in spite of acknowledged harm, by setting them apart from illicit drugs.

Enforcing prohibition

'This war on terrorism is gonna *rule*. I can't wait until the war is over and there's no more terrorism.'

'I know. Remember when the U. S. had a drug problem, and then we declared a War on Drugs, and now you can't buy drugs anymore? It'll be just like that.'

'Right! God, if only that War on Drugs hadn't been so effective! I could really use some fucking marijuana right now!'

Get Your War On, comic strip by David Rees, 2002

The war on drugs is a phenomenon distinct from worldwide drug prohibition. The term was coined by US President Richard Nixon in 1971 to describe a US-led initiative to enforce drug prohibition in the round by attacking the production, supply, and consumption of illicit drugs. It is a phrase now often used sardonically, but the war continues nonetheless. It is not an inappropriate term to describe the approach of the US government to global prohibition since Nixon's time, involving as it does militarization of enforcement internationally, and the kind of abrogation of individual rights and extension of Federal government power over US citizens and others that are usually only justified in times of actual war. The defining feature of the drug war is the coordination of foreign and domestic US policies around drugs, implemented through the Drug Enforcement Administration and coordinated through the Office of National Drug Control Policy. The impact of the drug war domestically involves a huge expansion of the prison population, the development of paramilitary policing, and the limitation of judicial discretion with mandatory minimum sentences being demanded for certain drug offences.

In a tiny way in the story told at the start of this chapter I was being hindered by the war on drugs. The production, transport, buying and selling of drugs is a crime without a complainant. The state takes upon itself the role of substitute victim, and creates an apparatus of surveillance across and within borders that by necessity is highly intrusive of the person of the citizen. The war on drugs is a US innovation, but it is relevant to all countries, not least because it is exported to them. All countries around the world subscribe to the UN Conventions and share in the same ironies and injustices that it produces.

A few of these are: in 2005, two ten-year-old girls in Flagler County, Florida, USA, were arrested for pretending that a bag of parsley they had brought to school was marijuana. A Florida state law makes it an offence to claim that a substance is an illicit drug, whether or not there is any attempt to sell or distribute the substance. In other words, in the state of Florida it is an offence to make a particular kind of statement about a substance in your possession, regardless of any attempt to deceive or defraud, and regardless of the actual content of the substance. Drug-war limits on free speech are not confined to this case. In 2007, the US Supreme Court ruled in a separate case that school students could be disciplined for speech that promoted drug use. An Alaskan high school student, Joseph Frederick, had unfurled a banner saying 'Bong Hits 4 Jesus' outside his school, for which he was suspended. He filed a lawsuit against the school principal for violating his First Amendment rights to free speech. At the same time, the court ruled that students could not be punished for expressing their views on drug *policy*. This was not the case in Saskatchewan, Canada, where during 2007 a fifteen-year-old, Keiran King, was suspended from school as a result of arguing that cannabis was safer than cigarettes or alcohol.

The doctrine of 'acquitted conduct sentencing enhancement' was established in US sentencing practice in 1997. In effect, this means that if a person is charged with multiple offences, but only found guilty of some, the court can sentence them as if they were guilty of all. As with so many attenuations of legal principle and liberty, this was established in two drug cases (United States v. Vernon Watts; United States v. Cheryl Putra, No. 95-1906, 719 US 148, 1997). In the case of Watts, crack-cocaine was discovered in the defendant's kitchen by police, and two guns were found in his bedroom. He was convicted of possessing the drug with intent to distribute, but acquitted of another charge of using a firearm in relation to a drug offence. In sentencing him to twenty-two years inside, the sentencing court chose to consider on the preponderance of evidence (the balance of probabilities, in UK terms) that he had committed the other offence.

In *Putra*, the defendant was found guilty of aiding and abetting possession with intent to distribute one ounce of cocaine, and the same charge in relation to five ounces on a separate occasion. She was convicted of the first count and acquitted of the second, but again sentenced on the grounds that the preponderance of evidence pointed to her guilt in the second charge, resulting in her being given a sentence greater than the federally mandated maximum for that offence. Convicted as a small-time dealer, she was sentenced as a larger-scale distributor (Russell, 2001).

Both sentences were appealed, the Supreme Court finally upholding the sentencing principle by a 7–2 majority. The Supreme Court in its judgement argued that this is part of the normal process of taking a defendant's conduct into account when sentencing, in which the court has wide discretion. However, far from being normal, this affected three principles that are the basis for the American and other English common-law-derived legal systems. 'Preponderance of evidence' is the weaker standard of proof required in civil cases, as opposed to 'beyond reasonable doubt', required in criminal cases. One of the reasons for requiring criminal cases to be so proven is that a guilty verdict can lead to loss of liberty, and in some US states, of life. Here, the drug war has led to the mixing of the lower-order standard of proof with the higher-order punishment. It has also diluted double jeopardy, the principle that a person cannot be tried twice on the same charge, and partially reversed the principle of innocent until proven guilty.

Asset forfeiture laws allow law-enforcement agencies to confiscate property – cash, houses, farms, boats – if illicit drugs are found on or in it, and, in the case of cash, if there is suspicion by a police officer that it may be used in a drug trade. The drugs are deemed to 'possess' the property, which then becomes the possession of the state, and in the case of cash suspected of being for use in a drug trade, the belief by a law-enforcement officer is sufficient for it to become appropriated by the state. In the USA, by adding baking soda to your cocaine and freebasing it you will get a much longer prison sentence. Possession of crack-cocaine is more severely punished than that of powder cocaine. The federally mandated minimum sentence for possession of 5 grams of crack-cocaine is five years. A defendant would have to be found in possession of 500 grams of powder cocaine to trigger the same sentence. There is no pharmacological difference between the two – both are cocaine – so users are literally being punished for the baking soda involved in its production, but really because of the perfect storm of race, crime and urban deprivation that formed around crack during the 1980s.

The imperative to catch dealers in 'possession' has encouraged the use of paramilitary 'no nock' drug raids. These typically involve an unannounced night-time forced entry on a suspect's property by 'SWAT' teams, militarized, heavily armed police officers. As they are frequently based on anonymous tip-offs, errors are common. There is a sad record of innocent citizens being killed in botched raids of this type as they try and defend themselves against what appears to be a gang of armed men breaking into their house in the middle of the night (Balko, 2006a). The drug war is bound up with race – black and some other ethnic minority individuals are disproportionately affected, either on the receiving end of punitive criminal sanctions, or of collateral damage surrounding the drug business. Many hundreds of thousands of black Americans are disbarred for life from voting for drug felonies. A military maxim is that in war you should not reinforce failure. In this war, failure has not led to withdrawal, but to a ratcheting up of intensity, and consequent damage to individual lives, livelihoods and due process.

The proverbial Martian dropping down to planet Earth might think that the entire drugs-war paraphernalia is set up purely to manage the production of drugs, punish some unlucky producers, and regulate or punish some consumers. It certainly does not reduce drug-related harm; the opposite, if anything (Stimson, 2000). Does the evidence suggest that these laws are unenforceable, like those on gambling and prostitution (Woodiwiss and Bewley-Taylor, 2005: 6)? First, this may not be a wholly relevant way of framing the question. Many laws are not intended to be 100 per cent enforced. They exist to express the dominant values of a society. That, in itself, is not reason to get rid of them. Law is a symbolic order and futility is as much a vice of lawmakers as sensation-seeking is of lawbreakers. The endless failures of laws to work in this area can suggest that the laws are not designed to 'work' in their explicit sense, of creating a society in which nobody uses scheduled substances for anything other than sanctioned medicinal purposes. There are other senses in which laws work. These can be: to keep a problem within manageable proportions; to convince the voting public that 'something is being done'; to assert symbolic or practical dominance of one group over another (Gusfield, 1963); and to restrict the severest harms to marginalized and voiceless groups in society, where most social problems, but few influential people, reside. It is the latter sense in which the war on drugs has been most effective and, like the war on poverty, and the war on smoking, has done the job of concentrating the most intractable social problems amongst those worst placed to deal with them.

Perspectives on prohibition and the 'drug problem'

Few scholars on either side of the debate appear to seriously accept that the drug war can be 'won' in any final sense. Outside university debating societies, most arguments rely on balances of cost and risk, consequences and principles, with much speculation, analogy and guesswork in the equation by necessity.

There are broadly three perspectives in commentary on the drug war, not all of which are mutually exclusive. These are, first, that there is a drug problem and prohibition prevents it from being very much worse than it otherwise would be (Edwards, 2004; Inciardi, 1999; Wilson, 1990a, 1990b). Weighing the cost and benefits of prohibition, they broadly argue that on balance criminalization helps more than it hurts. On one side of the equation are the costs of policing, maintaining many hundreds of thousands of mainly low-level drug criminals in prison. On the side of the benefits are keeping drugs out of the hands of the majority of the population, with consequent lower levels of addiction and overdose than otherwise might have been the case. One argument made is that the uptake of heroin in Harlem, New York, in the early 1970s had been reduced as heroin users died of overdoses, poisoning by adulterated heroin, or hepatitis caught from infected injecting equipment (Wilson, 1990a). This would not have been the case had heroin been freely, legally available. It is rare but refreshing to see a government policy being explicitly defended on the grounds that it will kill some of its citizens, although this is not in fact uncommon in morally absolutist discourses on human behaviour. Some anti-smoking activists have opposed smoking harm-reduction measures on the grounds that encouraging safer tobacco use discourages quitting attempts and legitimizes tobacco use (Sullum, 1998). Better a few should die, than many live in sin.

One of the concerns raised is of having children exposed to cocaine, heroin and so on, and the moral and physical risk this would represent. As I write, I sip from a glass of whisky, a very potent substance. The glass is barely wet at the bottom. If I filled the tumbler to the brim and drank that, I would be very ill, and possibly die. Yet I am happy to have this hideously risky substance lying around my house, within the reach of children and my binge-drinking friends. But we are, if not happy with that situation, at least capable of finding it tolerable, because we think, again often in the teeth of the evidence, that children will avoid hard liquor, or not like it if they try it. Furthermore, the fact that children are exposed to illicit drugs in their most dangerous form is a consequence, and not a cause, of prohibition. My point here is not that these arguments are representative of proponents of prohibition, or that they discredit them, but that they are representative of the impact the drug war has had on academic and popular debate.

Like all wars, it implies that the lives of some can be sacrificed in the service of the greater good, and that illicit drugs have a power that similar, legitimate, substances do not.

Since prohibition is the status quo, its supporters have an advantage in the debate. They can point to the unknowable risks involved in taking other paths, such as harm reduction, decriminalization and legalization. Legalization – the end of prohibition – by its nature is a speculative gamble, based on finger-crossing about the likely consequences. There is a problem common to many liberal and libertarian perspectives in that commentators have a tendency to propose policy positions which they will not have to suffer the consequences of, as they can be sure there is no likelihood of them ever being implemented. Proposing the legalizing of all drugs is a safe proposition as it seems very unlikely to happen, so any downside is purely theoretical, and a morally satisfying position can be safely taken. It is also the case that prohibitionists never face the problems caused by drug prohibition, as they are by definition 'drug problems'.

A common thread in prohibitionist arguments comes into play here, where the problems caused by criminalization are used as arguments against decriminalization. For instance, the criminal organizations that are supposed to control the drug trade will not shut up shop, but undercut the new legal drug markets, encouraging much higher levels of use (Edwards, 2004: 251). The fact that criminal organizations are involved in the drug trade in the first place is of course a product of criminalization, and, given that an ecstasy pill is cheaper than a pint of beer in Britain, it appears to have had little effect on the price. Prohibition is as speculative as its opposite number. There is no way of telling whether it in fact delivers the goods. As illegal drug industries do not publish accounts or sales projections, our information on them is frequently sketchy and unreliable. Prohibition is itself risky as new products like crack-cocaine and methamphetamine are introduced on to the market without any testing or regulation. Again, these developments are then quoted as evidence for the prosecution, rather than indications of the failure of prohibition to protect users from drug-related harms.

The harm-reduction perspective is that there is a drug problem and the war on drugs is a barrier to effective treatment. Harm reduction is a catch-all term to cover the application of strategies which mitigate drug-related harm, without judging the user morally or demanding that they abstain from use. The war on drugs diverts resources from harm reduction to prohibition, and stigmatizes harm reduction as back-door legalization. Proponents of this perspective sometimes take a neutral stance on the question of prohibition, arguing that, as a drug problem exists, the humane response is to try and mitigate it. Others feel that, as they are frequently involved in reducing the harm caused by the war on drugs, rather than by the actual drugs, they cannot really be neutral about the root causes. Proponents of the drug war tend to lump harm reduction and decriminalization with legalization – for instance, spokespersons for the US Drug Enforcement Administration deliberately lump all three together (Marshall, 1999). Harm-reduction advocates often write from experience of working in the drug field, with those affected by drug problems, and of the cognitive dissonance that comes from the gulf between the rhetoric of abstinence and the reality of drug users' lives.

Additionally, libertarians take the view that there may be a drug problem, but that it is not the main issue, as the war on drugs is ineffective and indeed immoral, since humans have always used and will always use drugs of one sort or another (Sullum, 2003). Furthermore, the distinction between licit drugs and illicit drugs is artificial and has no basis in objective analysis of risks and harms of various psychoactive substances. From this viewpoint, there would not be a drug problem at all without the drug war, or it would be substantially mitigated. Like female hysteria or frigidity, both formerly psychiatric diagnoses, the existence of the problem is dependent on powerful forces in society making it into one. The libertarian perspective is that humans have a right to choose to use drugs, and that drug-war hysteria means that we must include on the benefit side of the equation the pleasure that may accrue to users of drugs. A more measured approach would be to state that there are many drug problems, but the war on drugs, in seeking to create one overarching 'drug problem', makes it more difficult to address the problems individuals and groups may have with specific substances. In enforcing a divide between drugs and alcohol, it also arguably makes alcohol problems less visible and hence harder to address humanely. 'Prohibition, as the USA discovered in the course of its disastrous experiment with alcohol, is in fact closer to the free market than to regulation,' states Desmond Manderson (2005: 37).

Amidst liberal worrying, social interventionism, anarcholibertarianism, and plain old handlebar-moustached, red-faced rage, the free-market *Economist* magazine recognized what the illegal drugs trade was – a business, and in its own terms quite a successful one to boot. It listed the characteristics that would bring it praise were it an above-the-board enterprise – it delivers high profits, selling its commodity for vastly more than the production costs; it is competitive, flexible, and it responds closely to demand. It does not fall prey to some of the common criticisms of globalized capitalism from the political left – it is not centralized, it disperses proceeds probably more equitably than other forms of global industrial agriculture, and it does not use manipulative advertising to push its product. There are no hidden persuaders (Cairncross, 2001). Indeed, it is one of the few remaining commodity industries in which the functional qualities of the product itself are the sole selling point, rather than secondary qualities like brand, design or style, so answering many intellectual criticisms of the consumer society where style trumps substance. Although physically insubstantial, illicit drugs are almost all substance. Consumers claim great skill in distinguishing between the qualities of different drugs, based on experience.

However, this position, although entertaining, is rather rosy-tinted. The production of cocaine, for instance, involves widespread corruption and subversion of the rule of law in producer countries. There is massive violence existing around the cocaine trade, together with the corruption of political and law enforcement systems in Latin America. Drug mules, the lowest rung of the smuggling hierarchy, are not brutally exploited, but the trade relies on the most vulnerable to take the biggest risks. Having said that, legal trades can be more exploitative and certainly often less lucrative for farmers in developing countries, and many of the risks exist because the trade is illicit. The major drug networks are kept free from competition in part through prohibition. Prohibition has globalized drugs networks and the attempts to interdict those networks are akin to censoring the Internet. The networks are stronger than any one node, so long as there are new recruits, which it seems there always are. The abolition of prohibition may in fact reduce cocaine and other drugs to the status of another cash crop, controlled by the same corporations that currently attract the ire of the anti-globalization movement. Many of those who propose drug liberalization, especially of cannabis, hold out a probably forlorn hope that the trade would continue to have these distributed elements to it, rather than being marketed by British American Tobacco, Anheuser-Busch and Diageo.

Alcohol, crowds and intoxication

> A person shall not be intoxicated or simulate intoxication in a public place.
> *The Code of Iowa*, Section 123.46

An inscription estimated to be from 5 BC in the ancient stadium at Delphi warns that those taking wine into the stadium will be fined 5 drachma (Mandelbaum, 1965), an early indication of the association between crowds, alcohol and danger. The war on illicit drugs is a war on users, those who possess drugs and are possessed by them. Control of alcohol presents a different proposition. Controls on alcohol and drinkers are targeted at a population or group level, and, whereas prohibition targets possession, controls of alcohol target place and time of use, and – in theory – degree of intoxication. The governance of alcohol is the governance of drinking as a practice. These principles are encapsulated in alcohol licensing regulations, and offences in various countries related to the crime of being intoxicated in a public place. Being drunk in public is a criminal act in itself, along with, in the state of Iowa, pretending to be drunk.

Football (soccer) has always been somewhat anarchic in Britain. The original football matches were big free-for-alls, involving, for instance, the populations of two villages fighting it out to get a football over one or the other village boundary. Violence and deaths were common. To this day, residents of Kirkwall, Orkney, and Ashbourne in England play a survival of these early games. In Britain, the connection between drunkenness and violence at football matches is explicitly drawn, although there is in fact not a great deal of evidence for a direct relationship (Marsh et al., 1996). In 1982 a social experiment-cum-con-trick was conducted on Aston Villa fans attending the Feyenoord Stadium in Rotterdam to watch their team play Bayern Munich in the final of the European Cup. Unbeknownst to them, the bar in their area of the stadium was serving alcohol-free lager. Observers noted that many of the fans, convinced that they had imbibed a skinful and were 'well lagered', as we say, did in fact act that way. Conviviality and aggression appear to vary with the fans and their environment, not drinking levels. We do not have to trespass on the territory of anthropology to see drunken comportment at work.

Control of alcohol in football grounds was a very localized response to a specific problem of disorder. More generalized responses are apparent when alcohol is established as a public problem, rather than a problem of a few members of identifiable groups in society. The response of Nordic countries was to socialize alcohol or, alternatively, alcohol drinkers. Alcohol use and regulation in Finland, Sweden and Norway was a live political issue from the mid-nineteenth century. In Finland, temperance education was included as an aim in Conservative Party programmes in the 1960s. Nordic countries frequently sought quite precise controls on the form and strength of alcoholic drinks. A debate over the introduction of medium-strength beer in Finland in the 1960s was couched in terms of switching people from spirits to milder brews, such as beer and wine, and the rights of citizens not to have their consumption controlled by the government. Proposals for nationalization of the means of intoxication were heard in Nordic countries throughout the 1970s and into the 1980s. They would have involved taking breweries into public ownership, and the re-establishment of state alcohol monopolies, as part of a backlash against the liberalization of the 1960s.

An innovative solution in Sweden was to nationalize the drinker, rather than the drink. The Swedish 'Bratt' system involved rationing alcohol, and also rationing drinkers. It was introduced in Sweden in 1914, as a kind of light Prohibition, and lasted until 1955. It was devised by Ivan Bratt, a Stockholm doctor. Alcohol was sold to those who possessed a ration book (*motbok*) which limited the amount of alcohol they could buy according to their age, sex, whether they lived in the countryside or a town, their social circumstances, marital status, social class, reports of drunken misconduct, criminal record and financial status. The system excluded beer, and wine was not generally rationed. Single men and women only obtained a *motbok* at age twenty-five. Single women could be sold no more than a gallon of spirits a year. Married women automatically lost their book and could not buy alcohol. The Bratt system was praised for reducing alcohol problems, and Bratt received grateful letters from women about their husbands not being drunk any more. It satisfied a number of constituencies, providing for limitations on alcohol consumption, socializing the sale of alcohol and giving the state a ready income stream.

What was important to Bratt was the way that alcohol was consumed and by whom. The Bratt regulations are a handy summary of most of the characteristics by which intoxication is deemed to be socially acceptable or not. Drinking by single people and women is potentially disruptive. The system effectively licensed some people to buy alcohol under various conditions (Nycander, 1998). It was supposed to operate as a kind of harm-reduction approach, although it denied alcohol to married women, not notably a problem-drinking category, except on their husband's say-so. In doing so, it would have reinforced the power of the patriarchal drunkard.

The story of the debates over alcohol control in Nordic countries should alert us to the distinction between political or civic libertarianism and free-market libertarianism. The success of the free-market capitalism in Britain and the USA has tended to blur the distinction between the two, or focus mostly on the latter. It has meant that often the debate on drug and alcohol control is characterized as one between relatively free-market legalization and prohibition. Socialization is a third option that has been little considered outside countries where it has been in use, where it appears to have been quite effective in some circumstances. Socialization makes apparent in explicit terms society's concerns with maintaining the boundary between licit and illicit leisure.

Illicit leisure: creating the drug menace

> The newspaper story also explained that one way to inhale glue is to soak a handkerchief with glue and hold it over the mouth and nose. A photograph accompanying the article showed a young man demonstrating how the glue-soaked handkerchief should be held. Interesting results were promised if the glue were sniffed as directed: 'The first effect of breathing the undiluted fumes is dizziness, followed by drowsiness. There is a feeling of suspension of reality. Later there is lack of coordination of muscle and mind.' In a word, it was like getting drunk.
>
> Consumers' Union Report on Licit and Illicit Drugs (Brecher, 1973)

If you were to intentionally go out to create a national drugs menace, there are a few basic rules to follow. You should begin by taking a leisure activity involving some kind of illicit substance use, engaged in by predominantly young people, which will not be immediately comprehensible to those not involved, particularly their parents and the media, and which involves a previously little-known drug whose powers can only be guessed at. Around this should be built scare stories, alternating fascinated repulsion about the kind of goings-on at these events, the writhing bodies, the sweat, the drug-crazed stares of youth out of their minds on god-knows-what substance, with the evil dealers and predators luring innocents to their corruption. These should be written in such a way as to ensure that the activity sounds as exciting and enticing as possible to any young person reading. In the example quoted above, regarding the use of solvents, it is probable that the practice was rare to non-existent before the press in the USA sensationalized it, helpfully providing detailed diagrams describing how household solvents could be used to intoxicate cheaply, using common household objects.

To ensure that harm to those involved is maximized, overreaction by police and politicians is necessary, thus preventing a rational assessment of risks and the development of pragmatic measures to minimize harm to the participants. Ideally, misinformation should be so widespread that participants come to distrust any authoritative source of information, correct or not, thus exposing themselves to unnecessary risks. If you have done your job correctly, this in turn will lead to deaths from what would have been the avoidable side effects of drug use, which can then be used to further sensationalize the drugs menace.

Drugs menaces form around illicit leisure. By the illicit is meant not just the illegal, although both words are frequently used interchangeably. The illicit is forbidden by rules and custom as well as law, but it forms a sphere with its own rules and customs. Illicit leisure contrasts with licensed leisure. The drug user takes him or herself outside the boundaries of society. They leave the world of deferred gratification, nine-to-five work, and steady relationships, for one of instant gratification, furtive behaviour, deceit and immersion in the illicit. Popular music was often treated like this, and regularly linked to drugs and unlicensed sexuality, as in the cocaine underground dance and jazz clubs of London that arose in the First World War and whose popularity and notoriety peaked in the 1920s. The existence of drug scenes – settings where drugs other than alcohol are used in a determinedly recreational manner – came about in the 1890s (Berridge, 1988), and were part of a long tradition of illicit, or unlicensed, leisure (Measham, 2004). The rave scene was the latest in this venerable tradition.

Rave first became a nationwide phenomenon in 1988. Raves or acid-house parties were all-night parties that were held in various locations away from the mainstream urban nightclub, such as warehouses, aircraft hangars, a tent in a field off a motorway. Their soundtrack was acid-house music, mixed by a DJ. Rave was initially quite separate from mainstream dance clubs and discos, in terms of the location of the parties, the type of music, and especially the codes of behaviour that were followed. Despite their differences, raves were a part of club culture, a long tradition of British leisure time that involved dancing to pre-recorded music in clubs and dance halls.

A major ingredient in the mix was the use of MDMA/ecstasy. It was used alongside LSD, speed, cannabis and cocaine, but on its own was highly symbolic of the new scene. MDMA had been patented by the German chemical company Merck in 1912, but not marketed at the time. It surfaced in 1953 when the US Army tried it out for psychological warfare – along with LSD, the US military and the CIA seem to have been responsible for introducing at least two major recreational drugs into common use. Ecstasy was closely associated with rave and the developing values of that club culture. Partly, it just oiled the wheels of an all-night dance party. It helped users to dance, or think they could dance, without looking or feeling like idiots. Its psychological effects developed in the setting of the rave included feelings of warmth, empathy and well-being, which helped promote the emotional ambience and forms of social interaction that were peculiar to raves. Raves differed from the common mainstream nightclub atmosphere. The atmosphere was best described as erotic rather than sexual. Predatory, sexually aggressive behaviour by men was off-limits, as was dancing round your handbag by women. Rave was centred around the act of involvement in the rave (Malbon, 1999).

Despite being more defiant than deviant, rave sparked off what appeared to be an old-fashioned moral panic in Britain and the USA. In Britain, there was a general sense of 'middle England' being violated, by ravers and New Age travellers, and the media responded with the combination of titillation and condemnation typical to its reporting of deviance (Young, 1973). Along with pressure from outraged residents of violated rural heartlands, this had a very real political impact and generated a response by the then Conservative government, in the form of the 1994 Criminal Justice and Public Order Act.

> 63.—(1) This section applies to a gathering on land in the open air of 100 or more persons (whether or not trespassers) at which amplified music is played during the night (with or without intermissions) and is such as, by reason of its loudness and duration and the time at which it is played, is likely to cause serious distress to the inhabitants of the locality; and for this purpose—
> (a) such a gathering continues during intermissions in the music and, where the gathering extends over several days, throughout the period during which amplified music is played at night (with or without intermissions); and
> (b) 'music' includes sounds wholly or predominantly characterised by the emission of a succession of repetitive beats. (Criminal Justice and Public Order Act, 1994)

This was a wide-ranging law covering terrorism, pornography, removing the obligation on local authorities to build sites for Gypsy-Travellers, removing the right to silence for individuals arrested and charged with a criminal offence, and targeting New Age travellers. It was intended to give police special powers to close down raves. Powers included ordering people to leave land if they were involved in a rave, or even suspected of preparing for one, or to stop them within a five-mile radius of the site if they were suspected to be on the way to a rave.

It was the first piece of legislation that attempted to def... and target a specific form of music. The lawyers drafting the Act had great trouble in finding a definition of acid-house music that would characterize it specifically, not simply as 'playing music very loud'. This rather awkward definition, persistent repetitive beats, spawned much mockery. Electronica two-piece Autechre released a track called 'Flutter', produced with a sequencer programmed so that each beat was very slightly different, and therefore would be technically allowable under the terms of the Act. It was also utterly impossible to dance to.

Despite the amusement, those drafting the Act in this way did in fact put their finger on a fundamental point about rave club culture that differed from other subcultures. The objections to it were not so much that it was subversive of mainstream cultural values. In comparison to previous subcultures, it wasn't particularly politicized, though some of its more radical spokespeople would have disagreed. Rave culture was about parties/clubs, dancing and drugs – it was primarily about leisure, and a particular 'episode' of leisure, the rave. The unintended consequence of its suppression was that rave, acid house, and the use of ecstasy and other club drugs became mainstream. The outcome was that rave was incorporated into mainstream club culture. Raves moved into nightclubs and spawned the superclubs like the Ministry of Sound in London and Cream in Liverpool.

The CJA helped destroy rave as a separate entity, but it did not mean a reduction in drug use at clubs; quite the opposite. The draconian response to rave fuelled a shift towards a renewed city centre nighttime economy that took on some of the aspects of rave space – standing room only, loud music, strobing lights – entering into new bars, along with a range of branded drinks designed to appeal to a sweet tooth. These developments were key elements in creating a licit leisure culture focused around the rapid consumption of alcohol, which is associated with the phenomenon of binge drinking. It could be argued that the destruction of illicit rave culture contributed to the latest manifestation of alcohol as a public order nuisance (Hadfield, 2006). Free and illicit parties have started to return in Britain (2008) and have faced a fierce crackdown, but the main legacy of rave is its accidental contribution to the experience economy.

Twenty-four-hour party people: the experience economy

This isn't life. This is just stuff.
The character of Lester Burnham, *American Beauty* (Sam Mendes,
Dreamworks SKG, 1999)

Western societies, in particular the free-market democracies of the USA and the UK, are based around an experience economy and culture. Consumption is increasingly about generating experiences rather than having things. We do not pay to buy objects and services so much as to buy sensations and memories, although these may be objectified or located in objects (Pine and Gilmour, 1999). Sensations, rather than services, are sold. This is not simply 'entertainment', like movies, theatre or music hall. In a sense, the consumer is consuming him or her self, or, rather, consuming his or her own experiences. This is particularly true of the night-time intoxication economy, which has driven the regeneration of British town centres throughout the 1990s and into the twenty-first century.

Up until the late twentieth century, pubs in Scotland, like most bars in Britain and the USA, were traditionally divided into a bar and lounge area; these used to be the men's and women's sections. In Britain, this gender order has radically changed since the 1990s. There are still 'feminine' and 'masculine' drinks but the design and atmosphere of many pubs has been deliberately altered to make them more women-friendly. There are now pub chains explicitly designed to appeal to women, with large windows, high ceilings, uncluttered pine surfaces, mood lighting and relatively large selections of wine, rather than the traditional pub's 'red or white' choice. What is being consumed along with the alcohol in these environments is the feminized atmosphere and, crucially, other clientele, who are screened formally or informally for their suitability in contributing to that atmosphere.

The experience economy is a political economy of experience. Political economy is the way in which law, politics and environment influence each other in the context of power, all three being as important as the formal workings of the monetary exchange economy. Some individuals and institutions can group together and act to shape these processes to their advantage. For instance, when marijuana was made illegal in the USA, hemp growers and the American Medical Association did not have the power to seriously challenge the Federal Bureau of Narcotics. However, alcohol has a legitimate, lucrative, organized industry speaking for it at a national level. Illicit drugs do not.

The industry's power in this process is not absolute. That of the tobacco industry has been successfully challenged to some extent in many countries, and the political economy of smoking has been dominated by an ongoing clash between it and anti-smoking bodies. Alcohol producers have been successful at avoiding this fate, tagging drinking problems as the fault of irresponsible drinkers.

The political economy of experience involves the government-controlled licensing of leisure. The state licenses people and places. Power works in a capillary manner, through, for instance, the configuration of space and material objects. Medical methadone is configured to make it supposedly uninjectable. Cigarettes are designed to burn for the optimal length of time for the smoker to start to need another. Bars are designed to encourage certain kinds of interaction. This economy of objects and spaces creates the cultural and material settings for intoxication. It is big business, serious partying. In the case of the night-time economy, leisure time and space is highly organized so as to get the effect of disorganized fun.

The reorganization of licit leisure has involved a transformation and corporatization of drinking spaces. If you can picture having a drink in a British pub in the 1980s or early 1990s, you would see a careful arrangement of regulars who drink mostly the same drink day in and day out. All are men. They are all known to the barman/landlord, who along with the regulars operates an informal vetting procedure for would-be customers. Those who might threaten the order of the place are quietly made to feel that it is not for them (Social Issues Research Centre, 1998). There might be a special area for women, 'the lounge', which has more comfortable, lower seating and more elaborately homely décor. It is separate from 'the bar', where men sit on stools in the yellow light and contemplate the pub's extensive collection of stuffed animals. Women were served feminine drinks in feminine glasses. Women who went into the bar were prostitutes. Every pub had its gender order. This ordering was often quite precise – men could stand at the bar, women would sit at tables, when they were not excluded altogether (Lupton, 1979). Women, if they had to get drunk, were meant to do it in private, and discreetly, although they often subverted this, taking advantage of low-surveillance spaces like snugs, much to the outrage of the authorities and moral guardians (Kneale, 1999).

By the 1990s, many British towns and cities, especially those in Scotland and northern England, the Midlands and Wales, had been blasted by suburban flight and post-industrial deprivation. When not completely empty of people, town centres at night were dominated by either groups of teenagers hanging out in the street or old men's pubs. Bar takings were in steady decline, as young people eschewed the delights of beer and sawdust for the burgeoning rave scene. Between 1987 and 1992, pub attendances fell 11 per cent, and the industry predicted further falls to come of 20 per cent over five years. Today, or rather tonight, the average British town centre will be dominated by branded superpubs and superclubs, with names like J. D. Wetherspoons; O'Neills; All Bar One; and Firkin. The clientele will be young, professional and gender balanced, if not female dominated. They are decorated from warehouses full of old Guinness adverts, Irish green paint, railway station signs, and brass pipes

This change was not just generated by random shifts in consumer demand. It was created as part of a strategy by the drinks industry, combined with government deregulation of licensing, the disintegration of rave, and the nightlife-driven regeneration strategies that municipalities were encouraged to adopt. The aim was to create urban areas with round-the-clock activity, from the business day to the evening and night-time economies. The city itself became a product to be sold. For the young professionals providing the consumer backbone to this, work, shopping, leisure and home would be located in the same place.

High-volume vertical drinking spaces were created, in place of the old 'local' pub. Pubs were redesigned to encourage high throughput of customers and alcohol. For instance, it was found that customers drink more if they cannot talk easily, and if they are standing. So the pubs have loud music, and few seats. This chimes with past ethnographic observation that in urban bars people tend to 'mill' in an open-plan area round the bar, even if there are seats available (Cavan, 1966). The identity of pubs changed. The female-friendly design – with large windows, open plan and polished wood – says what the superpubs are not. They are not the working-class men's pub, but they are also not traditional 'female' sections of pubs, the lounge areas.

Customers' behaviour is closely managed to ensure a high volume of product consumption. Techniques like upselling are applied to 'sell to customers already in spending mode'. Image management is involved, creating queues to give the impression of popularity. Rave culture involved unlicensed premises, unlicensed leisure and low alcohol consumption. Dance culture was not destroyed but coopted, in a commercialized, clean form. Dressed up nicely and given a glass of beer. The drinks industry took the opportunity presented by the crackdown on raves, developing 'rave' pub brands, with new drinks like alcopops imitating the popularity of soft drinks sold at raves. As mentioned, when the Criminal Justice Act helped destroy rave as a separate entity, and as an independent experience economy, the gap was quickly filled by the breweries.

These developments were key in creating a licit culture of intoxication focused around the rapid consumption of alcohol, which is associated with the phenomenon of binge drinking. The new venues do not have the informal social controls of the old, so must create the 'illusion of order'. There is a tension in these premises. They are aiming for maximum alcohol consumption, without the regulators of drunken comportment established in traditional pubs, such as the presence of older adults, with talking, pacing, mutual oversight and the power of the regulars. Order is maintained through very basic harm-reduction techniques, such as selling drinks in plastic glasses, which handily saves time washing real glasses, and through removing or preventing entry to undesirables by controlling entry and monitoring the internal space of the pub. Camera surveillance is used. There are no 'regulars' to keep an eye on things and back up the barman, but bouncers instead. There is no sense in which informal controls are allowed to or able to emerge. Bars have a front-of-house area through which customers have to pass, a filter for troublemakers and others who would spoil the atmosphere by being too old, too drunk or too ugly. In this experience economy, customers are themselves consumed both by and in the experiences they have, and they become objects of surveillance.

Knowledge, surveillance and rhetoric

> The fight to curb Idaho's meth problem stepped into uncharted territory Wednesday: The wombs of pregnant mothers. A proposal that would make it a felony offense for a pregnant woman to take certain drugs passed a legislative committee despite the concerns of pediatricians who fear the get-tough measure could lead to more abortions and less pre-natal care.
>
> 'Proposal to crack down on pregnant drug users gathers steam', *Idaho State Journal* (16 February 2006)

In July 2005, the Sat-1 German television channel swabbed for traces of cocaine in the European Parliament in Brussels, repeating an exercise conducted in the German Parliament five years previously. As in the previous exercise, most locations tested were positive for traces of cocaine. In the same month, a member of the Welsh Assembly, William Graham, invited his colleagues to try out a new drug 'sniffer' machine, designed to test suspects for traces of illicit drugs. It came up trumps with its first test subject, finding traces of cannabis on Mr Graham's hands. Minister Edwina Hart likewise tested positive for cannabis. The explanation given was that the results were due to cross-contamination. Cannabis was so common in society that it was effectively present everywhere, instantly undermining the rationale for these detection systems being used in a criminal investigation. Information of this sort only becomes 'evidence' when the person is already suspect in some way.

The use of illegal drugs is a crime without a complainant, since only the user and the seller know drugs have changed hands, and neither has an incentive to inform the authorities. The use of informers and surveillance is the only way of gathering evidence in these circumstances. The aim in this section of the chapter is not to explore the use of surveillance in criminal justice regimes, but to examine how drug surveillance has been incorporated into treatment and management regimes, and to realize how surveillance has been extended into the workplace and public places in order to produce managed and manageable populations. The new surveillance regimes survey what is in the body, and what is on the mind. The horizons of surveillance are thrust deeper into the body through monitoring what is in the body, what it does, and what it might do.

There has been much written recently about the surveillance society, mainly in relation to the most visible (literally) form, closed circuit television, which is used to monitor public and semi-public space. There are many other disciplinary/surveillance technologies being embedded, or that have been embedded, in the many transactions that take place every day. In my wallet I carry seven cards, which collectively register where I am and what I am doing, depending on the situation. My gym pass, university staff card, credit and debit cards, library card, and supermarket loyalty cards provide a matrix of data from which can be told what pubs I socialize in, if I exercise as much as I claim to, and what most of my leisure activities are. Supermarket loyalty cards alone are enough to take a guess at income, relationship status, smoking habits, drinking patterns, education or employment status and many other 'personal' pieces of information that we are reluctant to divulge to survey-wielding strangers and even those known to us, but will give freely to a corporation's customer management department.

The emergence of this kind of surveillance is an important feature of modern life. What is distinct about drug use is the combination of surveillance with coercion, sometimes manifested as a form of tough love, or coercive compassion. Nancy Campbell (2004) examines this in the context of drug-use monitoring technologies. These technologies of suspicion or mistrust produce (or create) independent proof that a person is free of illicit chemicals. They are often used as conditions of drug users entering treatment programmes, sometimes as an alternative to custody. When used in drug maintenance, this kind of bio-surveillance promotes the notion that users cannot be trusted and must be checked up on – an aspect that addicts are sometimes complicit in, such as in accepting addict identity, demanding that they be subject to coercive treatment. Testing for biochemical 'markers' of drug use, as in methadone-maintained addicts, extends the surveillance gaze inside the body. They also lengthen it, across time, for some substances, so that it is possible to tell if a person has used cannabis within the past month or longer.

Population drug testing has been used in schools, prisons and the armed forces. It is no magic way of ensuring a drug-free population. Where it has been used on static populations, such as in prisons or armies on active duty, it has perversely led to the use of potentially more dangerous, but less detectable, substances. Mandatory drug tests in prison reduce the incidence of some types of drug use, but often lead to drugs being used that disappear more quickly from the bloodstream. In some cases, this has involved users switching from cannabis to heroin and cocaine, the latter leaving the system quicker and being more likely to escape detection.

Surveillance always implies a power relationship, in which it is the vulnerable who are scrutinized, as in the example of suspect pregnant women at the start of this section. These bioassays encode bias – or, rather, the social processes that lead to their development encode bias in the technologies. Societies do not develop tests for substances that are not considered to be problematic. Surveillance involves the production of knowledge about individuals and populations, and this is used to manage them. Surveillance produces the drug taker as a subject amenable to risk management and other reflexive disciplinary techniques. This moves us away from a focus on addiction, on drug use as slavery of the will, and towards the establishment of the self-governing subject, to be discussed in chapter 6. It also involves changing the social space for substance use, binding it subtly within a web of regulations.

Drug maintenance as discipline

> Why is it that the poor kids get parked on methadone while the rich kids
> get sent to the Priory?
>
> Former heroin addict to Rosemary Byrne, Member of the Scottish
> Parliament (Scottish Parliament Official Report, Col. 24760, Thursday,
> 20 April 2006)

When we ask for help we want two things: someone to acknowledge
our suffering; and a promise that something will be done. Treatment
incorporates morality, that of the treated, as well as that of the person
giving the treatment. This is particularly apparent in the use of sub-
stitution or maintenance programmes for the treatment of drug addiction. Maintenance of iatrogenic or medical addicts has a long history.
In pre-First World War USA, these addicts were maintained quite
happily. Heroin maintenance in Britain during the post-war period
consisted in simply providing the drug to those who had become
addicted to it – mainly doctors and nurses. There seems to have been
little or no expectation that this was a way of reducing their dependence. They had a need, without the drug they would suffer, and sympathetic doctors did not have any ethical qualms about providing it. In
preventing suffering this fell under the rubric of treatment. In both
instances, it was only when the profile of addicts changed, becoming
younger, male, and having deviant/outsider status, that heroin maintenance was abandoned. Methadone maintenance was eventually
substituted in its place.

Methadone is an artificial opiate, originally developed as an anal-
gesic. Its use for the maintenance of opiate – mainly heroin – addicts
was identified in the 1960s by Marie Nyswander and Vincent Dole
(Courtwright, 1997). Oral methadone is longer acting than injected or
smoked heroin and so allows for a more steady maintenance. It also
'blocks' heroin so that users supposedly no longer get a euphoric effect
from the drug. Nyswander and Dole found that addicts they treated
with it no longer craved heroin or spent every waking minute waiting
for their next fix. The metabolic model of addiction they built, using
their experience with prescribing methadone, contributed to the
remedicalization of opiate addiction and the biochemicalization of its
treatment.

Methadone maintenance has been called a form of discipline,
'chemical parole' (Edward Jay Epstein, quoted in Moss, 1977: 144).
The intention is to manage addicts in a medical environment, rather
than to make them opiate free. The ethnographer Phillipe Bourgois

(2000) examines how medical methadone constructs both the user and the drug as a certain kind of subject. The addict prescribed methadone is a vulnerable, but also untrustworthy, patient, the institutionalized distrust of whom requires regular tests of his or her adherence to the programme and pledge to get 'clean'. Methadone clinics in the USA require the addict to 'perform', to show that previous detox attempts have failed, and to prove a certain period of heroin use. Urine samples have to be given, showing that the user has stayed off illicit drugs and sometimes alcohol also. The addict is required to come in daily and drink their methadone in front of the pharmacist. Good behaviour is rewarded. Dosage can be changed as a form of retribution for a dirty sample.

Methadone has some notably nasty side effects – constipation, psychological problems, aches and pains, and sexual disruption. Despite this, it is a cure: a legitimate medication, with side effects that may be unfortunate but are a price worth paying; and heroin is a poison. One of the reasons methadone blocks heroin is that it is more physically addictive, the user developing a rapid tolerance. Heroin is dope, a 'drug', with harms that are a central part of the drug's operation. Bourgois calls attention to the way that methadone is constructed as a good drug, heroin a bad one, when the only difference seems to be that heroin is more euphoric. Like any other drug, methadone has no consistent behavioural effect. Some users stabilize on it, and are able to carry on normal lives. For many, this is not so. A large number of people resist its effect, or find euphoria with it, sometimes in conjunction with other drugs. A black market exists, indicating it has its own street niche. Methadone is intended to solve the problem of heroin addiction, a problem that has emerged because heroin itself is illegal. It therefore functions as a chemical solution to a social problem.

Disciplinary practices do not just reside in the prescription of maintenance treatments, but also in the provision of facilities for addicts. The cover of the Joseph Rowntree Foundation's report on *Drug Consumption Rooms* (Independent Working Group on Drug Consumption Rooms, 2006) has a picture of one of these rooms, where users can take drugs they have bought elsewhere and consume them in clean, supervised conditions. Almost a caricature of Bentham's Panopticon, the picture is of a row of identical, numbered booths, rather like polling booths. Each has a seat, a desk shelf, and a large mirror. The user is both atomized – separated from other users – and visible, to staff. In the parlance, there is axial visibility and lateral invisibility. The mirror ensures that the action of injecting can be easily observed. Drug consumption rooms manage the behaviour of the user and their impact on others – for instance, reducing unsightly public injections, needle and other litter. This definitely takes some of the fun out of drug use, radically revising the setting the user will be accustomed to. However, the apparent disciplinary imperative of maintenance should not obscure the power struggles that exist within the application of this and other harm-reduction strategies, and the broader criminal justice context which frames it and with which it is ambivalently related. Drug consumption rooms are mostly intended for homeless users or those who inject in public places, whom it is presumed will find this preferable to the risks of violence and robbery they are exposed to. In these disciplinary regimes, heroin users are produced as disciplined, in stark contrast to smokers, who are considered incapable of discipline but who are globally disciplined.

No smoke: marginalization and manners

> It was easier to mount a more consistent attack on the existence of a habit associated primarily with women and the poor.
> Virginia Berridge, 'Passive Smoking and its Pre-History in Britain: Policy Speaks to Science?' (1999)

Smoking in the US, Canada, Western Europe and much of the rest of the world is surrounded by a set of encroaching customary stigmas and legal restrictions that are steadily eroding its acceptability. There have been several historical high points of cigarette control, one early in the twentieth century when fifteen US states prohibited cigarettes entirely (Alston et al., 2002). The current peak is distinguished by its globalized form and reach. Many countries ban smoking in the workplace and in public places. Some US states are seeking to ban smoking in private vehicles. The World Health Organisation in 2005 decided to refuse smokers employment. Cigarette packets carry graphic warnings of the dangers of smoking. In a successful attempt at European harmonization, these are required to be consistent throughout all European Union countries. One general warning must be displayed covering 30 per cent of the packet, normally on the front, saying 'Smoking kills/smoking can kill' or 'Smoking seriously harms you and others around you'. A further sign must cover 40 per cent of the pack and select one of fourteen further warnings, including 'Protect children: don't make them breathe your smoke', 'Smoking is highly addictive, don't start', 'Smoking can damage the sperm and decreases fertility', and 'Smoke contains benzene, nitrosamines, formaldehyde and hydrogen cyanide'. A company offers spoof signs to stick on packets, such as 'Smoking is Cool', 'Social smoking doesn't count', 'It's OK, I'm not pregnant', and 'You could get hit by a bus tomorrow'. Changes in smoking norms constitute a remarkable shift in accepted manners and practices, in developed countries at least. Rather more important than the harm-reduction impact of these regulations, which is debatable, is what they signify. Smoking is now seen by many as a contaminating, disgusting practice that justifies the segregation of smokers while they engage in their reprehensible habit.

The anti-smoking wave of sentiment has gone far beyond the marginal evidence of risk from passive smoking, nonetheless deployed as a scientific justification for cutting smoking out of daily life. What is it about smoking that has attracted such repulsion? There are some elements in smoking itself, the fact that it involves smoke for a start. Smelly, invasive, it lingers in the mouth and in the nostrils well after the last cigarette has been stubbed out. 'Like kissing an ashtray' is a more frequently heard comment from those who have had the misfortune of exchanging saliva with a smoker. Then there is the apparently compulsive element – heavy smokers never without a cigarette give the whole business a bad name. When restrictions began to be introduced these factors reinforced themselves. Segregating smokers makes them appear even odder, as they cluster in small groups outside offices, pubs and restaurants. It is quite difficult to smoke surreptitiously when around non-smokers.

The regulation of smoking is quite unusual for an otherwise legal product. I can sip a whisky while delivering a lecture without any comeback, except perhaps from my students thinking that I am a caricature from a 1960s campus novel. If I light up a cigarette, that becomes a sacking offence, not to mention setting off the fire alarm. These changes have not been introduced without some resentment, but remarkably little resistance is in evidence. Norbert Elias explored the changing nature of the acceptable in his *History of Manners* (Elias, 1978). Just as one no longer relieves oneself at the table, or vomits into the communal food bowl, one no longer smokes around others who do not. What has happened is a visceral change. Non-smokers find smoking as disgusting as moderns would find someone who blew their nose on their sleeve.

The changes in manners around smoking might be of little consequence were it not for the fact that public health policies and changes in smoking patterns have tended to concentrate smoking amongst those least able to deal with its harmful effects. Smoking has become concentrated among low socio-economic status (SES) groups (Action on Smoking and Health, 2006). Public bans on smoking do not reduce overall population exposure to passive smoking, but tend just to shift that exposure from bar staff and bar customers to children in the home (Adda and Cornaglia, 2006). It is a source of bafflement to many that those least able to bear the financial and health costs of this habit would continue with it, in the face of constantly rising prices and continual exhortations regarding the damage it is doing to them. This only adds to the stigmatizing of smokers, who it is assumed must therefore be dim, ignorant or such slaves to their addiction that nothing else matters.

Conclusion

> Had the government deprived Coleridge of opium, he might have been happier. Then again, there might have been no 'Kubla Khan'.
>
> *The Economist* (8 April 2006)

There are many logics of governance of intoxicants. Alcohol licensing laws, self-help groups, models of intervention, all operate on their own, and are operated by very different sets of people with different aims and interests. There is no singular regime of intoxication, but there are many sites and methods of intervention, each with its own practical, and often formal, logic. There are many fields of regulatory practice which intersect at each point in the production, distribution and consumption of intoxicants. They locate the body of the user, which is their object, but they target the self. They know the myriad ways in which subjects are regulated and produced, subjects that are not sober but manageably intoxicated. The regulation and control of the many intoxicants that are available in our societies is of interest to more than lawyers and law enforcers concerned with their everyday work. The governance of what we put in our bodies is really about the government of us as subjects. The many rules, laws and customs that surround the production, distribution and consumption of intoxicants both enact norms and values about what we can legitimately do with our minds and bodies; and also change the shape of what intoxication is. They set up boundaries between legitimate and illegitimate intoxicants, but also alter the practices of intoxication within those boundaries. This happens both directly – for instance, in altering the kinds of substances used, their purity and quality, though certainly not merely in a restrictive way – and also indirectly, say, in narrating women's drinking in terms of risk from sexual violence and threats to femininity. These are not just negative regimes. They operate also by strategic deployment of some substances in ways that productively regulate intoxication.

It might be assumed that there is no other way of limiting the harms from illicit drugs than prohibition. However, for hundreds of years drugs like opium and cannabis were used around the world without requiring prohibition. Other systems of regulation are possible, such as that involving a mature, largely self-regulating drug culture of the type that exists around alcohol. An analogy might be useful here. Traffic lights are supposed to exist to ensure the smooth flow of traffic, keep pedestrians safe and avoid congestion. When the traffic lights are out at a junction, as they occasionally are, does the traffic snarl up? Do cars crash headlong into others coming in the opposite direction? Do drivers become aggressive maniacs aiming to run down pedestrians? In fact, just the opposite happens. Drivers use common sense, communicate with other drivers and pedestrians with subtle nods and hand signals, accidents are reduced, and the traffic continues to flow based on a mutual cooperation that emerges largely spontaneously. However, an entrenched bureaucracy and professional class has built itself around the idea that cars are dangerous and can only be made less so by the imposition of technological controls backed up by escalating penalties. It is the lack of a normalized culture around illicit substances, because they are illegal, alongside the absolutist treatment of smoking, that makes it difficult for us to manage them and the problems they cause in a rational and coherent manner that minimizes harm and does not marginalize those with substance-use problems.

6 Lifestyle Medicines and Enhancement

From the Daily Dose website, 'The World's leading drug and alcohol news service', www.dailydose.net, 26th October 2006:

UK army tested 'stay awake' pills Dr Anna Casey told the Science and Technology Committee the MoD [Ministry of Defence] funded research into stimulant and performance-enhancing drugs and dietary supplements. 'One is always looking for something that would give military personnel an extra edge,' she told the committee which is investigating the use of such drugs in sport [BBC, UK, 26-10-06].

Military drug tests making sure soldiers clean, sober Drug tests have started for Canadian soldiers preparing to head to Afghanistan.

Chronicle Herald, USA (26 October 2006)

Dispassionate drugs

The above juxtaposition that appeared by chance on the Daily Dose website encapsulates the key argument of this chapter. There are some drugs whose use is illegitimate, and individuals caught in possession may be punished. In the example quoted, possession includes having the drug or its metabolites in one's bloodstream or urine. There is another set that may be used in a medical context, which may be the same substances but in different form, rebadged or rebranded. A growing category of drugs is that of pharmaceuticals that are used to enhance, and that are not restricted to the treatment of illness. Militaries around the world have tested and are continuing to explore the use of battlefield pharmaceuticals that will give their soldiers, sailors and airmen an edge, in staying awake, staying focused and promoting endurance. Some pharmaceuticals may become ritually obligatory for performance as a successful 'self' in work and personal life.

Many chemical substances that affect mind and body have been made into commodities, whether in the hands of a drug dealer, a tobacconist, a pub or a pharmacist. Vast industries are devoted to the production and distribution of such substances – the illegal drugs trade, breweries, tobacco companies and pharmaceutical corporations. Lifestyle medicines have been a major growth area for pharmaceutical corporations. They are premium products, developed for and mainly sold in affluent markets. Companies are spending heavily on research into new drugs and conditions to be treated, creating new markets and new demand. Research and development resources go as much into identifying or, more accurately, constructing conditions as into developing pharmaceutical products in response to clinically identified needs (Coe, 2003). There is a systematic alteration in the place of the self in the world, making some personal problems into sicknesses. This is the other side of the construction of public problems, the constructing of others as private problems, legitimated troubles that are expected to be dealt with on a private, individual basis.

There is a new generation of pharmaceutical drugs in development that will allow users to forget past wrongs and bad habits, alter their bodies' response to nicotine, cocaine and other drugs, allow them to stay sharper and more focused, and stave off sleep. Many of these qualities in past times have been attributed variously to opium, cocaine, tobacco and alcohol. It seems as if society may be renewing its acquaintance with functional intoxication, although in a targeted, medicalized form. Here we are getting away from substances as *genußmittel* (Schivelbusch, 1992), objects consumed for pleasure, instead emphasizing their directed use to change the self in the world, to alter, manage and enhance an individual's efficacy in the social world. These are dispassionate drugs, which are used to moderate the self into the rhythms of modern life and to blunt the edge of stresses and strains caused by its conflicting demands on the individual. Once, the palliatives for life's miseries were laudanum and patent medicines; now they are Paxil, Ritalin and Viagra, so-called lifestyle medicines.

Feeling sad, anxious, tired? Lifestyle medicines and branding illness

Whereas the people of rank, who must have something prescribed for every ailment, and believe that we have a cure for every symptom, grow impatient if the physician does not abate their cough, and give them some rest in the night. Opium, and nothing but opium, will do this; they take it in many different shapes, and find it of service in making them cough less and sleep more; therefore they continue it, become slaves to it.

George Young, *A Treatise on Opium, Founded Upon Practical Observations* (1753)

Although a common term in scientific and popular literature, there is no agreed definition of which pharmaceutical drugs are 'lifestyle medicines', and which are not (Moldrup, 2004). Different studies include in the term treatments for sexual dysfunction, depression, cholesterol control, baldness, social phobia, anxiety addiction and obesity, and also oral contraceptives (Gilbert et al., 2000). Various rationales lie behind these choices. They are conceived as medicines used to intervene at the boundary between health and illness, to enhance lifestyle goals, or to treat conditions that are associated with lifestyle choices (Flower, 2004). The advertising tagline in the above subtitle ('Feeling Sad, Anxious, Tired?') was used to market Zoloft, an anti-depressant, and clearly promotes this understanding of the medication's purpose. The term is also often used rather disparagingly, particularly by social commentators. These are not perceived to be proper medicines, but chemical crutches for a risk-averse, mollycoddled, healthicized society that desubjectifies individuals (Furedi, 2004). The term is used here to describe pharmaceuticals taken to alter or manage the user's interactional relationship with others, a function that is to some extent shared with non-pharmaceutical drugs, taken in response to perceived problems of interaction, and to conform to interactional norms.

In the light of their popularity, especially in affluent Western societies, concerns have been voiced about the potential for the creation of a society in which any deviation from the norm is defined as a medical pathology, and in which an ever-expanding sphere of human experience is medicalized. A recently articulated critique, developed from the medicalization critique but with its own distinctive aspects, is of the pharmaceuticalization of the human condition, encapsulated in the phrase 'a pill for every ill'.

Disease marketing is the term given by critics to an increasingly common practice among pharmaceutical corporations. The market for lifestyle medicines is expanded by encouraging consumers to think of what previously would have been considered to be personal problems as potentially medical, treatable problems, carried out through advertising, sponsoring of patient groups, known as 'astroturfing', sponsoring of research to establish that there is a problem, and promotion of medical conditions directly to doctors, making patients into consumers. Illness is big business. Telling healthy people that they are or might be sick is lucrative. Pharmaceutical companies have an interest in defining diseases – defining them as conditions that are widespread and amenable to chemical treatment. They also have an interest in promoting awareness of those diseases they can provide treatments for. In case this sounds paranoid, it is worth looking at how this is described within the industry itself.

An article by the trade journal *Medical Marketing & Media* entitled 'The Art of Branding a Condition' (Parry, 2003), addressing industry insiders, gives a good summary of common practice. It eulogizes the power of branding, of making a version of a condition popular, in a form sympathetic to a cure with a course of pills. The key is imbuing the commodity with the power to solve the consumer's difficulties, difficulties they may not have been aware they had. In an early instance, the company Warner-Lambert, maker of Listerine antiseptic mouthwash, was unhappy with its sales, which (in the 1920s) were flat at $100,000. The company created and promoted the condition of 'halitosis', turning bad breath into a scary-sounding, anxiety-promoting condition nobody could want to have, and for which Listerine was the treatment. Sales rocketed to $4 million.

Three strategies are involved in branding a condition. First, an existing condition can be expanded and elevated in importance. So, Pre-Menstrual Tension (PMT) becomes Pre-Menstrual Dysmorphic Disorder (PMDD), turning a common experience among women into a disorder that can and should be treated. This is not to say that there are not women with serious, debilitating menstrual symptoms, but the process inverts this, so it takes the most severe conditions as representative of the whole. Consumers are encouraged to think of personal difficulties as potentially medical, treatable problems.

Second, many medical conditions have stigma attached to them, so the branding effort should redefine an existing condition to reduce a stigma. For instance, in promoting Viagra, its manufacturer, Pfizer, successfully changed the language of male sexual problems from impotence to erectile dysfunction (ED). Impotence was associated with physical problems or loss of sexual desire and libido, and was highly stigmatizing, with its connotations of loss of power.

Third, a new condition may be developed to create a need. For instance, social anxiety disorder, or social phobia, developed over twenty years until it was first accepted into the DSM-III, the third edition of the American Psychiatric Association's *Diagnostic and Statistical Manual of Mental Disorders*. The anti-depressant Paxil was successfully promoted as a treatment for it after its maker, SmithKline

Beecham (now GlaxoSmithKline), gained the approval of the US Food and Drug Administration to market it. Promotion campaigns for the anti-depressant Aurorix in Australia claimed that as many as 2 million Australians might be suffering from the disorder.

The process of branding vertically integrates the condition and the treatment in a very effective commodification process, which goes right down to the precise form and colour of the medicines themselves. Each pill is intricately designed for its ill (Moynihan and Henry, 2006). PMDD is treated with Sarafem, made by Eli Lilly. Sarafem is the same dose and formula as Prozac, fluoxetine, an established anti-depressant drug. The new indication for fluoxetine allowed the company to breathe new life into the product, whose Prozac patents ended in 2001 and 2003, exposing the company to competition from generic medicine manufacturers. It was able with this new condition to market the same formula as a different medicine. The names and forms of these pills are not randomly chosen. For instance, Sarafem pills are pink and lavender. It is frequently assumed that the colour of the capsule is the colour of the drug it contains, but this is not the case. The name is likewise not some technical term but a brandname chosen to give the pill a reassuring personality – in this case, Sara, like a women's best friend, and fem, feminine, not clinical or cold.

Lifestyle drugs stand accused of contributing to a culture of individuated selves and diminished subjects (Beck and Beck-Gernsheim, 2002), where enhanced pharmaceutical selves medicate away the first signs of unhappiness or dissatisfaction. For their part, pharmaceutical companies and some patient groups argue that there is massive under-diagnosis and undertreatment of a range of major disorders, including diabetes, depression and asthma, of which they are raising awareness. It does appear that the boundaries between health and illness, and between therapeutic treatment and enhancement, are being redrawn in the way that lifestyle drugs are promoted and prescribed. They are undoubtedly commodities as much as they are medicines. The rise of psychopharmacology and the commodification of mental well-being has fundamentally altered the role of medicine in the day-to-day lives of millions.

Psychopharmacology and Big Pharma

> In the 60s, people took LSD to make the world weird. Now the world is weird and people take Prozac to make it normal.
>
> Anon.

The history of psychopharmacology – medicines used to treat and manage mental illness – is only a small part of the history of psychoactive substances. It is a growing part of psychoactive substance use, driving the development of new psychoactive substances, and it is a key technology in the psychiatrization of everyday life. Psychiatry came late to pharmacology. Heroin was initially prescribed in order to tackle what was seen as a widespread problem of morphine misuse, and cannabis was used in psychiatric practice. However, these substances were outlawed following the First World War. Psychiatry in the inter-war period was largely focused around the asylum. There were few psychiatrists in private practice. In 1951, the US Food and Drug Administration made all new medicines only available on prescription. This meant that the control of psychoactive substances shifted from the pharmacist and the consumer to the doctor (Healy, 2002).

This was crucial in shaping the development of chlorpromazine and reseprine for use in psychiatry in the early 1950s, which began the widespread incorporation of drugs into psychiatric practice, integrating psychopharmaceuticals into medical practice and temporarily establishing professional medical control over them. Although drugs had been used before in psychiatry, for instance, in insulin coma therapy, this was the first time that medicinal drugs were targeted to specific mental disorders, in this case psychosis. Their use pictured the brain as a biochemical mechanism that medicines could fix, a fundamental change in the understanding of mind. This is usually termed 'medicalization', in a process that defines an ever wider sphere of human behaviour and experience as medically problematic and subject to professional control, although it is a multithreaded process that has eventually demedicalized and consumerized some aspects of mental health care.

A second major development, which was supported and made possible by the availability of psychiatric drugs, was the movement of treatment outside the hospital environment and, to an extent, outside a clinical context. There was both a de-hospitalization and a de-institutionalization of psychiatry, which gathered momentum into the 1980s. The combination of de-hospitalization and partial de-professionalization pushed the locus of psychiatric medicalization outside the hospital. It became a multicentred process. There are now multiple locations of medicalization processes, which do not necessarily work in the same manner or in the same direction. Psychopharmacology became established as separate from psychiatric medicalization, and the psychiatric profession began to lose its exclusive position with regards to psychopharmacological medication. To some extent, medication started to become once again about pharmacy rather than professional medical practice.

The emphasis on medicinal substances highlights changing concepts of what medicine and medical practices consist of. The shift from clinical experience to evidence-based medicine as the foundation of expertise (Evidence Based Medicine Working Group, 1992), the rise of surveillance medicine (Armstrong, 1995) and the expert patient (Armstrong, 1984), aforementioned marketization and globalization of health care (Lewis and Dixon, 2005), and the promotion of healthy lifestyles (Fitzpatrick, 2001), have all contributed to a de-institutionalization of medicine and the emergence of neo-liberal health-care systems.

Along with these institutional changes went the reorganization of Western pharmaceutical industries, analogous with the globalization of the illicit drug trade discussed in the previous chapter. Financial pressures, global competition and an emphasis on the pursuit of shareholder value required the pursuit of markets which provided a high return on investment; in other words, premium products, blockbuster drugs for chronic conditions (Triggle, 2005). Pharmacy took precedence over chemistry. The cost and time involved in developing and gaining regulatory approval for a new drug, which the pharmaceutical industry claims amounts to $800 million and around ten years, means that returns have to be high and guaranteed. A huge investment is made into researching and testing/proving new drugs, not only lifestyle drugs. The pressures to make that investment pay off are intense, and so pharmaceutical companies expend a vast amount of effort to market their products and the conditions they are designed to treat.

However, the statistic of $800 million per drug is partly manufactured, for instance, through treating expenditure as an opportunity cost. It is also artificially inflated, for example, by including pharmaceutical companies' own investment in post-approval clinical trials, which has more to do with adding to the claims they can make about efficacy in comparison with rival products than safety testing. Other estimates put the clinical cost at $108 million, pre-tax. Further, much drug development consists of 'me too' medicines (Goozner, 2004), products which are sufficiently differentiated from others to be patented, but which are at best incremental improvements on existing treatments, and at worst more expensive and no more effective than those already in use. Product differentiation of this type is the sign of a mature, saturated commodity market where companies attempt to make up for similarities in products with differences in branding. This would not matter so much were they producing games consoles or cola, but given the large proportion of health budgets consumed by their products, and the relative neglect of widespread, and severe, but less profitable conditions, then cynicism about Big Pharma's public service motives is understandable.

There have been some criticisms of the market and mindshare dominance enjoyed by Big Pharma, from within and without the medical profession (Smith, 2004). Medical professionals are concerned about their subordination to the priorities of pharmaceutical corporations' marketing departments. Medical journals, it is argued, have become marketing devices for pharmaceutical corporations. For instance, a significant source of their income derives from pharmaceutical corporations ordering huge numbers of offprints of articles reporting on favourable trials of their products, trials that are funded by the same companies. The medical profession stand in an ambivalent relationship to psychopharmacology in the form it has taken. It involves the location of privileged professional knowledge being shifted away from doctors, and although it articulates medical knowledge and relies on their professional validation, medical knowledge becomes another aspect of the product to be consumed, and doctors become more like technicians of the self.

> [Prescribing solely on the basis of evidence from randomized control trials] in the 1980s and 1990s handed over to pharmaceutical companies the power to decide when and for what drugs work . . . a prescribing that transferred the magic of the therapeutic act from the healer to the brand name of the drug being administered by a technician. (David Healy 2002 : 314)

The location of valued knowledge about these drugs has shifted from individual clinical experience to the publicly available results of randomized control trials (RCTs), clinical trials which assess the effectiveness of a drug or other treatment. Pharmaceutical companies' attempts to use that RCT evidence to establish and maintain brand value has made the knowledge base available to and accessible by the patient/consumer. Yet this apparently neutral and objective knowledge base is deceptive. It may be distorted, for instance, by the desk-drawer effect, in which trials that show no effect are not published, by the construct of RCTs, for instance, comparing the company's new drug to a placebo rather than to the best available treatment (Lexchin et al., 2003).

This alerts us to another key element in psychopharmacology: its position in systems of reflexive consumption that characterize late modernity (Lash and Urry, 1994). Lifestyle drugs, along with other medications, and knowledge about them have been reshaped by neoliberal health-care strategies and the marketization and globalization of health-care provision (Lewis and Dixon, 2005). There has been a shift in treatment from clinical encounters involving professional 'embrained' knowledge to organizational 'encoded' knowledge (Baines and Whynes, 1997; Department of Health, 2000; Ruston, 2006). Lifestyle medicines exist at a juncture between lay self-diagnosis and self-care practices, partial de-institutionalization of medicine, and the production of healthy, self-monitoring citizens (Petersen and Lupton, 1996). Jennifer Coe (2003) writes: 'The lure of easy-to-swallow pills that promise to cure impotence, obesity, hair loss, wrinkles, and even sadness, has captured the public imagination.'

A common trope in commentary on lifestyle drugs is to make reference to the soma of Aldous Huxley's *Brave New World*, the state-sanctioned transport of delight used by citizens of Huxley's dystopia (Triggle, 2005). There have been many dire predictions about the dangers of a society in which people's minds and bodies are fine-tuned to live up to societally validated standards of sociability, sexual performance and socially useful behaviour. This is linked to medicalization and also health-ism, meaning the dominance of a health-based moral narrative intended to modify behaviour (Fitzpatrick, 2001). This critique is sometimes extended so that health-ism and medicalization constitute part of a web of regulative powers that produce risk-reflexive subjects. Yet we limit our analysis of lifestyle drugs if we subsume their use within the category of medicalization, as a decreasing proportion of their use is medicalized. Psychopharmacology is contributing to the production of a new form of subjectivity, the stimulated subject, which exists within a system of reflexive consumption, a self who uses medicinal and non-medicinal drugs to shape, enhance and extend subjectivity, although often not in conditions of their own choosing.

Viagra: sorting men

Viagra, although not the first 'lifestyle medicine', is one of the pinnacles of the art. It is used to treat erectile dysfunction, the condition formerly known as male impotence. Viagra has been used by more than 16 million patients, and it is thought to be one of the medicines most frequently used off-label (Alpert, 2005). It has an enormous cultural presence. It is a referent for jokes, and for metaphors of power, age and masculinity. It has great brand strength. It is often held up as evidence of further medicalization of human experience, and of an emerging pharmaceuticalized society where enhancement supersedes treatment in medical intervention. The promotion of Viagra generated positive associations with virility and sexual performance. Few previous medications were considered signs of potent health and masculinity. It enables a particular sexual act, inscribed in terms of a particular kind of intimacy that privileges plastic sexuality and mutual pleasure as its organizing principles (Giddens, 1994). However, in practice, its use extends well beyond this inscription.

Sildenafil citrate, to give it its technical name, was developed to treat angina in men, by enhancing blood supply to the heart. Trials for this purpose were stopped in 1992 due to lack of success. However, in a story made for Pfizer's public relations department, some of the volunteers in the trial had found that they had a marked improvement in erectile function and, it is claimed, refused to return their remaining samples of the drug. Pfizer had begun investigating this effect in 1989 and by 1998 was ready to launch sildenafil, branded as Viagra, on the market. It faced a major challenge, in that, despite the media hype about the drug, there was resistance among men to talking about or consulting about impotence.

It could be said that Pfizer chose its moment well. Public and academic debates in the 1990s reserved a special place for the 'problem male'. The problem male came in many forms. Young men were portrayed as out of control, joyriding stolen cars and turning on their own communities in a riot of rampaging masculinity (Campbell, 1993). Middle-aged men were said to be unable to cope with the crisis of masculinity brought on by the loss of their privileged and unquestioned position in the workplace and the home. The male of the ruling classes was represented by an unfaithful, emotionally dysfunctional heir to the British throne who drove his wife to self-harm. Problem men were viewed as dangerous, to women, children, families, communities and to themselves; serial abusers, emotionally constipated, brittle and fragile.

There is a long-standing cultural stereotype of women's minds and bodies being complex, fuzzy, and governed by hormonal cycles and emotions, and of men's as being simpler and governed by logic and reason, underscored by a strong separation between the mental and the physical. A large-scale cultural change that became readily apparent during the 1990s was that, while this dichotomy was retained and reaffirmed, the female side of it became more and more valorized and validated as in tune with the times. However, this presented a problem; if men were so simple, then why were they acting (up) with such complexity? In that moment, Viagra helped provide a narrative that reduced men back to a few simple things. The problem male was matched and superseded by the male problem, impotence. This served a useful cultural purpose. Morphing the many problems of and with men into one single male problem allowed both sexes to reassure themselves that men are not complex in all ways.

Viagra and its associated narrative of erectile dysfunction reaffirmed the notion that there is a single on/off switch for a man's sexuality. It restates the male side of the dichotomy; the idea that men's minds are starkly separate from their bodies, especially when it comes to intimate sexuality. The way Viagra was promoted deliberately downplayed, or ignored altogether, psychological causes of impotence or disappointing sexual performance in favour of a biological cause that could be simply treated (Loe, 2004). It also reaffirmed the conception of the male body as an instrument. The difficulties reported in developing a female 'Viagra' have been put down to the relative complexity of women's sexuality. These challenges have been reported on with a certain satisfaction in some quarters. It further underscores the dichotomy between male and female sexuality, and restores the 'invisibility' of the context-specific nature of male sexuality (Tiefer, 2003). Pfizer engaged in some smart promotion, engaging mature men such as former senator and US presidential candidate Bob Dole and footballer Pelé, promoting a certain mature, heterosexual virility. They downplayed the term 'impotence', with its connotations of loss of manhood, in favour of the less stigmatizing and, as it turned out, much more malleable 'erectile dysfunction' (ED). Following the product launch, Pfizer encouraged a steady expansion in the consumer profile, modifying what it promoted as ED to include younger men with mild erectile problems, such as a general dissatisfaction with hardness or staying power (Loe 2004: 59). Viagra was presented as a lifestyle drug, a drug for managing intimacy. The kind of intimacy being imagined in Pfizer's definition of ED is heterosexual, centred around vaginally penetrative sex, this being affirmed as the most satisfying form of sex. Users' accounts do not entirely accept this narrative, however. Some give enthusiastic endorsements of Viagra sex; others find the Viagra-induced erection to be false and alien. The relentless focus on the erection can leave male users feeling like a robotic appendage to it (Potts, 2004).

Viagra very quickly leaked beyond boundaries of gender, age and the categorized disorder of erectile dysfunction. Pfizer created and dominated the Viagra narrative for a long time, but experiences with Viagra are not confined to that narrative, nor to the medicalized category of erectile dysfunction. There are two forms of off-label use of Viagra. First, it is being used without prescription for the purposes of enhancing sexual potency; second, it is being used for its psychoactive effect. A simple separation of 'physical' (sexual potency) and 'mental' (psychoactive stimulation) is problematic here. Most studies are of gay men using it; they tend to problematize this, associating it with unprotected sex. It is used on its own or in combination with other psychoactive drugs. Sexstasy or erectstasy are the street names for the combination of Viagra and ecstasy.

There is a sense in which pharmaceutical companies have moved on from managing sexuality, perhaps due to the failure to create and crack the market for female sexual dysfunction, to the production of what are not so much mood modifiers as feeling modifiers. Viagra was a cultural phenomenon for the 1990s, a metaphor for troubled masculinity and sexuality without intimacy. Ritalin has shown some signs of attaining a similar metaphorical status for the twenty-first century, of out-of-control children and demand-laden adults.

Ritalin: cramming pills

Attention Deficit Hyperactivity Disorder (ADHD) is defined as a disorder involving inattention, impulsivity and hyperactivity, usually manifesting in more than one domain. It is estimated to affect 8–12 per cent of children and is much more common in boys than girls (Biederman and Faraone, 2005), although diagnosis varies significantly between countries. It is increasingly diagnosed in adults. Stimulants have been used to treat ADHD-type disorders since 1937. Ritalin (methylphenidate), a central nervous system stimulant, is used for ADHD. Ritalin operates by elevating dopamine levels, much like cocaine, although it does this both more efficiently and more slowly, like 'cocaine dripped thought molasses' (Vastag, 2001). ADHD is controversial. The medical profession has been criticized for medicalizing bad behaviour and Ritalin has in some quarters been scapegoated as a chemical cosh for dissatisfied children. ADHD is one condition where the diagnosis follows the drug, an inversion of medicalization. There is no agreement on the causes of the disorder, but if Ritalin is effective on the child, then he or she has the condition (Crister, 2005).

Off-label use of Ritalin and similar medications like Adderall, which is also used for ADHD, is widespread. During the 1990s, Ritalin leaked into the illicit drug market in large quantities, in proportion to the increased prescription of it. Prescription users sell or share their pills, and quantities are stolen from pharmacies. Ritalin is not marketed as a lifestyle product in the manner of Viagra but is being used as a lifestyle product by some recreational users, in school and college, who are using it to help them through exam revision, for example. Ritalin is known as the 'cramming drug' on some US university campuses. Both Ritalin and Adderall have also reportedly been used by businesspeople to maintain concentration and stave off fatigue.

Accounts of off-label use of Viagra are more ready to allow for its informal use as partly legitimate; in contrast, use of Ritalin outside a medical context is only represented as abuse. Viagra is intended for use as a lifestyle-management tool; Ritalin as a behaviour modifier. Both have been subject to a similar cultural process of substance–disorder displacement. Viagra has come to partially stand for ED; and Ritalin for ADHD. The substance becomes a sign of the disorder; engagement with ED or ADHD is mediated through that sign. The substances are appropriated reflexively into off-label use, and so are not simply attached to their respective disorders or dysfunctions.

> Ritalin should be given cautiously to emotionally unstable patients, such as those with a history of drug dependence or alcoholism, because such patients may increase the dosage on their own initiative. (Ritalin package insert, 2001)

It is hard to get product information on Ritalin from manufacturer Novartis' website, but the quote from the information sheet above is typical of the direction of responsibility established by pharmaceutical companies for problems arising from use. People abuse it because they are addiction prone. As with alcohol and alcoholism, the problem is presumed to be theirs, the attitude of dependence they bring to the drug.

> Nervousness, insomnia; Loss of appetite, leading to serious malnutrition; Nausea, vomiting; Dizziness, headaches; Changes in heart rate and blood pressure (usually elevation of both, but occasionally depression); Skin

rashes, itching; Abdominal pain, weight loss, digestive problems; Toxic psychosis, psychotic episodes, drug dependence syndrome. (Indiana Prevention Resource Centre, 2008)

Above is a list of possible side effects of using Ritalin recreationally. Some of these side effects might be effects that are sought – loss of appetite; staying awake for long periods; faster heart rate. They are listed under effects of Ritalin *abuse*. Prescription use presumably guards the user against these harmful effects.

Ritalin is intended to encourage the user to adapt to the demands of structured institutional environments, and interacting in an accepted manner with family members and in various social settings such as school (Singh, 2004). It could be argued that Ritalin and Viagra both manage masculinities. ADHD is mainly diagnosed among boys, and it could be said that it is part of the stigmatization of traditional masculinity – troublesome boys. Prescription drugs can be powerful blame-shifters, for instance mothers of boys prescribed Ritalin describe a shift from pre-diagnosis blame for the mother, to post-diagnosis blame on the brain (Singh, 2004). Pharmaceuticals are powerful as they ward off blame.

The pharmaceutical society

When I visited the prescription pricing agency in Newcastle, it had a number of interesting examples of items that GPs had prescribed. You, Mr. Deputy Speaker, might consider it unusual if, when you next visited your GP, he prescribed you a pint of Guinness, but it has been done – and done within the letter of the rules. Another example involved a prescription for a Christmas pudding.

Minister for Health Gerald Malone, MP, House of Commons Hansard, 19 February 1997, Col. 1022

What is a medicine? Are Christmas pudding and Guinness medicines when prescribed by a doctor? Is whiskey? Are opiates? Is any substance used in a medicinal way a medicine? In an episode of the medical drama, *House*, which features the eponymous crotchety senior doctor and his troupe of cameragenic juniors, Dr House prescribes cigarettes to a patient who has an irritable bowel (smoking has a positive effect on the symptoms of one form of the condition). The patient protests that cigarettes are addictive and dangerous. House counters that this is no different from most of the drugs he prescribes, the difference being that this one is legal, stylish and cheap to boot.

The development of new medical treatments is increasingly led by the commercial priorities of pharmaceutical corporations. This means the prioritizing of health problems for which there are high-value medicines available or with the potential to be developed; and prioritizing medicinal treatments over other methods of health/illness management and disease control, such as public health interventions. For instance, HIV/AIDS was an opportunity to develop expensive antiretroviral therapies for sale to an affluent, mainly Western, market which constitutes a small minority of the overall disease burden from it (Bancroft, 2001).

It also feeds a process whereby an aspect of human experience becomes defined as suitable for intervention with drugs that are medicinal but decreasingly medicinalized. The focus of pharmaceuticalization on a particular chemical substance is an important element of the process. The substantive aspect of medicinal drugs – their existence as physical objects – allows them to be produced as commodities which can be, and have been, displaced from their position within a system of medicalized production and re-placed within a system of reflexive consumption. This aspect creates the potential for the substance to move outside the medicalized sphere. It becomes leaky and unstable.

Their nature as *pills* (strictly, tablets and capsules) helps make these substances so seductive. Some types of drug delivery are stigmatized and considered suspect; and others are more accepted. Pills are more validated because their composition and dosage is regulated and controlled; smoking, injecting or snorting the same substances that can be obtained in pill form is highly stigmatized and often presented as evidence of abuse. Smoking in Western societies is a pathologized form of consumption. The US Drug Enforcement Administration (DEA) makes a clear distinction in its publicity between legitimate and illegitimate delivery methods of the same substance, stating that 'Smoked Marijuana is not Medicine' ('Marijuana: The Myths Are Killing Us', DEA News Release, 26/4/05).

In Western society we are used to taking pills as the delivery mechanism for many treatments, not all of which are medicalized, including prescription drugs, some alternative medicines, dietary supplements, and the enormous number of over-the-counter medications that are sold and consumed. This fact eases the incorporation of lifestyle drugs, which come in this form, into processes of reflexive consumption. If Viagra came in the form of injections or suppositories, then it would not in all likelihood have taken off as successfully as it did, partly because of the convenience but also because those methods of ingestion are more medicalized and treated as indicative of pathology. The pill is a drug delivery mechanism with high levels of trust and validation, which has the advantage of being easily consumed, in a literal sense. Pills constitute for the companies producing them brandable, identifiable, controllable products. Hence pills have significant value as commodities, being both clearly identifiable *things* apparently with stable, reliable, consistent qualities, and generally accepted for frequent use.

As a process, pharmaceuticalization commodifies and alters status; in this case, producing a commodity that, while containing the active agents of cannabis, or synthetic derivatives of them, does not have its status as an illicit drug. The re-statusing does not necessarily work in reverse. Cannabis used for the purposes of recreation or self-medication is not legitimated simply because it now has an accepted medicinal derivative, whatever its therapeutic qualities may be. The pharmaceuticalization of cannabis is a process of legitimation of a processed form of the substance only.

Reflexive consumption, deviant consumers

> How happy is the blameless vestal's lot! The world forgetting, by the world forgot. Eternal sunshine of the spotless mind! Each pray'r accepted, and each wish resign'd.
>
> Alexander Pope, *Eloisa to Abelard* (1717)

Medical knowledge about a drug presented by a doctor to a patient in a consulting room is just one source, and often not the most important source, of a patient's understanding of that drug. The media, advertising, the Internet, lay networks and other sources of knowledge may be equally or more important. The development of psychopharmacology is increasingly appropriated within systems of reflexive, knowledgeable consumption. This applies both to the presentation of lifestyle drugs as commodities, and to the demand-led nature of their consumption.

Some criticisms of medical marketing have focused the promotional practices of pharmaceutical companies, in particular on 'Direct to Consumer' (DTC) advertising and the closely intertwined relationship between doctors and drug companies (Moynihan, 2003). DTC advertising is legal in the USA and New Zealand, but not elsewhere in the world. In 2004, pharmaceutical companies spent $4 billion on DTC advertisements (Lenzer, 2005). The complaint is that these campaigns increase public anxiety, encourage healthy people to think that they are ill, and encourage demand for new, branded treatments over established and equally effective treatments (Mintzes, 2002). For their part, defenders of DTC practices say that there is large-scale under-diagnosis of treatable conditions that DTC helps to address. A more widespread practice is the promotion to consumers of a condition through the media; what are presented as public service informational adverts about erectile problems, social phobia, depression and other conditions are sponsored by various companies touting treatments for these conditions.

Although relevant, these criticisms do not take into account the reflexive nature of consumption, and tend to assume that patient/consumers are pushing the panic button in response to the media presence of lifestyle conditions constructed by cynical pharmaceutical corporations. The criticisms of 'disease mongering', as it is called, also rely on a fairly stable and coherent separation of legitimated medical conditions from non-medical ones. It assumes that, because the sphere of life being opened to medication is expanding, people must be thinking of themselves as sick even when they are healthy. These are the notorious 'worried well', young, healthy, anxious patients apparently cluttering the waiting rooms of GP surgeries (Fitzpatrick, 2001). Yet lay and professional conceptions of health and illness are situational and relational constructs. Anxiety or illness is not necessarily always seen as debilitating. Either can be deployed positively as part of the production of identities and subjects.

Disease mongering impacts on subjectivity. At first sight, its object appears to be deviant subjects. They are highly individualized, abhorring deviance from a cultural norm of healthy, self-regulating consumption. It constructs two kinds of deviant. There are the deviant consumers, who eat, drink and smoke too much. Then there are the interactional deviants, such as depressives, attention-deficit hyperactivity disorder sufferers, men with erectile dsyfunction, and women with female sexual dysfunction, who are unable to function and to perform adequately as subjects that are sufficiently chirpy, attentive and orgasmic.

Medicalization is mostly viewed as de-subjectifying, as making the individual the object of the medical gaze; and likewise psychopharmacology is usually subsumed into this critique (Szasz, 2001). Yet lifestyle drugs are appropriated by knowledgeable subjects. In other words, this may positively enable and generate a particular form of subject, as shown by the use of Viagra and Ritalin, and other examples. This does not mean the process is unproblematic – far from it – but we have to start working on understanding why and how individuals might take this up and incorporate it into their narratives, their sense of subjectivity as reflexive consumers.

Dominant approaches foreground the kinds of uses of lifestyle drugs being made, pathologizing some (as addictive, abusive or medicalized, depending on the perspective); and accepting others as normalized. This closes off an important element of lifestyle, and other drug use, which is, how substances are being deployed actively to generate localized subjectivities. There is no stable set of medications that are lifestyle drugs. The drugs cannot be separated from their habitus, the generative context in which the drug is taken, that produces it as recreational or medicinal, stimulating or sedating, and so on.

There are many critiques of diminished subjectivity in late modern society (Heartfield, 2002; Malik, 2001; Nolan, 1998). These appraisals identify very powerful phenomena; but in connecting such developments as the decline of the private and the rise of the therapeutic narrative to diminished subjectivity they reproduce a broader sociological assumption, which is that subjectivity equals the conscious self. Sociological theories of subjectivity assume a sober, autonomous consciousness, although they recognize this as produced, for instance, through the incorporation of regulative discourses and technologies of the self (Foucault, 1979). Like theories of addiction, they tend to pay obeisance to the autonomous self. Other forms of consciousness are mentioned in the literature, but only as negative forms. The subconscious sometimes makes its appearance in sociological writing, although mostly with little consideration, if any, as to what it means except for 'not consciousness'. Theories that rely on the concept of false consciousness treat it as a departure from what people really should think; another constraint upon the subject, to be excised through consciousness raising.

A growing concern is that psychopharmacology medicalizes intimacy and other aspects of private life. The baleful role the pharmaceutical corporations are presumed to have can be exaggerated with regard to lifestyle drugs. Although profitable and carrying much media cachet, these drugs are not the only and often not the main source of revenue for these companies. Nonetheless it is this aspect of lifestyle medication that has drawn much ire and criticism; the pharmaceutical corporations, along with some doctors and patient groups, are accused of inventing and propagating spurious medical conditions that serve to draw an ever wider range of human experience into the medical sphere. Nobody, it seems, ever went out of business overestimating the public's propensity to define itself as sick. However, this argument is limited as it conceives of the medications being prescribed as static objects in a process of medicalization, rather than malleable objects in a system of reflexive consumption, as I argue.

The use of psychopharmaceuticals is defied by the practices of users, which do not make this absolute distinction between being well and being ill, or between medicines and non-medicinal substances. These medications are part of a set of tools that are used to manage interaction, and that are generative of specific subjectivities. These substances are tools for practical action and, like any technological artefact, are employed as part of a technoculture in which their use is not programmed in to the substance itself. The widespread use of medicinal and recreational drugs generates a certain kind of subject, the stimulated subject, who is both self-regulating but who employs intoxicants and recreational drugs within a framework of 'reasonable use', reasonable in terms of local situated rationalities that are appropriate to their context. Users navigate these contexts and may use the same or similar substance in very different ways, recreational, self-management, self-care and so on.

Pharmaceuticalization is particularly apparent, it is claimed, in the commodification of branded prescription medication. Yet this is an incomplete critique because it treats the substances being prescribed as stable entities. It relies on a distinction between acceptable use, dispassionately sanctioned by doctors, and lifestyle use, the outcome of the shameless manipulation of needs in the marketplace. Lifestyle medicines are leaky and unstable, leaking out of the bounds of medicalized discourse, and unstable, undergoing unpredictable shifts in use and meaning. Pharmaceuticalization is treated as an aspect of medicalization; as an element of a process outside of the subject, that objectifies the user. The stimulated subject, who makes use of medication, intoxicants and other stimulants is often given the same chemical substances employed in different circumstances, as practices for developing an effective subjectivity, and, into the future, involving new forms of regulation and control through the distribution of drugs.

Better than life

Eyeing future developments in the normalized use of psychopharmaceuticals involves one part prediction to five parts speculation.

Nonetheless this speculation can usefully indicate how we currently perceive the relationship between self, subjectivity and chemistry. On 13 July 2005, the British Department for Trade and Industry published a set of reports exploring the future for drug use in the UK, under the common title of *Drugs Futures 2025?* This was part of its Foresight programme, which has been running since 1994 with the aim of identifying opportunities for UK industry in exploiting scientific developments predicted beyond the normal business horizon. Current projects are obesity; intelligent infrastructure systems; detection and identifying of infectious diseases; and brain science, addiction and drugs. The last of these projects put forward a variety of scenarios and future possibilities regarding illicit drugs, licit intoxicants, mental health medication, lifestyle or enhancement drugs, and addictions/ dependencies that some presented as moral and political choices (Office of Science and Technology, 2005). The reports themselves are in many ways refreshingly non-judgemental, extensive and thought-provoking, although any predictions of future development in human society have to be taken critically, to say the least. The futurology of the 1980s and 1990s produced some rather overexcited predictions about the impact of communications and information technologies on society, few of which came to pass in anything like the manner foretold. So the reader might be advised to assume that every speculative prediction that follows has all the validity of pronouncements made from the vantage of the saloon bar. Having said that, the trends identified are relevant to how we should conceptualize and theorize drug use and in particular our understanding of medicalization processes.

A major theme of the reports is the expectation of a continued and sustained shift in the focus of pharmaceutical medication in affluent countries from therapy to enhancement. Drugs will be developed to enhance normality; making people happier at home, more able to maintain a focus on work tasks for extended periods of time, and less prone to temptations by vaccinating them against illicit forms of enjoyment. As said previously, enhancement drugs are already a fact in practice. Viagra is now used not just to treat impotence, but also to improve on dissatisfactory sexual performance. Its maker, Pfizer, markets it to men who are less than happy with their erections. Ritalin is used, illicitly, by college students for exam cramming, and medication for mood management is widespread, particularly in the USA.

Some of the predictions are on the sinister side. A future is painted full of happy, contented citizens with all negative traits medicated out of them. Children deemed to be at risk of developing cocaine or smoking habits can be vaccinated against enjoying either. Vaccines are in fact already under development for nicotine and cocaine. They work in two ways; by inserting antibodies into the bloodstream that bind to the substance and prevent it acting as an agonist for the relevant brain receptor; or altering the body's own immune system so that it produces these antibodies itself. Here we have an example of the already established de-legitimation of certain chemically induced pleasures being inscribed on the body. This is a regulative discourse that includes much public health practice, and which might be called the governance of euphoria. Some pleasures are legitimated; others pathologized. Society has always pathologized some pleasures, usually by recoding them as addictions or vices; the process is currently ongoing with smoking. Public health medicine and other social sciences have had a role in this, as they are part of this regulatory system. It may be that public health will become ever more closely concerned with the regulation of pleasure.

The focus of these interventions on pleasure indicates that hedonists might be a future site of ethical debate and conflict. Vaccinating children is a decision taken by their parents, often under considerable institutional and moral pressure. Parents are normally allowed to act in the best interests of the child, within limits set by law and customary practice. The state claims this role when its agents deem it necessary. If the definition of 'in the best interest' extends to deciding what the child will be capable of enjoying in the future, then effectively the parent or the state is writing the child's future choices into their bloodstream.

> You've just had a heavy session of Electro-shock therapy, and you're more relaxed than you've been in weeks. All those childhood traumas magically wiped away, along with most of your personality. (The Orb, *Pomme Fritz*, 1994)

As well as managing or limiting certain acts of euphoria, there is the possibility of drugs being used to manage memory, for instance, allowing people to forget addiction, or traumatic experiences. Without downplaying the miseries of past traumas or current dependences, there are some ethical issues that become salient if this were to be normalized. Bad memories are unpleasant, but they are part of who we are; furthermore, painful experiences can teach us to avoid the same set of circumstances, or people, again. One can imagine unscrupulous uses for 'forgetting' drugs, even if they only work when the person taking them wants to forget. I might decide to wipe my memory of the promise I made to marry you when I got my promotion, giving me a guilt-free get out. More sociologically, this practice may change how we conceive of memory as a collective, social endeavour. Struggles over memory and denial have informed representations of the Holocaust, and continue to have salience. Let us imagine that the survivors of a future holocaust had their trauma treated by 'forgetting' therapy. Where then would be the museums and memorials? The slogan 'never again' has been honoured far more in the breach than the observance, but it remains more powerful than 'never remember again'. In contrast to what I wrote earlier, experience may become reversible.

There are also implications for the self in society. The true, knowing, aware self has been presented as the ideal subject in our society, supported by therapeutic discourses and narratives of authenticity that are located around identities. The predicted widespread employment of forgetting as an active social practice, assisted by drugs and therapy, may presage a move away from this self as an ideal. If self-knowing is deliberately limited, then what remains? It is likely that new concepts of the self will be formulated in response to this, that are not entirely based on the certainty of the autonomous, knowing, consciousness. There are some implications for social theory. Most mid-range social theory has of late incorporated the concept of reflexivity, the requirement placed on members of our society to continually remake themselves in the light of new knowledge, experiences, and demands. Reflexivity is called into question when knowledge is deliberately abandoned and destroyed. One might think of this as a higher order of reflexivity, one that acts on the subconscious and the non-reflexive elements of self, that actively shapes habitus and then forgets the act of shaping.

The reports' authors predict that it will become normal practice to take enhancing drugs; for better memory, concentration, alertness and so on. Ritalin-type drugs, it is envisaged, would be available from your local chemist and you would take them with as little thought as the morning-after-the-night-before paracetamol. Most ways of conceiving medicalization have incorporated the notion of pathologization; of bodies, behaviours, practices and identities. The pathological is the object of medical practice; but since these medicines are being used to enhance normality, then we may have to develop a theory of normalized medicalization, where pathologization plays a diminished role. There are significant social, cultural and political implications to the enhancement of normality. For instance, much art, philosophy and literature has been produced by people who would today be defined as depressives or compulsive-obsessives like Van Gogh. Anger and dissatisfaction can be resources for social and political change, not just problems of the self. Normality is produced; it is produced in the actions of individuals as well as in the advertising campaigns of drug companies promoting cures for shyness and traumatic memories. However, the likelihood of creating a society composed of chemically neutered shiny happy people is limited.

Looking back at the history of drug use, we can see how substances do not have effects that are fixed in their chemical make-up. The effects of drugs are produced in the interaction of self and place; this does not just apply to psychoactive drugs, but to all drugs that intervene at the level of being in the world. If past experience is at all relevant, then the predicted cognition enhancers, addiction vaccines and future recreational psychoactives that are being cooked up in pharmaceutical companies' research departments and illicit chemists' laboratories will be malleable, leaky, entities, whose use will very quickly extend beyond the intentions of their makers. The drugs on which these predictions are based have indeed not been used in the way that their manufacturers intended. Lifestyle drugs are being used off-label and also recreationally. It may be that users of drugs, whether medicinal, recreational or otherwise, will incorporate their use into a developing 'chemical subjectivity' that does not correspond to any official idea of normality or ideal healthy subjectivity. It may also be that the popularity of enhancement drugs will produce a backlash in favour of the authenticity of incurable sadness, uncertain sexual performance, and bitter memory.

The predictions made in the DTI reports rely on a well-established historical narrative, that of ever greater targeting and precision. There is a narrative of medicinal drug use that combines technology (syringe, refinement) and knowledge (about the function of drugs on the brain) to produce a steadily more refined targeting of drug impacts on the user. Developments in the understanding of how drugs act on the brain and interact with genetic predispositions will allow those prone to addiction or adverse reactions to be identified. Pharmacogenetics promises even more fine-tuning, although whether the promise of this will be borne out is hard to say.

BARBARELLA: On Earth when our psycho-cardiograms are in harmony for lovemaking . . . we take an exaltation transference pill . . . and remain like this. Here let me show you. For one minute or until full rapport is achieved.

MARK HAND: I don't care for that. This is what I mean . . . the bed!

BARBARELLA: That? But nobody's done that for centuries! Except the poor.

(*Barbarella,* dir. Roger Vadim, Dino de Laurentiis Cinematografica, 1968)

In the 1967 film *Barbarella,* Jane Fonda's title character informs a lustful Mark Hand (Ugo Tognazzi) that on Earth sex is performed through the use of exaltation transference pills, and the physical act of lovemaking has long been abandoned as distracting and inefficient. The 1997 movie *Gattaca* presents a society in which well-off parents select the genetic characteristics of their children. The genetic elite differentiates within itself ever more finely. The tiniest flaw, such as a heart murmur, acts as barrier to advancement. Whether the affluent will be able to buy their way to perfection is another question. It is the case that public displays of health are already markers of social status. Smoking is stigmatized and patrons of fast-food restaurants are mocked in art-house documentaries.

Inhibiting the self

There is an ambivalence present here, since the subject that the healthy society is presumed to create is sober, but worried and anxiety-stricken. The implication is that illicit drug users or binge drinkers are subverting or resisting this subjectification; maybe. But they could be incorporating intoxication into this subject. There is the potential for a social divide emerging here. There are the rational, consuming stimulated subjects whose on- and, with increasing frequency, off-label use of lifestyle drugs is incorporated into a stimulated subjectivity. The flipside of this is the creation of addict subjectivities, which is a proliferating practice.

Western society emphasizes choice and agency, expressed through consumption; at the same time, a growing range of consumption practices are pathologized as addiction (Reith, 2004). Addiction, however, is no longer located in a dangerous object, or the habits of specific social groups, but lies in the interpretation of the individual as having lost control over his or her consumption practices, whether it be gambling, sex, shopping or eating chocolate. Addiction is the revenge of the object on those who will (literally) consume it. There was a contradiction in the nineteenth-century notion of the addict identity, though. Addiction was a disease of the will; but it was also too much will, a will to consumption, will to forgo every other need – for food, respectability, sleep – in order to pursue its object. The concept of addiction current today places the addiction outside the will of the subject, and in a combination of the chemical structure of the object and the brain structure of the subject.

A problem with this thesis is that it can sound as if drugs were about restoring to function or ensuring that functions continue unimpeded. They can be 'in themselves' about the exploration of or toying with consciousness, the pursuit of pleasure and so on. They are interactive, and will take the user in directions they may not have intended to go ('the trip' encapsulating this). Plenty of research from the addiction side of things indicates that drug users employ situated rationality, that drugs have uses for them; they are not slaves of the will. This description is mostly accepted by critical sociologists and drug libertarians; but, funnily enough, we do not recognize this when it comes to medicinal drugs, which are presumed to beat the user about the head with a pharmaceutical persuader.

Patients are knowledgeable consumers, however, just as much as recreational or problem users are. The subject is only stable within its place; the subject is produced and producing. We also have to consider how this is different from other tools of subjectivity, such as the narrative, which are universal. The stimulated subject clearly is not universal. Some elements of it can be drawn on by anyone, user or not, and are pervasive; for instance, the therapeutic, medicalized narrative. It is partly situational, relying on skilfulness. Another proviso has to be mentioned: these drugs are still a small part of the market and it could be seen as very ethnocentric to assume otherwise, in particular, regarding their use for individual self-development. They correspond to a culturally specific concept of subjectivity.

There are two senses in which the term 'drug normalization' can be used; the first, that illicit drugs are being used without any particular pathology or stigma attaching to them (Measham et al., 1998; Parker, 2005); and the second, used here, that drugs are used to help people achieve normality. Achieving normality is a large part of medicine these days. There was a debate in the 1980s and 1990s about treating children with growth hormone to correct short stature. When the availability of the hormone was limited, its use was restricted to children who were identifiably deficient in growth hormone. Once artificial hormones became available, it became possible to prescribe it to children who were not deficient in the hormone, but who happened to be short. The debate then moved to whether it was acceptable for doctors to 'correct' what was part of normal human variation in order to ensure children conformed to a society that values and rewards height (Lexchin, 2001). By implication, this validated and reinforced societal prejudice against short people. Addiction medication changes how users think of their selves and bodies, making addiction real. New lifestyle medicines will generate as many problems as they solve.

Conclusion

> It is easy to get a thousand prescriptions but hard to get one single remedy.
>
> Saying

There is extensive use of lifestyle drugs. Many more are in the development pipeline, intended to intervene ever more precisely in the self. Drugs are promised, or being tested, which enhance memory, which encourage forgetting, which immunize against craving. The form, function and use of medicinal drugs have changed markedly, and will change more in the future. I had intended to write this chapter largely in terms of the pathologization of aspects of the human condition, which I thought was at the heart of the drive towards pharmaceuticalization; although this is an element of it, a perhaps more significant factor, for this chapter at least, is the extensive use of drugs to *enhance* and *direct*, rather than to treat. Perhaps because of our interest in pathologization, sociologists of health and illness have had trouble theorizing a form of medicinalization that is not wholly a medicalization; I have attempted to make some progress towards doing so here, coining the term 'stimulated subject'. The term is perhaps a bit of a misnomer as stimulation is just one element of the effects being sought, but it captures the fact that this is not simply a diminished or circumscribed subjectivity. The subject so generated is not a stable entity; indeed, a descriptive term might be better phrased in terms of subjectivities that are generated in particular places.

Is it merely a trivial point that recreational or medicinal drugs are sometimes used in non-recreational ways? The statement perhaps makes better sense in reverse – recreational ways of using drugs are a part of intoxication in practice. It is the establishment of medicine on a professional footing, and apothecary as an industry, together with the rise of illicit and licit recreational drugs industries, that have generated the distinction between the two, downgrading recreational use as the suspect, delinquent, part of the relationship. Samuel Hahnemann, in 1803, complained that coffee created an artificial being; that it disrupted nature's rhythms of tiredness and rest, producing a wakefulness that was contrary to nature. In his statement there is a conservative dislike of modernity, with its departure from nature's rhythms, which were really the rhythms of pre-industrial society. All drugs, medicine and recreational, could be and are criticized for this. Pharmaceuticals are never as far as their makers would like to pretend from illicit recreational drugs, in formula or in usage.

7   Drugs in a Culture of Intoxication

Branches they bore of that enchanted stem,
Laden with flower and fruit, whereof they gave
To each, but whoso did receive of them,
And taste, to him the gushing of the wave
Far far away did seem to mourn and rave
On alien shores; and if his fellow spake,
His voice was thin, as voices from the grave;
And deep-asleep he seem'd, yet all awake,
And music in his ears his beating heart did make.
[. . .]
To dream and dream, like yonder amber light,
Which will not leave the myrrh-bush on the height;
To hear each other's whisper'd speech;
Eating the Lotos day by day,
To watch the crisping ripples on the beach,
And tender curving lines of creamy spray;
To lend our hearts and spirits wholly
To the influence of mild-minded melancholy;
To muse and brood and live again in memory,
With those old faces of our infancy
Heap'd over with a mound of grass,
Two handfuls of white dust, shut in an urn of brass!
(Alfred Lord Tennyson, 'The Lotos Eaters', 1833])

The moral economy of 'drugs'

A life in boundless pursuit of pleasure makes one blasé.
Georg Simmel, 'The Metropolis and Mental Life'
(1995 [1903])

Academic discussions of pleasure are rare, and are rarely examinations of how it may be increased. More usually, they expose the malignancy and exploitation hidden behind apparently everyday habits and enjoyments, be they sex, smoking, relationships, cooking the Christmas turkey, singing in the shower, eating a hamburger, going shopping or taking the children to a theme park. Our precautionary society hungers for technological progress but also treats every new discovery as a threat, and its vision of the future is one of impending doom. In our moral economy, every enjoyment today will be paid for with misery tomorrow.

Intoxicants upset this moral economy. Our societies tend to be ambivalent about them as apparently unearned pleasures, and therefore unethical or distorting (Young, 1971). Ambivalence, or outright condemnation, stems from the ways that intoxication does not appear to involve interaction or exchange with others, and therefore is profoundly anti-social. It puts the beneficiary outside the moral exchange. This is usually summarized in a statement to the effect that the pleasures of drugs are 'not real'. They are, so we tell ourselves, insubstantial, fleeting and meaningless. Even if the organic mechanisms by which pleasure is felt are the same, the means and the meaning are not.

Such a judgement depends on the standpoint. Wrestling with a thorny problem of how to reconcile the design for this book, I came up with what I thought was a solution – immediately, I was overcome with a profound sensation of satisfied relief. At the same time, I can guess, my brain was flooded with 'reward chemicals'. Was that pleasure earned, real or not real? What if the solution was in fact a 'magical' one, an apparent solution that did not in fact change anything, leaving an unstructured mess to be cleaned up later? A poor crack-cocaine user goes to enormous effort and takes huge risks to obtain money to buy crack – hustling, dealing and putting themselves in serious danger (Bourgois, 1989, 1995, 1998, 2003; Maher, 1997) – while all the time I am sitting comfortably at my desk. Is theirs then not a 'justified' reward? The answer may be that, contrary to the drug user, I was not aiming for the pleasure itself which was purely a 'reward' for hard work, but that is slightly disingenuous. Many drug users could be said not to be aiming for pleasure, but something more like satisfaction, self-reflection and avoidance of ennui. The illicit drug user, and in some cases the alcohol user, puts a foot outside the door of the ethical trading floor, but they remain, as a physical being, within the chemical world.

The chemical world and the stuff of enlightenment

We live in a chemical world. Our bodies generate chemical substances to regulate our mood and behaviour, for instance, to facilitate fight or flight responses to threatening situations. The world we live in is made up of and saturated with chemicals, natural and artificial. Long ago in the story of humankind we learnt to manipulate the chemicals we found in the natural world in order to alter our sense of being in that world – to the extent that we were able to create our own. Much of the ingenuity of humanity has gone into refining the natural and developing the artificial. Indeed, that largely describes our relationship to our environment. Once a cause for celebration, the human dominance of the environment is now questioned by the self-doubting, environmentalist ethic that has come to predominate in many Western societies. Humanity's chemical production is increasingly defined in terms of pollution, of the body, the mind, the earth, sea and air. This profound mistrust of human potential has increased in line with our increasing dependence on chemistry.

From the growing of fruit for fermentation into alcohol that may have been the foundation of the earliest agriculture, to the development of a range of mind- and mood-altering drugs that keyed into brain chemistry, in the twentieth and twenty-first centuries, one drive towards greater chemical refinement has involved seeking after intoxication. This is as much a common feature of our history, and our humanity, as the ability to directly and consciously shape the natural environment; which is what is more usually taken to be the aspect of life differentiating human from animal. The chemical make-up of new drugs was not deduced from observations of the workings of the brain. Knowledge of the workings of the brain in many cases followed well after the discovery or development of these substances and their effects, when at all. It was the effect of old and new drugs that shaped our understanding of the workings of the brain, and the relationship between the organic brain and the mind, and how to change it, feeding into the modern, reflexive cast of mind.

This faculty for intoxication is developed and worked on at different historical periods and cultures, shaped by the specific frames of mind pertaining in each place and time. It is as worthy of sociological study in itself as any other element of human life, and not just for the indubitable problems that are part of it. The role of chemistry in the modern world was asserted by Wilkie Collins in *The Woman in White*, where one character describes how the art of chemistry would make a babbling fool of Shakespeare, a mild kitten of Nero, and a coward of Alexander. The self is not so easily subverted, not unwillingly at least. Yet there remains some ambivalence, reflected in the term 'intoxicate' which means both to poison and to slip the bounds of dour sobriety.

Ambivalence about the unreality of intoxication stretches back into history. Many Ancient Greek cities, before 600 BC or so, kept groups of the chronically ill and disabled housed just outside their main gates, at public expense, with food and board paid for. At times when a natural disaster threatened the city – famine or pestilence, which was not a rare occurrence – one of the unfortunates would be chosen to be stoned to death in order to appease the gods. He or she was called the *pharmakos* – which means the poison and the cure. The word came to mean any medicinal drug that cured, and retained for a time its curious double meaning. Here, it was recognized that drugs which can cure can usually kill if given in the right dose. The arts of the healer and of the poisoner were not very different, involving similar knowledge, skills and tools. The distinction was a matter of degree of application. This reflects ambivalence about those who hold the power of curing, which is also the power of killing.

To accept this ambivalence we need to put human agency at the forefront, without which the question 'what is a drug?', asked in chapter 1, is an irrelevance. A drug is a substance used in a drug-like way, a medicine is the substance applied to cure, and a poison the substance used to kill. The end point is that any object or relationship to an object is only formed by the way humans relate to it. Psychoactive substances become 'drugs' only when they take on socially active characteristics, which incorporate human agency. Opium was a medicine when drunk and eaten by white Americans, Australians and Englishmen, and a corrupting luxuriant when smoked by, or in the company of, Chinamen (sic). They do, however, have solidity, in that they can never be uninvented. Technology is, within the timescale of a civilization, generally irreversible. Partly because of that, but also because so much power is invested in them, drugs come to be seen as objects outside human control; in fact, ones that can control people.

Sensual objects in material culture

Drugs are objects of material culture – objects that are commodified, scarified, stigmatized, but that are never without symbolic and economic value. The substantive, chemical, material, aspects of drugs are what allow intoxication to be generalized beyond the individual experience while retaining its specificity, which is why the paradigmatic metaphor of addiction is mostly just a metaphor when generalized in terms of other experience. Love is a form of intoxication, as perhaps is self-loathing. One might be addicted to a love, but despite the claims of pop songs, one is not really addicted to love, as such. Love is, after all, ideally fulfilling and fulfilled. Love is not greater than itself. Attainment of the object of love is the end of intoxication, and its loss the beginning of suffering. Those who say they are unable to function without coffee, who gasp for a cigarette, who live the working week for the weekend alcohol and ecstasy binge, are not claiming to be addicted to a particular cup of coffee or a particular pint of bitter, although coffee, cigarette and beer manufacturers try their best to inculcate the impression that the effects so derived are peculiar to a particular brand.

It is the repetition of the experience that is the delightful and destructive aspect of it, and this repetitive aspect is located within the forms of the substance itself. In this respect, the desire for intoxication bears closer resemblance to spiritual hunger than to love. Love is valued in the singular. There is never more than one love object. Drugs, like religious observances and self-mortification, are valuable in repetition. This is the fact that gifts them with the potential to be addictive, to be abused, to create madness and serenity. Here, we come to the difference between molecules and chemicals, and close to the question 'what is a drug' – a drug is an object that changes being in the world at an individual and potentially a group or societal level.

Drugs are acquired within systems or forms of life and within institutionalized regimes of control and surveillance. They can be hedonistic, mundane and/or medicalized. When used as a medicinal drug, cocaine was acquired as an anaesthetic within a particular social system and institutional setting, medicine. The patient, or rather the patient's body, is also acquired within that system as an object of it. These are modern systems, and their acquisition of psychoactive substances and patients' bodies is part of their modernity. For cocaine to be a recreational drug also presupposes a whole set of socio-economic structures and relationships, some of which are shared with medicine: the existence of leisure time; a group of friends or colleagues who will either join you in taking it, and not mind, or not notice, when you do; a set of distanced, globalized networks and technologies that can deliver the drug at a price the user is prepared to pay, and in a form in which he or she can swiftly and surreptitiously consume. This last element is shared between cocaine as a leisure drug and as a tool of medicine; indeed, would not have come about without it.

Intoxicating chemical substances become objects through culture, and those objects can be ordered according to various principles, some of which are more powerful than others in the experience of the user. When asked to list 'drugs', people will come up with a range of answers: marijuana, MDMA, heroin, methadone, LSD, alcohol, Ritalin, anti-depressants, sugar and more. Some are brand names. Heroin is the brand name for diacetylmorphine that was coined and later disowned by Bayer, the company that developed it. Ritalin is one brand of drug that contains methylphenidate, currently used in the treatment of attention-deficit hyperactivity disorder. Some names are descriptors of chemical structure; MDMA is 3,4-methylene-dioxymethamphetamine, a mouthful known more commonly by its street name, ecstasy. LSD is D-lysergic acid diethylamide, or acid. Some are categories based on effect, that include a very wide range of substances. Anti-depressants, medically defined, would include the SSRI class of drugs such as Prozac, and the tricyclic anti-depressants developed in the 1950s, named after the drugs' characteristic three-ring structure. Marijuana is the name given in the USA to the psychoactive product of the cannabis plant. It was a Mexican word popularized in the USA by the newspapers owned by William Randolph Hearst, as it sounded much more frightening than 'hemp', as it was known at the time (Booth, 2003).

Each term embodies assumptions about that particular drug; and, more generally, what drugs are; about which are legitimate medications, and which illegitimate 'drugs of abuse'. The category of 'drugs' could consist of: substances that have a narcotic or psychoactive effect; substances that alter the body's chemistry; illegal substances; something you buy from a pharmacist's; any substance taken with the intention of altering one's mental/physical state; substances used for the pursuit of pleasure; dangerous substances. There are various statuses given to substances according to which category they are placed in. The most common two are medicinal and legal status. There are socially dominant categories, which are explicit, and that come ready made. Other categories would be the effect of the substance: depressant, stimulant or hallucinogenic; and the form it comes in – as a pill, smokable, drink, or inhalant. These categories are not mutually exclusive, which is exactly the point. The same substance may appear in each of them, sometimes in a different guise. For instance, Ritalin when prescribed to a child by a doctor is legitimate. Failure to take the drug as required is defined as patient non-compliance. The same substance taken by a businessman before a meeting because it helps him to improve concentration is illicit, off-label use, although it is not something that will likely lead to severe penalties, and indeed would evoke sympathy for the pressures he is under. The same substance, again, crushed and snorted by a young woman for the purposes of getting off her face is drug abuse, and would invoke much more severe condemnation and sanctions, possibly legal.

These are not merely matters of description. Ritalin seems to calm down hyperactive children, but when crushed and snorted gives the user a speed buzz. Drugs are substances that have effects on individuals but these effects are not stable. They are also observable effects only in relation to something else – sobriety, consciousness, normality – and are divided between subjective and observed. They alter the body's chemistry, but some drugs appear to or are intended to restore balance, to make the body or brain normal. Anti-depressants are supposed to correct an imbalance of serotonin, whether or not the person receiving treatment is born with that chemical imbalance in their brain. Taken with the intention of altering mental/physical states, they are often used for the pursuit of pleasure. Many are not taken for pleasure, but out of felt necessity – for instance, a 'wake-up' coffee to feel normal, or the first cigarette of the day.

The image from 'one try and you're hooked' anti-drug messages is that heroin, cocaine, crack and similar drugs are so seductive that one try will give an incomparable euphoric high that will forever after be unobtainable. The hallucinogen Ibogaine is used ritualistically by the Bwiti religion in West Africa, and has recently been used in the UK to treat drug and alcohol addiction. Nobody who has taken it says it was pleasurable. Then, again, pleasure is often something that has to be learnt. Further, altered states presume that the original state one is being altered from is the true one, and that the user is entering some fake state; whereas many users are of the opposite view – that a drug like heroin makes them feel normal and human, supporting the autonomous self.

Autonomous consciousness

Consciousness was upon him before he could get out of the way.
                    Kingsley Amis, *Lucky Jim* (1961)

Drugs reveal the nature of consciousness. Intoxication is not the opposite of consciousness, but in altering conscious states it shows us what the processes of consciousness are, a balanced equilibrium of sensual experiences. The sublime elements of intoxicant experience are enacted in practices of intoxication and embedded in the substances themselves. They are substances that are in material form but have a solipsistic effect. Intoxicants directly connect our selves to consciousness; they make consciousness apparent, and they make the physical/material element of mind apparent – showing through intoxication that our minds are in part chemical and biological entities.

Enlightenment thought emphasized the foregrounding of explicit, reflective consciousness (Locke, 1689). It is in some ways a limited view of the human mind. Decisions taken without conscious reflection can be more satisfactory than those with (Dijksterhuis et al., 2006). It is recognized in some societies that altered consciousness is a source of authority; indeed, that those entering the altered state are not leaving the real world for an illusion, but are moving from one world to another, with its own rules and reality. Many in such societies – the shaman; the mystic; the visionary; the ascetic; the sadhu – have a status and power that derives directly from their access to this other world (Crapanzo, 2001). In modern society it seems we have gone to great lengths to treat these altered states as objects of study rather than places to go to. For instance, the analysis of dreams defines them as expressions of the subconscious; such uninhibited expression is defined as madness, an intimation of pathology .

Intoxication has been held suspect in post-Enlightenment societies for this reason. It appears to interfere with that process of explicit reflection and deliberation, subverting the self. Calling intoxication a form of distorted consciousness or impaired perception defines it as deviant. Even when sympathetically put, it devalues intoxication, defining it as degraded consciousness which departs from the norm of self-aware, sober, self-actuating consciousness. This approach reflects the way that, in Western societies, and in the social sciences, we privilege *autonomous* consciousness as the seat of self-hood. Any other kind is treated as either disturbed, repressed, inadequate or an anthropological curiosity. Nothing is to be had from the heroin addict except urine for a toxicology report and an account of the social and personal factors that keep him or her addicted.

The perspective that intoxication is deviant consciousness makes an assumption about the state of sobriety. It assumes that it is a state of static equilibrium – a steady-state theory of consciousness – which intoxication then pushes over. It divides and walls off intoxication from uninhibited consciousness. Our sober and intoxicated states of mind could in fact be more like the dynamic equilibrium that comes from constant movement of forces. When we walk we are in a state of constant dynamic equilibrium – where balance is maintained through constantly changing disequilibrium – which may explain why I can usually make it home when blind drunk. Intoxication, and perhaps sobriety, is not therefore a *particular* state of mind or balance of forces within the organism, but a dynamic that is enacted under the influence of psychoactive substances. Intoxication is the mind in a dynamic of disequilibrium.

Intoxication by necessity includes both positive and negative experiences – some sought after; some endured. It is not a quality inherent in the substance itself; nor in the personality of the individual using it. In that sense, intoxication can be many things. It can be a vehicle for greasing the palm of social intercourse, and an occasion for the flattening of social hierarchies with the lightening of inhibitions, while also asserting one group's claim to moral superiority over another. It is frequently a site for the temporary suspension of norms and the enactment of the most sacred values. It is a productive and active part of social life for more than its well-attested ability to make the intolerable bearable – in both people and situations. It also integrates and remoulds the self.

Practices of the plastic self

Mad desire and errant fancy are exquisite expressions of the self.
Ralph Turner, 'The Real Self: From Institution to Impulse',
The American Journal of Sociology, 81 (1976: 992)

Uninhibited consciousness is privileged because of the demand in modern society for self-control with a self-surveillance that requires continuous self-awareness and self-monitoring. At first glance, intoxication would appear to challenge this and so be inherently deviant, but it is reincorporated into this concept of self, although not fully so. Intoxication is not just a form of pleasure or a consciously altered state of mind, but rather an altered state of *self*. In the relationship between the individual agent and the social formations encountered, there is a dynamic of conscious and unconscious selves, of which the intoxicated self is one part of that dynamic. So we create social worlds with intoxication. Selves are stimulated. Self becomes known through consciousness and action. Intoxication is experienced and understood as an altered state of consciousness, but because consciousness cannot be observed, only reported on, it tends not to be taken seriously. The implications of this have remained opaque, perhaps because the rule of consciousness in modern society means that we resist accommodating its apparent subversion into an account of self in the world. This is the Enlightenment legacy – the Enlightenment self – self as I, as aware, acting subject, *homo sociologicus*, the rational self, the ego and superego. Transforming the self is subsumed into everyday life. Advertisements promote the transformative potential of their products, which will revolutionize our lives, our place in the world or the way others see us. Intoxication can be seen as being used to transform the self; but also conversely to assert it.

Intoxication will affect the self in several ways other than altering explicit consciousness. Emotional responses are changed when intoxicated and this will affect how the individual interprets the signals and motivations of others. Paranoia, maudlin sentimentality, rage, loving the stranger – these will all change both the nature of the situation and the individual's perception of it. Intoxication also changes the individual's physiognomy, causing dilated pupils, slurred or rapid speech, relaxed or tense posture. This will affect how others interact with the individual – so the form of interaction has altered. Their reaction of course depends on how they interpret these signals.

Intoxicants are deployed creatively to constitute and control spaces and subjects in this manner. The act of smoking a cigarette can mark time and space, the boundary between insider and outsider, and embody sociability, or stigma. This can be used on others: the drinking game used to initiate a newbie into the experience of getting very drunk very quickly, that can also of course be used to punish or embarrass an outsider; the party host over-eager to fill up your glass is trying to oil the wheels of social interaction. These are both ways of producing socially appropriate intoxication, socializing intoxications. They mark who is in charge, who has to defer to whom – refusing a drink can be a delicate matter in some circumstances, just as having one or several can be delicate in others.

An important element of this self-concept is its plasticity. It changes according to situation, so one can pride oneself on one's accountancy work, and on the recognition of friends at one's spliff-rolling ability (Duff, 2004). Ralph Turner (1976) suggests there are two sets of judgements by which people recognize their real self as in evidence – the institutional and the impulsive. Institutional self-concepts would consist of feelings and actions that are socially recognized and affirmed on the basis of status recognition, and of qualities demanded of the individual, such as self-sacrifice, or humanitarianism, or loyalty – in other words, self-conceptions that are primarily based on social roles. This does not hold only for dominant categories. Subcultural or subordinate identities are similarly institutional, but negatively or only locally valued – for example, in the case of subordinate sexual identities. Aspects of their real self are placed in institutional terms and others locate these aspects within the expressions and actions of impulse. The one involves the desire to achieve socially sanctioned goals; the other, the finding of true being through the uncluttered expression of impulsive desire. Turner argues that there is a shift away from the institutional towards the impulsive as the fountainhead of self. Feelings and behaviours that reveal or reflect the true self are those judged to emanate from the person. People accept some feelings and actions as part of their real self; others, they absolve themselves of.

It might appear to follow, then, that increased levels of recreational drug use in Britain and the USA from the 1970s onwards, and the binge-drinking phenomenon, are part of a shift from institution to impulse as the measure of the true self. Certainly, the evidence that there has been such a shift is strong. Whole industries of the self exist, and claim to be about breaking the bonds imposed on us – by our roles, our careers, our repressed sexual desires, our meaningless loyalty to relationships long rendered void of desire – and continuously enjoin us to find the inner child, express, impress; always condemning inhibitions, especially when it comes to sexuality. However, this does not mean that the institutional locus has disappeared. There are very strong institutional demands on the self, which are articulated through this impulsive medium. Some impulses are reincorporated into institutional life and affirmed as institutionalized values, the new morality of our time. Those that can perform to these demands may get a pat on the back.

Psychoactive substances – including illicit drugs, alcohol, tobacco and prescription drugs – have the potential to be used in either way. They appear at first glance to be more suited to the impulsive end of things, and many people do speak of their experience in that way. Yet there are plenty of instances of drugs being used to shore up institutional behaviour: the use of institutional medication; the soldier reliant on amphetamines to cope with life in wartime; the coffee-swilling cubicle rat. What I mean is a less directly institutionalized form of intoxicant use, but one that is subsumed into a form of life where the impulsive me-in-myself has displaced the accountable I-in-the-world as the ultimate attainment of being. What is more significant is that many of them consider their intoxicated state to be their true, ideal or least unpleasant state of being. 'The fake is simply more intoxicating' (Dahlia Schweitzer, 2000: 66).

Intoxication could be seen in part as a method of changing our being in the world, our 'ontological position'. For instance, we might like to be a merry, loquacious personality, but are in fact, or perceive ourselves to come across to others as, slightly dull and repressed. Intoxication alters one's own ontological state – people talk of 'being themselves', or 'not being themselves', when intoxicated. There is a deeper sense of being in the world to be understood here, more than altering the distance between self and behaviour. Drugs can transport us beyond the parameters of everyday life. The mixing, blurring and downplaying of gender boundaries in rave clubs is one instance.

Intoxication has a slippery relationship to the senses, appearing to heighten some and dull others, creating audio, visual and perceptual hallucinations, neatly illustrated by this quote from Georg Simmel's *The Sociology of the Senses* (1997 [1907]): 'The social question is not only an ethical one, but also a question of smell.' Sight and sound can be abstracted, according to Georg Simmel, but smell remains within the subject. Smell can be cultivated in the name of social taste, as part of the sense of taste, but it is never rendered objective. Smell is of the subject, and smell remains within the subject. The smell of a beautiful woman's perfume lingers in the mind long after it has dissipated in the air; and it is inextricably linked to that woman. Intoxication is like smell in that it remains within the subject. It dissipates and cannot be maintained, at least, not without great personal cost and the eventual revolt of the organism.

Partly because of this quality, intoxication is always localized. No experience of intoxication is precisely the same. It can only be imperfectly appropriated through telling or writing or creating visual or aural pictures of the experience that never really correspond to it. The closest we come to obtaining this is probably through music, which for those who are not intoxicated by it merely sounds alien. It is fundamentally an experience of the subject, and although the mechanisms of this experience can be described through pharmacology and neurology they cannot capture what it is, only why it is, which might be why it often induces paranoia and suspicion even of those close to you. Can you really be sure that your fellow stoners are seeing what you are seeing? Perhaps this is an outcome of the tension between our society's emphasis on individual experience, and the nature of much intoxication as collective emotionality.

The organization of pleasure

It is not for kings, O Lemuel, it is not for kings to drink wine; nor for princes strong drink:

Lest they drink, and forget the law, and pervert the judgment of any of the afflicted.

Give strong drink unto him that is ready to perish, and wine unto those that be of heavy hearts.

Let him drink, and forget his poverty, and remember his misery no more.

Proverbs 31, 4–7

Intoxicants are held to be bad for some, but necessary for others. As pleasures, they may be reserved for the elite. As intoxicants, that will numb the mind and reinforce the spirit, they are necessary for those who are bruised by the world. The logic is that intoxication takes the self out of the world; therefore, there must be something wrong with the subject's world to make him or her want to get out of it. Nihilism, deprivation and desperation are all quoted along these lines as causes of the desire for intoxication. Intoxication is the means for escaping one state, criticized as a false and deceptive 'escape', as if impermanence equals unreality.

This is the social organization of displeasure. First, the pleasures of the lower classes, black people, gays and other marginalized groups in society have always been treated with suspicion. They are disordering pleasures, disruptive and destructive. From London's underground jazz clubs in the early twentieth century to the rave parties strung out along motorway exits at its end, intoxication provokes the displeasure of authority. Second, it is assumed by the research-led social analyses that pleasure and pain is unevenly distributed – there is certainly plenty of evidence for that – and that one of the primary motivations for anyone from one of these groups doing anything socially disapproved of has to be in order to correct this imbalance. This second perspective, although usually profoundly liberal in its expression, does to some extent rely on the first, yet also tends to deny there being an element of pleasure-seeking involved.

There is also the pleasure deficit – that some lives are supposedly all spills and no thrills (O'Malley and Valverde, 2004). Drug use in social science and health promotion is perceived to be undertaken as an individual response to pleasure deficits – a mental crutch for those who cannot cope with the world and their life in it. This is the model for understanding many, if not all, social problems, such as crime, anti-social behaviour and educational underperformance. They are seen as the expression of other problems, of poverty, discrimination and hopelessness. Drug use is thrown into the same pot with these phenomena, as a way of topping up a person's pleasure deficit. Certainly, personal problems – loneliness, depression, stress and the need to self-medicate

– do push people towards drugs and alcohol problems. The burden of these problems falls harder on socio-economically disadvantaged groups, partly because they have fewer resources for dealing with any drug/alcohol problems that emerge. This makes their difficulties more visible, more likely to come to the attention of police or social services or surveillance regimes. A celebrity with a cocaine habit might find him or herself being checked into an exclusive clinic – some detox centres have taken on the aura of gentlemen's clubs – and emerge with a lucrative 'before and after' photo-story and book deal.

Pain is socially distributed in a literal sense. The experience of physical and mental pain is shaped by class, gender, race and other social factors. The prevalence of illness at the bottom end of the social scale is balanced by a 'mustn't grumble' attitude to pain and disability (Cornwell, 1984). The better off in society have freer access to the luxuries of life, and a cushion against its difficulties; and a more demanding, consumerist attitude does not see discomfort as a burden to be borne with stoicism.

There is then a subtle division between the rational pleasures of the middle classes, the racially superior, the healthy, or whatever happens to constitute the currently privileged and idealized group in society, and the intoxications of the lower classes, the degenerate races, the unfit. As discussed in chapter 1, intoxication, in particular alcohol use, can be used to confirm or enhance the power of one group, or to exclude another (Morgan, 1981). Classes, ethnic groups, sexes; the same or similar drinking patterns are validated in one group while used as evidence of another's inferiority. Intoxication in socially subordinate groups is taken as evidence of deviance or inferiority, physically, mentally or morally.

One can contrast the different interpretations given to the behaviour of a drunken young man and a drunken young woman. The first is an acceptable, masculinizing instance of cutting loose from the restricting or feminizing bonds of work and family. It can be safely indulged, and excuses behaviour that would normally be highly sanctioned, such as public violence, urination and damage to property. The second constitutes a regrettable and repulsive fall from grace, and makes the woman fair game.

The ban on wine propagated in early Islam was a way of asserting the values of a new elite over those of a vanquished, older civilization and its soon-to-be bygone elites (Sherratt, 1995). Powerful groups can reserve the right to inebriation for themselves, and use instances of the same inebriation amongst lower orders as evidence of their inferiority. Few techniques work better in symbolically reaffirming the social order than evidence that those lower down it are simply incapable of handling their drink. They either have to be protected from themselves (women, Native Americans in the USA, Canadian Inuit), or the higher group has to be protected from them (blacks in the Southern USA, British working-class men and women). More powerful groups could also deploy alcohol, and other drugs, in order to shatter internal social bonds of a subordinate group or to bind its members to the social hierarchy in a weakened position. For instance, white settlers of the Americas found alcohol very useful in controlling Native Americans. Intoxication can also involve resistance (Mitchell, 2004) – against the routines of formal work, and the obligations of family and community.

From deviant pathologies to social problems

An army of rapists stalks the land, spiking women's drinks with sedative drugs and taking advantage of drunken women. An advert aired during 2005 in the USA on Adult Swim, a TV channel segment showing satirical cartoons appealing to a young adult audience, shows a young girl alone in a mall. The caption tells the viewer that her carer – you – was so stoned that she was forgotten about and left there. A 2006 Home Office-funded advert about ecstasy warns that 'you don't know what you are getting'.

I grew up in the UK with anti-drug adverts in the 1980s that emphasized the life-destroying effects of highly stigmatized drugs like heroin. Images were presented of pale, ill-fed young men and occasionally women, living in doorways, cut off from friends and families by the evil substance. At the same time, in the USA, the crack epidemic was in full swing; images of crack-houses, crack-mothers and crack-babies were presented in the media as if crack embodied its own twisted family values. The fact that these images were and are partial, inaccurate, and in some cases completely without foundation, has been demonstrated time and again. African-American 'crack-whores' were supposedly so diminished by their addiction to the substance that they would submit to any degradation and ill treatment to get it. *Crack Pipe as Pimp* was the title of one academic collection on the topic (Ratner, 1993); although the actual pimps were as they had always been, men capable of employing violence to control women made vulnerable by conditions of extreme poverty and marginalization.

There has been a shift in the orientation of societal concern about intoxication from then to now. Previously drink and drug problems were the preserve of minorities or those who could be designated as sick – the enslaved minds and desiccated bodies of the alcoholic and the drug addict were to the fore. Although that has not been lost, it has been generalized to the whole of society; many, perhaps all, forms of intoxication are suspect, impairing and with the potential to spiral out of control unless some higher power steps in to save us from ourselves. A group of young professional women enjoying a few beers after work would have once been celebrated as a sign of growing affluence and leisure opportunities, of women's liberation, with their financial and personal independence, and their freedom from past cultural and material constraints. Instead, it is one more thread in the story of intoxication as a nightmare from which society is having difficulty waking up.

There is in these stories a tension being played out; between what we want and what we wish we would want. For much of modern history, the problem of controlling wants applied to what other people did – the lower orders, gin-swilling inebriates; Chinese immigrants, opium-puffing inscrutables; black men, cocaine-fuelled beasts. The intoxications of people who were not white, not middle class, not truly British or American or whatever, were suspect. If only their wants could be controlled, then the problems of social conflict, threats to the racial hierarchy, of the contamination of white space, would disappear. In Western societies now this has been generalized to the whole population; all are dangerous, all at risk. The risk comes less than it used to from illicit drugs, and more from dangerous others, although there is still a powerful set of interests promulgating the view that a particular chemical substance becomes deadly for the individual and society on the basis of its legal classification.

Abstinence and living above the influence

> But how ought we to define courage? Is it to be regarded only as a combat against fears and pains, or also against desires and pleasures, and against flatteries; which exercise such a tremendous power, that they make the hearts even of respectable citizens to melt like wax?
>
> Plato, *The Laws*, Book I (*c.*360 BC)

The propaganda of the drug war that portrays illicit drugs as supremely seductive and transforming has seen to it that drugs are thought of as capable of working vast magic on the organism. After all, what magical substance is it that commands the resources of entire government agencies to keep it in its box? Adverts showing neophytes being seduced by one touch of the destroying angel – while being in the same arena of accuracy as those adverts claiming a direct link between the consumption of hair products and the attentions of desirable members of the opposite sex – are less amenable to the democratic criticism of the consumer forum, because they refer to a substance that very few members of the audience have, or are likely to have, experience with.

If intoxication is so tempting, why aren't we all at it, most of the time? What separates people who don't from people who do? 'Why don't we all use drugs?' (Correia, 2005). Given the strong reinforcing properties elaborated in neuroscientific studies, it is hard to see why the population of illicit drug addicts does not grow continuously year on year. Christopher Correia relies on behavioural choice theory for his answer – that there are constraints on the availability of drugs and there are competing drug-free activities open to people. Attempts to explain individual variation often boil down to statements of the obvious. Some people like it; some don't. Some really, really don't like it; some can't. They may not tell us that much about either intoxication or people. Everyone follows their own path; we need to know what lies in and along that path, but the knowledge that the path winds one way or another for each individual may not advance our knowledge that much.

Not doing something that others do carries with it almost as much suspicion and moral judgement as the reverse behaviour. In many societies, especially Anglo-Saxon ones, those who abstain from alcohol are generally thought a bit suspect (Room, 2000b). Drinking is pleasurable, so to abstain from it means that the teetotaller has some motivation for rejecting pleasure; either they have some physical intolerance for it, or they are a religious maniac, a health freak or a reformed alcoholic. In any case, an explanation is required and may change the opinion the non-drinker's companions have of him or her. Saying 'I don't like it' will not cut the mustard.

Traditionally, abstinence had a spiritual role. Those taking religious orders might be supposed to abstain from drink. The temperance movement saw it as a sacred duty to society, but also drew on a strong religious tradition. The idea that moderate non-harmful use might be possible was not allowed for by the temperance movement, and is not recognized in current official thinking on drugs in Britain, although it is allowed for in practice. So intoxicant saturated is our society that abstinence can be seen as a slightly odd or unusual choice. It is less often justified in religious terms, but more often in terms of health, which provides a justification for most things.

Some users of anti-depressants have reported finding the transformation engendered by the drugs disturbing. The miserable mope becomes a cheery, sunny individual. The experience suggests that his old self, the sad, shy, quiet, morose person he has been for twenty years, is just a neurotransmitter imbalance. This is a disturbing prospect, threatening to self-identity, suggesting as it does that the new self is simply another bundle of mental molecules. Objections to illicit drugs also sometimes come in terms of the drug's potential for 'making me someone I am not'. Abstainers desire to hold on to and be sure of the self. For users, the self is not a pharmacological either/or, and can be tamed, enhanced and explored by using drugs.

Suspicious pleasures

Pleasure has needed permission, in most societies. Indeed, in every society with a functioning state, pleasures have been denied to some or limited for all. Modern Western societies seem unique in demanding that all exhibit the control of pleasure. Pleasure has become the enemy of health (Luik, 1999) and of progress. Some on the political left disparage intoxication as coming in the way of class struggle, engagement and social change (Fitzpatrick, 2002). Intoxication substitutes for achievement in the 'real world'. Others on the political right disparage it as a cop-out from facing one's personal circumstances and failings. Drugs are defined as an escape from reality. Left and right both assume that 'drugs' are part of unreality, whereas they are a part of reality. And the use of drugs can involve self-discipline, effort and deferred gratification; it does not mean mindlessly slipping into a pool of delight.

Let me now summarize my main conclusions. First of all, the use of intoxicating substances has been a fact of life throughout social life and human history. We are adapted to use drugs and have adapted plants to encourage their psychoactive properties. From the late nineteenth century onwards, this ability has become more intensive with the development of artificial drugs, such as MDMA, LSD and the ever-growing range of pharmaceutical medications. What makes a substance an intoxicant is the way in which it is used, rather than its strict pharmacological classification. So cocaine was originally an effective local anaesthetic. It is a club drug used illegally but in a normalized way by many. In the form of crack-cocaine, it is heavily addictive and associated with other significant personal and social problems.

There is a shifting boundary between what is acceptable and what is not, which depends on whether a drug is used in a socially acceptable way. When a drug is associated with a subculture and illicit leisure it has been rendered morally beyond the pale and outlawed. In contrast, medicinal use is a socially acceptable and encouraged – but still controversial – form of use. There is a continuum of drug use from problem to recreational use, with most users of most drugs at the recreational end of things.

Drugs are experienced in terms of being, consciousness and the self – enhancing, altering or destroying. Drug users learn to experience a particular effect, and the nature of highs and lows attributable to drug use are very closely related to the social context in which they are taken. The very widespread prescribing and off-label use of anti-depressants and mood/behaviour modifiers like Viagra and Ritalin indicate a large number of people find a great discrepancy between the expectation of what they should feel like and what they actually feel like; or between how they perceive the world and themselves, and how the world perceives them. It could be said that recreational/normalized use, drug abuse, and medicinal use when relating to mental health or sexual dysfunction, are all attempts to address this discrepancy.

Drug problems are best dealt with by examining how they are constituted, which is to say they are socially constructed in effect, although material in form. This can help us illuminate blind spots in policy and practice, such the risk gradient, which problematizes agency and pathologizes coping strategies. The prohibition of any of the substances discussed here rests on the premise that they are so seductive that they will on exposure destroy all reason and autonomy; that they will make men and women behave in unexpected ways that they otherwise would not have (well, they do a bit). The potential harm to society and individuals is so great that humans and psychoactive substances simply have to be kept apart. The evidence, however, is that 'drugs' do not have this power, and that prohibition makes risks worse rather than ameliorating them.

Drug prohibition is on balance making drug problems more difficult to deal with, but legalization is not a magic bullet. We need to consider why prohibition came about and is maintained – to compare, for instance, the rigorous testing of pharmaceutical drugs to the suck it and see approach to bringing illicit drugs to the market, and, for that matter, new forms of alcohol delivery such as alcopops. The anti-prohibitionists use some of the same arguments as those who favour drug control: 'The phrase "getting out of it" springs to mind. Surely if "it" was better, then so many people wouldn't need to get out of it so often' (Kevin Williamson, 1997: xii).

The above argument, despite its liberal air, is another 'escape' theory that does not really look into what is being done with intoxication, beyond removing oneself from a state of sobriety. It rather suggests a lack of faith in life, as if life is something that needs to be coped with rather than lived – which it often feels like. It is sure enough an odd state of affairs where full-time socialists and concerned liberals appear to be arguing for the supremacy of the unfettered free market and extensive third-world cash cropping.

There is still a persistent high level of problem drug use, where drug use dominates an individual's life to the detriment of their mental and psychical well-being and that of those close to them also. Both ends of this continuum, and the points in between, have to be understood with reference to the factors mentioned above. This is the stimulated self, who is the rational consuming self in a drug-normalized society. It is also at the heart of a new social divide, or a reworking of an older social division. The relatively prosperous are cool rational consumers, caring for the environment, healthy, free-choosing, with the time and resources to make themselves so, and this is how they understand and narrate their drug use. The divide between themselves and pathologized users is made starker because it corresponds to this more general division. Pathologized users – drug addicts, smokers – are viewed as so helpless they require the state to step in and remove from them the ability to make a choice about their habits.

An increasing proportion – perhaps the majority – of drug users act as 'rational consumers', combining regular drug use with an otherwise normal life, with a regular job, family, mortgage and all the other accoutrements of orderly sobriety. They consider drug use a consumption choice that enhances their recreational lives. Many drugs in modern society are used to manage mood and emotion, rather than to take the user 'on a trip', as in the world of 1960s psychedelic drug use. If intoxication is a trip, it is usually one in which the traveller knows where they are going.

The emergence of 'normalized' drug-use patterns are usually greeted with some relief by liberals. Here at last is evidence that drugs can be taken by many people regularly without society collapsing about our ears; and an opportunity to focus objectively on the extensive harms of alcohol and tobacco. There is a barely concealed sense of relief among some that drugs are no longer, or not for very much longer, to be associated with youth subcultures and so are freed from the stigmatization and implications of rebellion and moral regulation carried by that. It is reasonable to hope that these developments would lead to a rational debate on the topic of drug and alcohol use, although there is not a great deal of evidence that it has to date. We should not de-theorize intoxicant use because one element of it is normalized and no longer regarded as deviant or subcultural. Indeed, the fact that some kinds of illicit drugs are becoming normalized would suggest that their social significance has changed markedly, but not that it is reduced. Illicit drug use is one element of the practice of intoxication. The less visible a practice is, the less problematic, the more normative it is, the more urgent it should be to investigate its meaning and consequences, and the greater the likelihood that we will find it is interwoven in subtle ways into reconstituted citizens, subjects and forms of life, encapsulated in the stimulated self.

Bathe the drooping spirits in delight

> One sip of this
> Will bathe the drooping spirits in delight,
> Beyond the bliss of dreams.
> John Milton, *Comus* (l. 811)

The medicine cupboard is restocked with paracetamol every Sunday morning, next to the prescription Ritalin and Lustral, and grey-market Viagra. A quarter ounce of cannabis resin is kept wrapped in plastic in a carved wooden box in the back of the sock drawer. A dozen ecstasy pills sit in a Fisherman's Friend tin, nestled next to a packet of Camel cigarettes in a handbag swinging from the bedstead. Champagne and beer sit cooling in the refrigerator. Intoxication is represented as consisting of ecstatic highs and gut-wrenching lows, ecstasy or addiction. Yet that is not the experience of most users, which is neither that of de Quincey nor Coleridge. Accounts of intoxication that deal with the mundane, the day to day – the arguing over whose round it is, who is available to score off and why won't they answer the phone, who the joint is passed to next, exactly what was in that pill and why the wallpaper looks like a scene from *2001* – are harder to come by in literature. Yet it is in these everyday elements that the experience of intoxication is reproduced. It is a particularly modern aspect of intoxication that it is subsumed into everyday life in the manner of unremarked consumption, rather than being a ritualized or hedonistic event, and this goes equally for coffee junkies and heroin addicts.

Intoxicants are social substances, and intoxication is a social practice. It takes on a particular character in modern society, in which psychoactive substances and the experiences had with them are closely bounded and subject to regulation and governance. These technologies of the self produce very different meanings, actions and experiences depending on the substance, its form and the conditions of its consumption. In every substance we can taste the traces of history; the long, slow creation of intoxicating plants through selection and breeding over generations; the trading empires that grew from a few ships bearing cargoes of exotic spices and plants over thousands of miles of ocean swell; the advances in human control over chemistry at a molecular level driven by hothouse industrial sciences.

Before the colonial period there were a handful of psychoactive substances in use around the world: alcohol; betel; opium; cannabis; tobacco; coca; tea; and coffee, and most were restricted to particular regions of the globe, with the exception of alcohol. Now, there are several thousand in use, and the number is projected to increase into the tens of thousands, far beyond any hope of cumbersome laws or bureaucracies to keep up with, still less control or prohibit. It is predicted that the next stage will be drugs that take advantage of the new genetics, tailored precisely to one's genetic make-up in order to give targeted, desired results without problem side effects. They will be as different from MDMA and Ritalin as those drugs are to the soft sledgehammer of opium. Perhaps. New ways of taking, using and experiencing intoxicants are as important in the history of intoxication as the development of new substances. So, too, are the development of systems of regulation, public problems, the marginalization and pathologization of some psychoactive substances and their users, and the persistence of substance-use problems, meaning that intoxication will never be quite as much fun as we may want.

Bibliography

Anon. (1674), *The Women's Petition Against Coffee: Representing to Publick Consideration the Grand Inconveniencies Accruing to their Sex from the Excessive use of that Drying, Enfeebling Liquor: Presented to the Right Honorable the Keepers of the Liberty of Venus, by a Well-Willer*, London [s.n.].

Abel, E. L. (2001), 'Gin Lane: Did Hogarth Know about Fetal Alcohol Syndrome?', *Alcohol & Alcoholism*, 36, 2: 131–4.

Action on Smoking and Health (1998), *Tobacco Explained: The Truth About the Tobacco Industry in its Own Words*, London, Action on Smoking and Health.

Action on Smoking and Health (2006), *Smoking Statistics: Who Smokes and How Much*, London, Action on Smoking and Health.

Adda, J. and Cornaglia, F. (2006), *The Effect of Taxes and Bans on Passive Smoking*, Bonn, Forschunginstitut zur Zukunft der Arbeit/Institute for the Study of Labor.

Advisory Council on the Misuse of Drugs (2005), *Khat (Qat): Assessment of Risk to the Individual and Communities in the UK*, London, Home Office.

Advisory Council on the Misuse of Drugs (2006), *Pathways to Problems: Hazardous Use of Tobacco, Alcohol and Other Drugs by Young People in the UK and its Implications for Policy*, London, Home Office.

Ainsworth, C. (2002), 'Ecstasy on the Brain', *New Scientist*, 2339: 26.

Allaman, A., Voller, F., Kubicka, L. and Bloomfield, K. (2000), 'Drinking Cultures and the Position of Women in Nine European Countries', *Substance Abuse*, 21, 4: 231–47.

Allchin, F. R. (1979), 'India: The Ancient Home of Distillation?', *Man*, 14, 1, 55–63.

Alpert, J. S. (2005), 'Viagra: The Risks of Recreational Use', *The American Journal of Medicine*, 118: 569–70.

Alston, L. J., Dupré, R. and Nonnenmacher, T. (2002), 'Social Reformers and Regulations: The Prohibition of Cigarettes in the United States and Canada', *Explorations in Economic History*, 39: 425–45.

Amis, K. (1961), *Lucky Jim*, Harmondsworth, Penguin.

Anon. (1886), 'Comment and Criticism', *Science*, 153: 23–5.

Arlacchi, P. (1998), 'Towards a Drug-Free World by 2008 – We Can Do It', *United Nations Chronicle*, 35: 2, 4–5.

Armstrong, D. (1984), 'The Patient's View', *Social Science & Medicine*, 18, 9: 737–44.

Armstrong, D. (1995), 'The Rise of Surveillance Medicine', *Sociology of Health and Illness*, 17, 3: 393–404.

Ashworth, A. (1990), 'Reckoning Schemes of Legitimation: On Commissions of Inquiry as Power/Knowledge Forms', *Journal of Historical Sociology*, 3: 1–22.

Association of Crown Research Institutes (2006), 'Winning Research Could Help More Smokers Quit' (ACRI Press Release 6th June 2006), Wellington, NZ, ACRI.

Bailey, W. J. (1995), 'FactLine on Non-Medical Use of Ritalin (methylphenidate)', Bloomington, IN, Indiana Prevention Resource Centre (IPRC).

Baines, D. L. and Whynes, D. K. (1997), 'Over-the-Counter Drugs and Prescribing in General Practice', *British Journal of General Practice*, 47, 417, 221–4.

Balko, R. (2006a), *Overkill: The Rise of Paramilitary Police Raids in America*, Washington, Cato Institute.

Balko, R. (2006b), 'Step Away from the Cold Medicine: Government's Drug War Fuels Meth Problem', *Reason*, December, <www.reason.com/news/show/117446.html>.

Bancroft, A. (2001), 'Globalisation and HIV/AIDS: Inequality and the Boundaries of a Symbolic Epidemic', *Health, Risk & Society*, 3, 1: 89–98.

Barnard, M. (2005), 'Discomforting Research: Colliding Moralities and Looking for "Truth" in a Study of Parental Drug Problems', *Sociology of Health & Illness*, 27, 1: 1–19.

Bates, C., Jarvis, M. and Connolly, G. (1999), *Tobacco Additives: Cigarette Engineering and Nicotine Addiction*, London, Action on Smoking and Health.

Beck, B. (1978), 'The Politics of Speaking in the Name of Society', *Social Problems*, 25, 4: 353–60.

Beck, U. and Beck-Gernsheim, E. (2002), *Individualization*, London, Sage.

Becker, H. (1953), 'Becoming a Marihuana User', *American Journal of Sociology*, 59, 3: 235–42.

Becker, H. (1967), 'History, Culture and Subjective Experience: An Exploration of the Social Bases of Drug-Induced Experiences', *Journal of Health and Social Behavior*, 8, 3: 163–76.

Becker, H. (2001), 'Drugs: What are They?', in Becker, H. (ed.), *Qu'est-ce qu'une Drogue?*, Anglet, Atlantica.

Berridge, V. (1988), 'The Origins of the English Drug "Scene" 1890–1930', *Medical History*, 32: 51–64.

Berridge, V. (1999), 'Passive Smoking and its Pre-History in Britain: Policy Speaks to Science?', *Social Science & Medicine*, 49: 1183–95.

Berridge, V. and Edwards, G. (1981), *Opium and the People: Opiate Use in Nineteenth-century England*, London, Allen Lane.

Best, J. (2008), *Social Problems*, New York, W. W. Norton.

Biederman, J. and Faraone, S. V. (2005), 'Attention-Deficit Hyperactivity Disorder', *The Lancet*, 366: 237–48.

Blazic-Cop, N., Seric, V., Basic, V., Thaller, N. and Demarin, V. (2001), 'Transcranial Doppler in Smoking Relapse Prevention Strategy', *Collegium Antropologicum*, 25, 1: 289–96.

Blumer, D. (2002), 'The Illness of Vincent van Gogh', *The American Journal of Psychiatry*, 159: 519–26.

Booth, M. (2003), *Cannabis: A History*, London, Bantam.

Booth Davies, J. (1997), *Drugspeak: The Analysis of Drug Discourse*, Amsterdam, Harwood Academic.

Bourdieu, P. (1980), *The Logic of Practice*, Cambridge, Polity.

Bourdieu, P. (1984), *Distinction: A Social Critique of the Judgement of Taste*, London, Routledge & Kegan Paul.

Bourgois, P. (1989), 'Crack in Spanish Harlem: Culture and Economy in the Inner City', *Anthropology Today*, 5, 4: 6–11.

Bourgois, P. (1995), *In Search of Respect: Selling Crack in El Barrio*, Cambridge, Cambridge University Press.

Bourgois, P. (1998), 'Just Another Night in a Shooting Gallery', *Theory, Culture & Society*, 15, 2: 37–66.

Bourgois, P. (2000), 'Disciplining Addictions: The Bio-Politics of Methadone and Heroin in the United States', *Culture, Medicine and Psychiatry*, 24: 165–95.

Bourgois, P. (2003), 'Crack and the Political Economy of Social Suffering', *Addiction Research and Theory*, 11, 1: 31–7.

Boyle, P., Gandini, S., Robertson, C., Zatonski, W., Fagerström, K., Slama, K., Kunze, M. and Gray, N. (2000), 'Characteristics of Smokers' Attitudes Towards Stopping: Survey of 10,295 Smokers in Representative Samples from 17 European Countries', *European Journal of Public Health*, 10, 3: 5–14.

Braidwood, R., Sauer, J. D., Helbaek, H., Mangelsdorf, P. C. and Cutler, H. C. (1953), 'Symposium: Did Man Once Live by Beer Alone?', *American Anthropologist*, 55, 4: 515–26.

Brecher, E. M. (1973), *The Consumers Union Report on Licit and Illicit Drugs*, New York, Little, Brown.

Brown, J. (1795 [1780]), *The Elements of Medicine [Elementa Medicinae]*, London, J. Jonson.

Brownstein, M. J. (1993), 'A Brief History of Opiates, Opioid Peptides, and Opioid Receptors', *Proceedings of the National Academy of Sciences of the United States of America*, 90, 12: 5391–3.

Buchan, J. (2003), *Crowded with Genius: Edinburgh's Moment of the Mind*, London, HarperCollins.

Budge, E. A. (1904), *The Book of Paradise Being The Histories and Sayings of the Monks and Ascetics of the Egyptian Desert by Palladius, Hieronymus and Others*, London, Lady Meux.

Bull, M. (2002), 'If Methadone is the Answer, What is the Question? A Genealogy of the Regulation of Opioids in Contemporary Industrialised Societies', Brisbane, Griffith University.

Byron, G. G. (1819), *Don Juan*, London, Thomas Davidson.

Cairncross, F. (2001), 'Stumbling in the Dark', *The Economist*, 360, 8232: 3–5.

Califano, J. A. (2007), 'Should Drugs be Decriminalised? No', *BMJ*, 335, 7627: 967.

Calkins, A. (1871), *Opium and the Opium Appetite*, Philadelphia, J. B. Lippincott.

Campbell, B. (1993), *Goliath: Britain's Dangerous Places*, London, Methuen.

Campbell, N. D. (2004), 'Technologies of Suspicion: Coercion and Compassion in Post-disciplinary Surveillance Regimes', *Surveillance & Society*, 2, 1: 79–92.

Campion, J., McNeill, A. and Checinski, K. (2006), 'Exempting Mental Health Units from Smoke-Free Laws would Worsen Health Inequalities for People with Mental Health Problems', *British Medical Journal*, 333, 7565: 407–8.

Camporesi, P. (1989), *Bread of Dreams: Food and Fantasy in Early Modern Europe*, Cambridge, Polity.

Cavan, S. (1966), *Liquor License: An Ethnography of Bar Behavior*, Chicago, Aldine.

Chesterton, G. (1905), *Heretics*, London, John Lane.

Christison, R. (1876), *Observations on the Effects of Cuca, or Coca, the Leaves of the Erythroxylon Coca*, London.

Clarke, S. W. (1919), 'The Rule of DORA', *Journal of Comparative Legislation and International Law*, 1 (3rd series), 1: 36–41.

Cobbe, W. R. (1895), *Doctor Judas, A Portrayal of the Opium Habit*, Chicago, S. C. Griggs.

Cockayne, E. (2007), *Hubbub: Filth, Noise, and Stench in England, 1600–1770*, Cambridge, MA, Yale University Press.

Coe, J. (2003), *The Lifestyle Drugs Outlook to 2008: Unlocking New Value in Wellbeing*, London, Business Insights.

Cohen, P. (2000), 'Is the Addiction Doctor the Voodoo Priest of Western Man?', *Addiction Research*, 8, 6: 589–98.

Coleridge, S. T. (1816), *Christabel &c*, London, John Murray.

Committee of Advertising Practice (2006), 'Smoking, Stopping', <http://www.asa.org.uk/cap/advice_online/advice_online_database/Show+Entry.htm?advice_online_id=120>.

Coomber, R. (1997a), 'The Adulteration of Drugs: What Dealers do to Illicit Drugs, and What They Think is Done to Them', *Addiction Research*, 5, 4: 297–306.

Coomber, R. (1997b), 'Vim in the Veins – Fantasy or Fact: The Adulteration of Illicit Drugs', *Addiction Research*, 5, 3: 195–212.

Coomber, R. (2003), 'There's No Such Thing as a Free Lunch: How "Freebies" and "Credit" Operate as Part of Rational Drug Market Activity', *Journal of Drug Issues*, 33, 4: 939–62.

Coomber, R. (2006), *Pusher Myths: Re-Situating the Drug Dealer*, London, Free Association Books.

Cornwell, J. (1984), *Hard-Earned Lives: Accounts of Health and Illness from East London*, London, Tavistock.

Correia, C. J. (2005), 'Behavioural Theories of Choice', in Earleywine, M. (ed.), *Mind-Altering Drugs: The Science of Subjective Experience*, Oxford, Oxford University Press.

Courtwright, D. (1997), 'The Prepared Mind: Marie Nyswander, Methadone Maintenance, and the Metabolic Theory of Addiction', *Addiction*, 92, 3: 257–65.

Courtwright, D. (2001), *Forces of Habit: Drugs and the Making of the Modern World*, London, Harvard University Press.

Courtwright, D. (2003), 'Drug Wars: Policy Hots and Historical Cools', *Bulletin of the History of Medicine*, 77: 440–50.

Crapanzo, V. (2001), 'The Etiquette of Consciousness', *Social Research*, 68, 3: 627–49.

Criminal Justice and Public Order Act (1994), London: Parliament of the United Kingdom, 1994, c.33.

Crister, G. (2005), *Generation Rx: How Prescription Drugs Are Altering American Lives, Minds, and Bodies*, Boston, Houghton Mifflin.

Davenport-Hines, R. (2004), *The Pursuit of Oblivion: A Social History of Drugs*, London, Phoenix.

Davis, J. (2006), 'Ecstasy and Cheerleading: A Basic Risk Comparison', *MAPS: Bulletin of the Multidisciplinary Association for Psychedelic Studies*, 17, 3: 21–2.

DeGrandpre, R. J. (2006), *The Cult of Pharmacology: How America Became the World's Most Troubled Drug Culture*, Durham, NC, Duke University Press.

Dennis, P. A. (1975), 'The Role of the Drunk in a Oaxacan Village', *American Anthropologist*, 77, 4: 856–63.

Department of Health (2000), 'Pharmacy in the Future: Implementing the NHS Plan', London, Department of Health.

Department of Health (2006), *Smoking Doesn't Just Affect You*, Department of Health Advertising Campaign.

de Quincey, T. (1886 [1822]), *Confessions of an English Opium-Eater*, London, George Routledge and Sons.

Dietler, M. (1990), 'Driven by Drink: The Role of Drinking in the Political Economy and the Case of Early Iron Age France', *Journal of Anthropological Archaeology*, 9: 353–406.

Dijksterhuis, A., Bos, M. W., Nordgren, L. F. and van Baaren, R. B. (2006), 'On Making the Right Choice: The Deliberation-Without-Attention Effect', *Science*, 311, 5763: 1005–7.

Dingelstad, D., Gosden, R., Martin, B. and Vakas, N. (1996), 'The Social Construction of Drug Debates', *Social Science & Medicine*, 43, 12: 1829.

Dudley, R. (2001), 'Fermenting Fruit and the Historical Ecology of Ethanol Ingestion: Is Alcoholism in Modern Humans an Evolutionary Hangover?', *Addiction*, 97: 381–8.

Duff, C. (2004), 'Drug Use as a "Practice of the Self": Is There any Place for an "Ethics of Moderation" in Contemporary Drug Policy?', *International Journal of Drug Policy*, 15: 385–93.

Duncan, D. F. (1994), 'Drug Law Enforcement Expenditures and Drug-Induced Deaths', *Psychological Reports*, 75, 1: 57–8.

The Economist (2006), 'The State is Looking After You', 378, 8472: 15.

Edwards, G. (2004), *Matters of Substance*, London, Allen Lane.

Elias, N. (1978), *The Civilizing Process, Vol.1, The History of Manners*, Oxford, Blackwell.

ElSohly, M. A. and Salamone, S. J. (1999), 'Prevalence of Drugs Used in Cases of Alleged Sexual Assault', *Journal of Analytical Toxicology*, 23: 141–6.

Emerson, R. W. (1904 [1870]), *Society and Solitude*, Boston, Houghton Mifflin.

ESPAD (2007), 'The European School Survey Project on Alcohol and Other Drugs', Stockholm, <http://www.espad.org/sa/site.asp?site=622>.

Etter, J.-F. and Perneger, T. V. (2001), 'Attitudes Toward Nicotine Replacement Therapy in Smokers and Ex-Smokers in the General Public', *Clinical Pharmacology & Therapeutics*, 69, 3: 175–83.

Evidence Based Medicine Working Group (1992), 'Evidence-Based Medicine: A New Approach to Teaching the Practice of Medicine', *Journal of the American Medical Association*, 268, 17: 2420–25.

Fagerström, K. and Balfour, D. J. (2006), 'Neuropharmacology and Potential Efficacy of New Treatments for Tobacco Dependence', *Expert Opinion on Investigational Drugs*, 15, 2: 107–16.

Fagerström, K. and Sawe, U. (1996), 'The Pathophysiology of Nicotine Dependence: Treatment Options and the Cardiovascular Safety of Nicotine', *Cardiovascular Risk Factors*, 6, 3: 135–43.

Fagerström, K., Schneider, N. G. and Lunell, E. (1993), 'Effectiveness of Nicotine Patch and Nicotine Gum as Individual Versus Combined Treatments for Tobacco Withdrawal Symptoms', *Psychopharmacology*, 111, 3: 271–7.

Fidler, J. A., Wardle, J., Henning Broderson, N., Jarvis, M. J. and West, R. (2006), 'Vulnerability to Smoking After Trying a Single Cigarette Can Lie Dormant for Three Years or More', *Tobacco Control*, 15: 205–9.

Fielding, H. (1824 [1751]), *An Enquiry into the Causes of the Late Increase of Robbers &c. with Some Proposals for Remedying the Growing Evil*, London, Otridge and Rackham.

Fillmore, M. and Vogel-Sprott, M. (1995), 'Expectancies About Alcohol-Induced Motor Impairment Predict Individual Differences in Responses to Alcohol and Placebo', *Journal of Studies on Alcohol*, 56, 1: 90–8.

Finch, E. and Munro, V. E. (2005), 'Juror Stereotypes and Blame Attributions in Rape Cases Involving Intoxicants', *British Journal of Criminology*, 45: 25–38.

Fischer, T. (2000), *I Like Being Killed*, London, Metropolitan Books.

Fitzgerald, J. L. (2005), 'Policing as Public Health Menace in the Policy Struggles over Public Injecting', *International Journal of Drug Policy*, 16: 203–6.

Fitzpatrick, M. (2001), *The Tyranny of Health: Doctors and the Regulation of Lifestyle*, London, Routledge.

Fitzpatrick, M. (2002), 'Drugs Debate: High on Myths', *Spiked!*, <http://www.spiked–online.com/Articles/00000002D196.htm>.

Flower, R. (2004), 'Lifestyle Drugs: Pharmacology and the Social Agenda', *Trends in Pharmacological Sciences*, 25, 4: 182–5.

Foucault, M. (1979), *Discipline and Punish: The Birth of the Prison*, Harmondsworth, Penguin.

Freud, S. (1885), *Über Coca*, Vienna, Verlag von Moritz Perles.

Friedman, J. and Alicea, M. (1995), 'Women and Heroin: The Path of Resistance and its Consequences', *Gender and Society*, 9, 4: 432–49.

Fuller, E. (2004), *Smoking, Drinking and Drug Use Among Young People in England in 2004*, London, NHS Health and Social Care Information Centre.

Furedi, F. (2004), *Therapy Culture: Cultivating Vulnerability in an Uncertain Age*, London, Routledge.

General Register Office for Scotland (2006), *Drug Related Deaths in Scotland 2005*, Edinburgh, General Register Office for Scotland.

George, T. P. and O'Malley, S. S. (2004), 'Current Pharmacological Treatments for Nicotine Dependence', *Trends in Pharmacological Sciences*, 25, 1: 42–8.

Gervais, A., O'Loughlin, J., Meshefedjian, G., Bancej, C. and Tremblay, M. (2006), 'Milestones in the Natural Course of Onset of Cigarette Use Among Adolescents', *Canadian Medical Association Journal*, 175, 3: 255–61.

Giddens, A. (1994), *The Transformation of Intimacy*, Cambridge, Polity.

Gilbert, D., Walley, T. and New, B. (2000), 'Lifestyle Medicines', *British Medical Journal*, 321: 1341–4.

GlaxoSmithKline (2006), *Nicorette Stop Smoking Gum*, <http://www.nicorette.com/>.

Goldstein, A. (1979), 'Heroin Maintenance – a Medical View: A Conversation Between a Physician and a Politician', *Journal of Drug Issues*, 9: 341–7.

Goozner, M. (2004), *The $800 Million Pill: The Truth Behind the Cost of New Drugs*, Berkeley, CA, University of California Press.

Gray, N. J. (2005), 'The Case for Smoker-Free Workplaces', *Tobacco Control*, 14, 2: 143–4.

Groman, E. and Fagerström, K. (2003), 'Nicotine Dependence: Development, Mechanisms, Individual Differences and Links to Possible Neurophysiological Correlates', *Wiener Klinische Wochenschrift*, 115, 5–6: 155–60.

Grund, J.-P. C. (1993), *Drug Use as a Social Ritual: Functionality, Symbolism and Determinants of Self-Regulation*, Rotterdam, Instituut voor Verslavingsonderzoek.

Gusfield, J. R. (1963), *Symbolic Crusade: Status Politics and the American Temperance Movement*, Urbana, IL, University of Illinois.

Gusfield, J. R. (1981), *The Culture of Public Problems: Drinking–Driving and the Symbolic Order*, Chicago, IL, University of Chicago Press.

Gusfield, J. R. (1996), *Contested Meanings: The Construction of Alcohol Problems*, Madison, University of Wisconsin Press.

Guy, P. and Holloway, M. (2007), 'Drug Related Deaths and the "Special Deaths" of Late Modernity', *Sociology*, 41, 1: 83–96.

Hadfield, P. (2006), *Bar Wars: Contesting the Night in Contemporary British Cities*, Oxford, Oxford University Press.

Hallstone, M. (2002), 'Updating Howard Becker's Theory of Using Marijuana for Pleasure', *Contemporary Drug Problems*, 29, 4: 821–45.

Hammersley, R. (2005), 'Theorizing Normal Drug Use', *Addiction Research & Theory*, 13, 3: 201–3.

Harding, G. (1986), 'Constructing Addiction as a Moral Failing', *Sociology of Health and Illness*, 8, 1: 75–85.

Healy, D. (2002), *The Creation of Psychopharmacology*, Cambridge, MA, Harvard University Press.

Heartfield, J. (2002), *The 'Death of the Subject' Explained*, Sheffield, Sheffield Hallam University Press.

Heath, D. B. (1962), 'Drinking Patterns of the Bolivian Camba', in Pittman, D. J. and Snyder, C. R. (eds), *Society, Culture and Drinking Patterns*, New York, John Wiley and Sons.

Henderson, S. (1993), 'Fun, Fashion and Frisson', *International Journal of Drug Policy*, 4, 3: 122–9.

Hochschild, A. R. (1983), *The Managed Heart: Commercialization of Human Feeling*, Berkeley, CA, University of California Press.

House of Commons (2006), *Science and Technology – Minutes of Evidence*, London, House of Commons, Select Committee on Science and Technology.

Hughes, J. R. (1999), 'Four Beliefs That May Impede Progress in the Treatment of Smoking', *Tobacco Control*, 8, 3: 323–6.

Idaho State Journal (2006), 'Proposal to Crack Down on Pregnant Drug Users Gathers Steam', <http://www.journalnet.com/> (16 February 2006; article no longer online).

Iowa General Assembly (2007), *Code of Iowa*.

Inciardi, J. A. (1999), *The Drug Legalization Debate*, Thousand Oaks, CA, Sage.

Independent Working Group on Drug Consumption Rooms (2006), *Drug Consumption Rooms: Summary Report of the Independent Working Group*, York, Joseph Rowntree Foundation.

Jarvik, M. E. and Henningfield, J. E. (1988), 'Pharmacological Treatment of Tobacco Dependence', *Pharmacology Biochemistry and Behavior*, 30, 1: 279–94.

Joffe, A. H. (1998), 'Alcohol and Social Complexity in Ancient Western Asia', *Current Anthropology*, 39, 3: 297–322.

Johns, A. (2001), 'Psychiatric Effects of Cannabis', *British Journal of Psychiatry*, 178: 116–22.

Johnson, H. L. and Johnson, P. B. (1995), 'Children's Alcohol Related Cognitions: Positive Versus Negative Alcohol Effects', *Journal of Alcohol and Drug Education*, 40, 2: 1–12.

Johnston, J. (1858), *The Opium Trade in China*, London, J. Heaton & Son.

Jones, C. (2001), 'Suspicious Death Related to Gamma-Hydroxybutyrate (GHB) Toxicity', *Journal of Clinical Forensic Medicine*, 8: 74–6.

Jonnes, J. (1996), *Hep-Cats, Narcs, and Pipe Dreams: A History of America's Romance with Illegal Drugs*, Baltimore, MD, Johns Hopkins University.

Keane, H. (2002), *What's Wrong with Addiction?*, New York, New York University Press.

Keats, J. (1998 [1816]), 'Ode on Indolence', in Elizabeth Cook (ed.), *John Keats: Selected Poetry*, Oxford, Oxford University Press.

Khurana, S., Batra, V., Patkar, A. A. and Leone, F. T. (2003), 'Twenty-First Century Tobacco Use: It is not Just a Risk Factor Anymore', *Respiratory Medicine*, 97, 4: 295–301.

Kish, S. J. (2002), 'How Strong is the Evidence that Brain Serotonin Neurons are Damaged in Human Users of Ecstasy?', *Pharmacology, Biochemistry and Behavior*, 71, 4: 845–55.

Kneale, J. (1999), 'A Problem of Supervision: Moral Geographies of the Nineteenth-century British Public House', *Journal of Historical Geography*, 25, 3: 333–48.

Knight, W. (2005), '"Info-mania" Dents IQ More Than Marijuana', *New Scientist*, <http://www.newscientist.com/article.ns?=dn7298>.

Lader, D. and Goddard, E. (2005), *Smoking-Related Behaviour and Attitudes, 2004*, London, Office for National Statistics.

Lash, S. and Urry, J. (1994), *Economies of Signs and Space*, London, Sage.

Leacock, S. (1964), 'Ceremonial Drinking in an Afro-Brazilian Cult', *American Anthropologist*, 66, 2: 344–54.

Lee, T. C. (1981), 'Van Gogh's Vision: Digitalis Intoxication', *Journal of the American Medical Association*, 245, 7: 727–9.

Leigh, B. C. (1999), 'Thinking, Feeling and Drinking: Alcohol Expectancies and Alcohol Use', in Peele, S. and Grant, M. (eds), *Alcohol and Pleasure: A Health Perspective*, Philadelphia, PA, Brunner/Mazel.

Lennard, H. L., Epstein, L. J. and Rosenthal, M. S. (1972), 'The Methadone Illusion', *Science*, 176: 4037, 881–4.

Lenzer, J. (2005), 'American Medical Association Rejects Proposal to Ban Consumer Adverts for Prescription Medicines', *British Medical Journal*, 331, 7507, 7.

Leshner, A. L. (1997), 'Addiction is a Brain Disease, and it Matters', *Science*, 278, 5335, 45–7.

Leshner, A. L. (2001), 'Addiction is a Brain Disease', *Issues in Science and Technology*, 17, 3: <http://www.issues.org/17.3/leshner.htm>.

Levine, H. (1978), 'The Discovery of Addiction: Changing Conceptions of Habitual Drunkenness in America', *Journal of Studies on Alcohol*, 39, 1: 143–74.

Levitt, R., Nason, E. and Hallsworth, M. (2006), *The Evidence Base for the Classification of Drugs*, Santa Monica, CA, RAND Europe.

Lewis, R. and Dixon, J. (2005), *NHS Market Futures: Exploring the Impact of Health Service Market Reforms*, London, King's Fund.

Lexchin, J. (2001), 'Lifestyle Drugs: Issues for Debate', *Canadian Medical Association Journal*, 164, 10: 1449–51.

Lexchin, J., Bero, L. A., Djulbegovic, B. and Clark, O. (2003), 'Pharmaceutical Industry Sponsorship and Research Outcome and Quality: A Systematic Review', *British Medical Journal*, 326, 7400: 1171–3.

Lindesmith, A. R. (1938), 'A Sociological Theory of Drug Addiction', *The American Journal of Sociology*, 43, 4: 593–613.

Little, R. (1850), 'On the Habitual Use of Opium', *Monthly Journal of Medical Science*, 10: 524–38.

Locke, J. (1689), *An Essay Concerning Human Understanding*, London, Thomas Basset.

Loe, M. (2004), *The Rise of Viagra: How the Little Blue Pill Changed Sex in America*, New York, New York University Press.

Lovell, A. M. (2006), 'Addiction Markets: The Case of High Dose Buprenorphine in France', in Petryana, A., Lakoff, A. and Kleinman, A. (eds), *Global Pharmaceuticals: Ethics, Markets, Practices*, Durham, Duke University Press.

Ludlow, Fitz Hugh (1856), 'The Apocalypse of Hasheesh', *Putnam's Monthly*, 8:48.

Luik, J. (1999), 'Wardens, Abbots, and Modest Hedonists: The Problem of Permission for Pleasure in a Democratic Society', in Peele, S. and Grant,

M. (eds), *Alcohol and Pleasure: A Health Perspective*, Philadelphia, PA, Brunner/Mazel.

Lupton, M. J. (1979), 'Ladies' Entrance: Women and Bars', *Feminist Studies*, 5, 3: 571–88.

McAllister, J. F. O. (2005), 'The British Disease', *Time Europe*, 11 December 2005.

MacAndew, C. and Edgerton, R. B. (1969), *Drunken Comportment*, London, Nelson.

McCann, U., Szabo, Z., Scheffel, U., Dannals, R. and Ricuarte, G. (1998), 'Positron Emission Tomographic Evidence of Toxic Effect of MDMA ("Ecstasy") on Brain Serotonin Neurons in Human Beings', *The Lancet*, 352, 9138, 1433–7.

McGlothlin, W. H. and West, L. J. (1968), 'The Marihuana Problem: An Overview', *American Journal of Psychiatry*, 125, 3: 370–8.

McKeown, T. (1976), *The Role of Medicine: Dream, Mirage or Nemesis?*, London, Nuffield Provincial Hospitals Trust.

Maher, L. (1997), *Sexed Work: Gender, Race, and Resistance in a Brooklyn Drug Market*, Oxford, Oxford University Press.

Malbon, B. (1999), *Clubbing: Dancing, Ecstasy and Vitality*, London, Routledge.

Malik, K. (2001), *Man, Beast and Zombie: What Science Can and Cannot Tell Us about Human Nature*, London, Phoenix.

Mandelbaum, D. G. (1965), 'Alcohol and Culture', *Current Anthropology*, 6, 3: 281–93.

Manderson, D. (1993), *From Mr. Sin to Mr. Big: A History of Australian Drug Laws*, Melbourne, Oxford University Press.

Manderson, D. (1997), 'Substances as Symbols: Race Rhetoric and the Tropes of Australian Drug History', *Social and Legal Studies*, 6, 3: 383–400.

Manderson, D. (2005), 'Possessed: Drug Policy, Witchcraft and Belief', *Cultural Studies*, 19, 1: 35–62.

Mann, J. (2000), *Murder, Magic and Medicine*, Oxford, Oxford University Press.

Mars, G. (1987), 'Longshore Drinking, Economic Security and Union Politics in Newfoundland', in Douglas, M. (ed.), *Constructive Drinking: Perspectives on Drink from Anthropology*, Cambridge, Cambridge University Press.

Marsh, P., Fox, K., Carnibella, G., McCann, J. and Marsh, J. (1996), *Football Violence and Hooliganism in Europe*, Brussels, The Amsterdam Group.

Marshall, D. (1999), *Testimony to Congressional Hearing*, Washington, DC. Congressional Subcommittee on Criminal Justice, Drug Policy and Human Resources.

Matt, G. E., Quintana, P. J. E., Hovell, M. G., Bernert, J. T., Song, S., Novianti, N., Juarez, T., Floro, J., Gehrman, C., Garcia, M. and Larson, S. (2004), 'Households Contaminated by Environmental Tobacco Smoke: Sources of Infant Exposures', *Tobacco Control*, 13, 1: 29–37.

Matthee, R. (1995), 'Exotic Substances: The Introduction and Global Spread of Tobacco, Coffee, Cocoa, Tea, and Distilled Liquor, Sixteenth to Eighteenth Centuries', in Porter, R. and Teich, M. (eds), *Drugs and Narcotics in History*, Cambridge, Cambridge University Press.

Measham, F. (2004), 'Play Space: Historical and Socio-Cultural Reflections on Drugs, Licensed Leisure Locations, Commercialisation and Control', *International Journal of Drug Policy*, 15, 5–6: 337–45.

Measham, F. (2007), 'The Policing of Pleasure and the New Culture of Intoxication: The Contrasting Fortunes of Ketamine and Alcohol', *Sociology Seminar Series*, Edinburgh: University of Edinburgh.

Measham, F., Newcombe, R. and Parker, H. (1994), 'The Normalization of Recreational Drug Use amongst Young People in North-West England', *The British Journal of Sociology*, 45, 2: 287–312.

Measham, F., Parker, H. and Aldridge, J. (1998), 'The Teenage Transition: From Adolescent Recreational Drug Use to the Young Adult Dance Users in Britain in the Mid-1990s', *Journal of Drug Issues*, 28, 1: 9–32.

Metropolitan Police Service (2004), 'Don't Let Drug Dealers Change the Face of Your Neighbourhood', <http://www.met.police.uk/drugs/advertising.htm>.

Meyers, J. E. and Almirall, J. R. (2004), 'A Study of the Effectiveness of Commercially Available Drink Test Coasters for the Detection of "Date Rape" Drugs in Beverages', *Journal of Analytical Toxicology* 28, 8: 685–8.

Milton, J. (1890 [1634]), *Comus: A Mask*, London, Macmillan.

Mintzes, B. (2002), 'Direct to Consumer Advertising is Medicalising Normal Human Experience', *British Medical Journal*, 324, 7342, 908–9.

Mitchell, T. (2004), *Intoxicated Identities: Alcohol's Power in Mexican History and Culture*, New York, Routledge.

M'laren, D. (1860), *An Inquiry Into the Results of the Opium Trade with China Including its Bearing on the Export of British Manufacturers*, Edinburgh, Andrew Elliot.

Moldrup, C. (2004), 'The Use of the Terms "Lifestyle Medicines" or "Lifestyle Drugs"', *Pharmacy World and Science*, 26, 4: 193–6.

Moore, D. and Valverde, M. (2000), 'Maidens at Risk: "Date Rape Drugs" and the Formation of Hybrid Risk Knowledges', *Economy and Society*, 29, 4: 514–31.

Moore, K. and Miles, S. (2004), 'Young People, Dance and the Sub-cultural Consumption of Drugs', *Addiction Research and Theory*.

Morewood, S. (1824), *An Essay on the Inventions and Customs of Both Ancients and Moderns in the Use of Inebriating Liquors: Interspersed With Interesting Anecdotes, Illustrative of the Manners and Habits of the Principal Nations of the World, With an Historical View of the Extent and Practice of Distillation Both as it Relates to Commerce and as a Source of National Income*, London, Hurst, Rees, Orme, Brown, and Green.

Morgan, P. (1981), 'Alcohol, Disinhibition, and Domination: A Conceptual Analysis', in Room, R. and Collins, G. (eds), *Alcohol and Disinhibition: Nature and Meaning of the Link*, Rockville, MD, US Department of Health and Human Services.

Moss, A. (1977), 'Methadone's Rise and Fall', in Rock, P. E. (ed.), *Drugs and Politics*, New Brunswick, NJ, Transaction Publishers.

Moynihan, R. (2003), 'Who Pays for the Pizza? Redefining the Relationships Between Doctors and Drug Companies', *British Medical Journal*, 326, 7400, 1189–96.

Moynihan, R. and Henry, D. (2006), 'The Fight Against Disease Mongering: Generating Knowledge for Action', *PLoS Medicine*, 3, 4: e191.

Musto, D. F. (2002), *Drugs in America: A Documentary History*, New York, New York University Press.

National Institute on Drug Abuse (1998), *NIDA Research Report – Tobacco Addiction*, Bethseda, MD, National Institutes of Health.

Nesse, R. M. and Berridge, K. C. (1997), 'Psychoactive Drug Use in Evolutionary Perspective', *Science*, 278, 5335, 63–6.

Newlin, D. B. (2002), 'The Self-Perceived Survival Ability and Reproductive Fitness (SPFit) Theory of Substance Use Disorders', *Addiction*, 97: 427–45.

Nolan, J. L. (1998), *The Therapeutic State: Justifying Government at Century's End*, New York, New York University Press.

Notley, C. (2005), 'Four Groups of Illicit Substance Users amongst the Adult "Hidden" Non-problematic Community', *Drugs: Education, Prevention and Policy*, 12, 4: 279–90.

Nutt, D., King, L. A., Saulsbury, W. and Blakemore, C. (2007), 'Development of a Rational Scale to Assess the Harm of Drugs of Potential Misuse', *The Lancet*, 369: 1047–53.

Nycander, S. (1998), 'Ivan Bratt: The Man who Saved Sweden from Prohibition', *Addiction*, 93, 1: 17–25.

Office of Applied Studies (2005), *Results from the 2005 National Survey on Drug Use and Health*, Rockville, MD, Substance Abuse and Mental Health Services Administration.

Office of National Drug Control Policy (2005), *Club Drugs*, <http://www.whitehousedrugpolicy.gov/drugfact/club/index.html?mark_id=cache%3A6&mark_low=0&mark_high=10>.

Office of Science and Technology (2005), *Drug Futures 2025? Executive Summary and Overview*, London, Department of Trade and Industry.

Office on Drugs and Crime (2007), *Drugs of Abuse: The Facts*, New York, NY, United Nations.

Oliver, F. E. (1872), *The Use and Abuse of Opium*, Boston, Massachusetts State Board of Health.

O'Malley, P. and Valverde, M. (2004), 'Pleasure, Freedom and Drugs: The Uses of "Pleasure" in Liberal Governance of Drug and Alcohol Consumption', *Sociology*, 38, 1: 25–42.

Orb, The (1994), *Pomme Fritz*, Island Records.

Parker, H. (2005), 'Normalization as a Barometer: Recreational Drug Use and the Consumption of Leisure by Younger Britons', *Addiction Research and Theory*, 13, 3: 205–15.

Parker, H., Williams, L. and Aldridge, J. (2002), 'The Normalization of "Sensible" Recreational Drug Use: Further Evidence from the North West England Longitudinal Study', *Sociology*, 36, 4: 941–64.

Parry, V. (2003), 'The Art of Branding a Condition', *Medical Marketing & Media*, 38, 5: 42–9.

Partanen, J. (1981), 'Toward a Theory of Intoxication', in Room, R. and Collins, G. (eds), *Alcohol and Disinhibition: Nature and Meaning of the Link*, Rockville, US Department of Health and Human Services.

Paton-Simpson, G. (2001), 'Socially Obligatory Drinking: A Sociological Analysis of Norms Governing Minimum Drinking Levels', *Contemporary Drug Problems*, 28, 1: 133–77.

Peele, S. (1999), 'The Persistent, Dangerous Myth of Heroin Overdose', *DPFT News (Drug Policy Forum of Texas)*, August, 5.

Peralta, R. L. (2007), 'College Alcohol Use and the Embodiment of Hegemonic Masculinity Among European American Men', *Sex Roles*, 56, 11–12: 741–56.

Petersen, A. and Lupton, D. (1996), *The New Public Health: Health and Self in the Age of Risk*, London, Sage.

Pine, J. B. and Gilmour, J. H. (1999), *The Experience Economy: Work is Theatre and Every Business a Stage*, Boston, MA, Harvard Business School Press.

Pirmohamed, M., James, S. et al. (2004), 'Adverse Drug Reactions as Cause of Admission to Hospital: Prospective Analysis of 18820 Patients', *British Medical Journal*, 329, 7456, 15–19.

Plato (1921 [c.360 BC]), *The Laws of Plato, the Text Edited with Introduction, Notes, etc. by E. B. England*, Manchester, Manchester University Press.

Pliny the Elder (1938 [c.AD 77]), *Natural History; With an English Translation by H. Rackham*, London, Heinemann.

Pollock, A. (2004), *NHS Plc: The Privatisation of Our Health Care*, London, Verso.

Pope, A. (1720 [1717]), *Eloisa to Abelard*, London, Bernard Lintrot.

Poppig, E. F. (1835), *Reise in Chile, Peru und auf dem Amazonenstrome, Während der Jahre 1827–1832*, Leipzig, F. Fleischer.

Portman Group (2004), *Don't Do Drunk*, Cinema and Poster Campaign.

Potts, A. (2004), 'Viagra Cyborgs: Creating "Better Manhood Through Chemistry"?', in Potts, A., Gavey, N. and Weatherall, A. (eds), *Sex and the Body* Palmerston North, Dunmore Press.

Quan Nicholls, J. (2003), 'Gin Lane Revisited: Intoxication and Society in the Gin Epidemic', *Journal for Cultural Research*, 7, 2: 125–46.

Raleigh, M. J., McGuire, M. T., Brammer, G. L., Pollack, D. B. and Yuwiler, A. (1991), 'Serotonergic Mechanisms Promote Dominance Acquisition in Adult Male Vervet Monkeys', *Brain Research*, 559, 2: 181–90.

Ratner, M.S. (1993), *Crack Pipe as Pimp: An Ethnographic Investigation of Sex–for–Crack Exchanges*, New York, Lexington Books.

Rees, D. (2002), 'Get Your War On', Brooklyn, NY, Soft Skull.

Reinarman, C. and Levine, H. G. (2004), 'Crack in the Rear-View Mirror: Deconstructing Drug War Mythology', *Social Justice*, 31, 1–2: 182–99.

Reith, G. (2004), 'Consumption and its Discontents: Addiction, Identity and the Problems of Freedom', *British Journal of Sociology*, 55, 2: 283–300.

Ribot, T. (1896), *The Diseases of the Will*, Chicago, IL, Open Court.

Richardson, D. and Campbell, J. (1980), 'Alcohol and Wife Abuse: The Effect of Alcohol on Attributions of Blame for Wife Abuse', *Personality and Social Psychology Bulletin*, 6, 1: 51–6.

Robbins, T. W. and Everitt, B. J. (1999), 'Drug Addiction: Bad Habits Add Up', *Nature*, 398, 6728: 567–70.

Roberts, M., Klein, A. and Trace, M. (2004), *Towards a Review of Global Policies on Controlled Drugs*, Oxford, The Beckley Foundation.

Robins, L. N., Davis, D. H. and Goodwin, D. W. (1974), 'Drug Use by US Army Enlisted Men in Vietnam: A Follow-Up on their Return Home', *American Journal of Epidemiology*, 99, 4: 235–49.

Robins, L. N. and Slobodyan, S. (2003), 'Post-Vietnam Heroin Use and Injection by Returning US Veterans: Clues to Preventing Injection Today', *Addiction*, 98, 8: 1053–60.

Room, R. (2000a), 'Rör inte helnykterhetsprincipen! Ny drabbingar i USA (Abstinence as the only treatment goal: new U.S. battles)', *Nordisk Alkohol– och Narkotikatidskrift*, 17: 149–51.

Room, R. (2000b), 'The More Drinking, the More Fun; But is There a Calculus of Fun, and Should it Drive Policy?', *Drug and Alcohol Dependence*, 60, 3: 249–50.

Roth, M. (2004), 'The Golden Age of Drinking and the Fall Into Addiction', *Janus Head*, 7, 1: 11–33.

Rowntree, J. (1895), *The Opium Habit in the East*, London, P.S. King.

Russell, F. (2001), 'Limiting the Use of Acquitted and Uncharged Conduct at Sentencing: Apprendi v. New Jersey and its Effect on the Relevant Conduct Provision of the United States Sentencing Guidelines', *California Law Review*, 89, 4: 1199–1229.

Ruston, A. (2006), 'Interpreting and Managing Risk in a Machine Bureaucracy: Professional Decision-making in NHS Direct', *Health, Risk and Society*, 8, 3: 257–71.

Schaler, J. A. (2000), *Addiction is a Choice*, Chicago, IL, Open Court.

Schivelbusch, W. (1992), *Tastes of Paradise: A Social History of Spices, Stimulants, and Intoxicants*, London, Vintage/Random House.

Schrad, M. L. (2006), 'Kicking the Vodka Habit', *The Moscow Times*, 3 November.

Schrad, M. L. (2008), 'Building the Transnational Temperance Movement, 1820s–1930s', *Transnational Communities Conference and Workshop*, Max Planck Institute for the Studies of Societies, Köln, Germany.

Schweitzer, D. (2000), 'Striptease: The Art of Spectacle and Transgression', *Journal of Popular Culture*, 34, 1: 65–75.

Scott, W. (1819), *The Bride of Lammermoor (Tales of My Landlord, Third Series)*, Edinburgh, Archibald Constable.

Scruton, R. (2007), 'The Philosophy of Wine', in Robinson, J. and Smith, B. C. (eds), *Questions of Taste: The Philosophy of Wine*, Oxford, Signal Books.

Secretary of State for Health (1998), *Smoking Kills: A White Paper on Tobacco*, London, Department of Health.

Secretary of State for the Home Department (2006), *The Government Reply to the Fifth Report From The House of Commons Science and Technology Committee Session 2005–06 HC 1031. Drug Classification: Making a Hash of it?*, London, The Stationery Office.

Sharfstein, J. (1999), 'Blowing Smoke: How Cigarette Manufacturers Argued That Nicotine is not Addictive', *Tobacco Control*, 8, 2: 210–13.

Sherratt, A. (1995), 'Alcohol and Its Alternatives: Symbol and Substance in Pre-industrial Cultures', in Goodman, J., Lovejoy, P. E. and Sherratt, A. (eds), *Consuming Habits: Drugs in History and Anthropology*, London, Routledge.

Simmel, G. (1995 [1903]), 'The Metropolis and Mental Life', *Readings In Social Theory: The Classic Tradition To Post-Modernism*, J. Farganis, New York, McGraw Hill, 149–57.

Simmel, G. (1997 [1907]), 'The Sociology of the Senses', in Frisby, D. and Featherstone, M. (eds), *Simmel on Culture*, London, Sage.

Singh, I. (2004), 'Doing Their Jobs: Mothering with Ritalin in a Culture of Mother-Blame', *Social Science & Medicine*, 59, 6: 1193–1205.

Slaughter, L. (2000), 'Involvement of Drugs in Sexual Assault', *Journal of Reproductive Medicine*, 45, 5: 425–30.

Smalley, J. and Blake, M. (2003), 'Sweet Beginnings: Stalk Sugar and the Domestication of Maize', *Current Anthropology*, 44, 5: 675–703.

Smith, R. (2004), 'Travelling but Never Arriving: Reflections of a Retiring Editor', *British Medical Journal*, 329, 7460: 242–4.

Snow, H. (1890), *The Palliative Treatment of Incurable Cancer with an Appendix on the Use of the Opium Pipe*, London, J. A. Churchill.

Social Issues Research Centre (1998), *Social and Cultural Aspects of Drinking*, Oxford, Social Issues Research Centre.

Sournia, J.-C. (1990), *A History of Alcoholism*, Oxford, Blackwell.

South, N. (2004), 'Managing Work, Hedonism and "The Borderline" Between the Legal and Illegal Markets: Two Case Studies of Recreational Heavy Drug Users', *Addiction Research and Theory* 12, 6: 525–38.

Stimson, G. V. (2000), '"Blair Declares War": The Unhealthy State of British Drug Policy', *International Journal of Drug Policy*, 11, 4: 259–64.

Suffolk Constabulary (2006), *Safe!* Ipswich, Suffolk Constabulary.

Sullivan, R. J. and Hagan, E. H. (2002), 'Psychotropic Substance Seeking: Evolutionary Pathology or Adaptation?', *Addiction*, 97, 4: 389–400.

Sullum, J. (1998), *For Your Own Good: The Anti-Smoking Crusade and the Tyranny of Public Health*, New York, NY, Free Press.

Sullum, J. (2003), *Saying Yes: In Defence of Drug Use*, New York, NY, J. P. Tarchers/Puttnam.

Surgeon General (2006), *The Health Consequences of Involuntary Exposure to Tobacco Smoke*, Washington, DC, Department of Health and Human Services.

Szasz, T. S. (2001), 'The Therapeutic State: The Tyranny of Pharmacy', *The Independent Review*, V, 4: 485–521.

Tennyson, A. (1901 [1833]), *The Lotos Eaters*, London, Gay & Bird.

The World Bank (1999), *Curbing the Epidemic: Governments and the Economics of Tobacco Control*, Washington, DC, The World Bank.

Tiefer, L. (2003), 'The Pink Viagra Story: We Have the Drug, but What's the Disease?', *Radical Philosophy*, 21: 2–5.

Tobacco Advisory Group (2000), *Nicotine Addiction in Britain*, London, Royal College of Physicians.

Triggle, D. J. (2005), 'Vaccines, Viagra, and Vioxx: Medicines, Markets, and Money – Where Life-Saving Meets Life-Style', *Drug Development Research*, 64, 2: 90–8.

Trocki, C. A. (1999), *Opium, Empire, and the Global Political Economy: A Study of the Asian Opium Trade, 1750–1950*, London, Routledge.

Turner, R. (1976), 'The Real Self: From Institution to Impulse', *The American Journal of Sociology*, 81, 5: 989–1016.

Valverde, M. (1998), *Diseases of the Will: Alcohol and the Dilemmas of Freedom*, New York, NY, Cambridge University Press.

Vastag, B. (2001), 'Pay Attention: Ritalin Acts Much Like Cocaine', *Journal of the American Medical Association*, 286, 8: 905–6.

Wallace, A. F. C. (1959), 'Cultural Determinants of Response to Hallucinatory Experience', *Archives of General Psychiatry*, 1, 1: 58–69.

Walton, J. (2000), *The Faber Book of Smoking*, London, Faber and Faber.

Wang, G.-J., Yang, J., Volkow, N. D., Telang, F., Ma, Y., Zhu, W., Wong, C. T., Tomasi, D., Thanos, P. K. and Fowler, J. S. (2006), 'Gastric Stimulation in Obese Subjects Activates the Hippocampus and Other Regions Involved in Brain Reward Circuitry', *Proceedings of the National Academy of Sciences*, 103, 42: 15641–5.

Warburton, H., Turnbull, P. J. and Hough, M. (2005), *Occasional and Controlled Heroin Use: Not a Problem?*, York, Joseph Rowntree Foundation.

Warner, J. (2004), *Craze: Gin and Debauchery in an Age of Reason*, London, Profile.

Warner, J., Gmel, G. and Rehm, J. (2001), 'Can Legislation Prevent Debauchery? Mother Gin and Public Health in Eighteenth–century England', *American Journal of Public Health*, 91, 3: 375–84.

Weil, A. T., Zinberg, N. E. and Nelsen, J. M. (1968), 'Clinical and Psychological Effects of Marihuana in Man', *Science*, 162, 3859: 1234–42.

Weinberg, D. (1997), 'Lindesmith on Addiction: A Critical History of a Classic Theory', *Sociological Theory*, 15, 2: 150–61.

Weitzman, E., W. DeJong and P. Finn (1999), 'Alcohol and Acquaintance Rape: Strategies To Protect Yourself and Each Other', Newton, MA, Higher Education Center for Alcohol and Other Drug Prevention.

West, L. A. (2001), 'Negotiating Masculinities in American Drinking Subcultures', *Journal of Men's Studies*, 9, 3: 371–92.

White, J. (2003), 'The "Slow but Sure Poyson": The Representation of Gin and its Drinkers, 1736–1751', *Journal of British Studies*, 42: 35–64.

Williams, G. P. and Brake, G. T. (1980), *Drink in Great Britain 1900–1979*, London, Edsall.

Williamson, K. (1997), *Drugs and the Party Line*, Edinburgh, Rebel Inc.

Wilson, J. Q. (1990a), 'Against the Legalization of Drugs', *Commentary*, 89: 21–8.

Wilson, J. Q. (1990b), 'Drugs and Crime', in Tonry, M. and Wilson, J. Q. (eds), *Drugs and Crime*, Chicago, IL: University of Chicago Press.

Woodiwiss, M. (1998), 'Reform, Racism and Rackets: Alcohol and Drug Prohibition in the United States', in Coomber, R. (ed.), *The Control of Drugs and Drug Users: Reason or Reaction?*, Boca Raton, CRC Press.

Woodiwiss, M. and Bewley-Taylor, D. R. (2005), *The Global Fix: The Construction of a Global Enforcement Regime*, Amsterdam, Transnational Institute.

World Health Organisation (2006), *Tobacco: Deadly in any Form or Disguise*, Geneva, World Health Organisation.

World Health Organisation (2007), *International Classification of Diseases*, Geneva, World Health Organisation.

Young, G. (1753), *A Treatise on Opium, Founded Upon Practical Observations*, London, A. Millar.

Young, J. (1971), *The Drugtakers: The Social Meaning of Drug Use*, London, MacGibbon and Kee.

Young, J. (1973), 'The Myth of the Drug Taker in the Mass Media', in Cohen, S. and Young, J. (eds), *The Manufacture of News: Social Problems, Deviance and the Mass Media*, London, Constable.

Zinberg, N. E. (1984), *Drug, Set and Setting: The Basis for Controlled Intoxicant Use*, New Haven, CT, Yale University Press.

Index